D0472522

Best of the Best from the

Southeast

Cookbook

Selected Recipes from the
Favorite Cookbooks of
South Carolina, Georgia, and Florida

PHOTO COURTESY OF NATIONAL PARK SERVICE.

Set aside in 1968, Biscayne National Park is the largest marine park in the National Park System, with 95% of its 173,000 acres covered by water. The park is only 30 miles from downtown Miami, along the extreme southeastern coast of Florida.

Best of the Best from the

Southeast

Cookbook

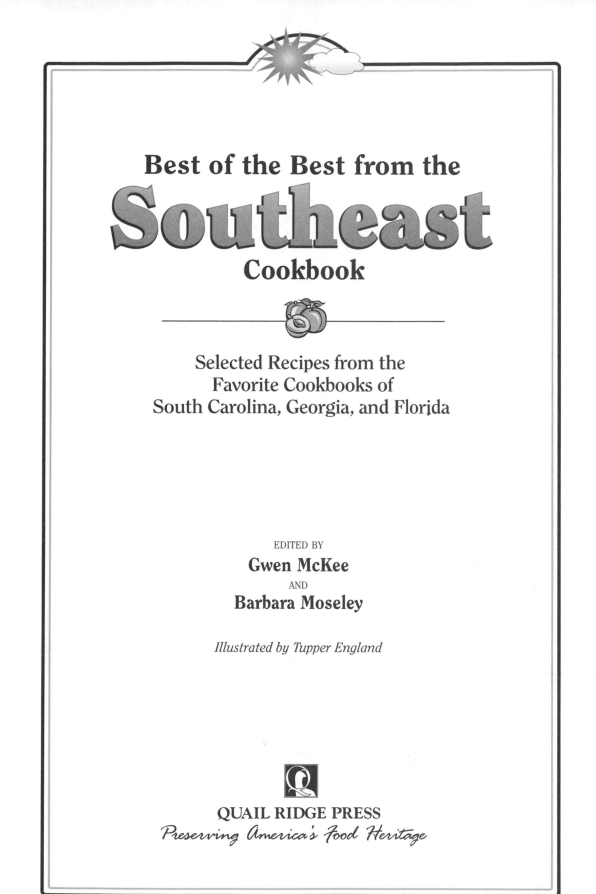

Selected Recipes from the
Favorite Cookbooks of
South Carolina, Georgia, and Florida

EDITED BY

Gwen McKee

AND

Barbara Moseley

Illustrated by Tupper England

QUAIL RIDGE PRESS
Preserving America's Food Heritage

Recipe Collection ©2009 Quail Ridge Press, Inc.

ALL RIGHTS RESERVED
Recipes reprinted with permission from the publishers,
organizations, or individuals listed on pages 267 to 274.

Library of Congress Cataloging-in-Publication Data

Best of the best from the Southeast cookbook : selected recipes from the favorite cook-
   books of South Carolina, Georgia, and Florida / Gwen McKee and
   Barbara Moseley ; illustrated by Tupper England. — 1st ed.
      p. cm. — (Best of the best cookbook series)
   ISBN-13: 978-1-934193-26-6
   ISBN-10: 1-934193-26-7
      1. Cookery, American--Southern style. 2. Cookery—Southern States.
   I. McKee, Gwen. II. Moseley, Barbara.
TX715.2.S68B4982 2009
641.5973--dc22   2008053205

ISBN-13: 978-1-934193-26-6 • ISBN-10: 1-934193-26-7

Book design by Cynthia Clark • Cover photo by Greg Campbell
Printed in Canada

First edition, June 2009

On the cover: Company's Coming Peach Pie, page 243

QUAIL RIDGE PRESS
P. O. Box 123 • Brandon, MS 39043
info@quailridge.com • www.quailridge.com

CONTENTS

PHOTO © BROOKGREEN GARDENS.

Brookgreen Gardens is the floral jewel of South Carolina's coastal community. In the heart of the gardens is Live Oak Allee, comprised of centuries-old trees lining the path that once led to the main plantation house. These inspiring matriarchs frame this garden space like a living cathedral.

Quest for the Best
Regional Cooking

It seems that everywhere Barbara and I travel, we find that people love to talk about food. Invariably they mention specific dishes that have been an important part of their family's heritage and tradition, and do so with exuberance and pride.

"My mother always serves her fabulous cornbread dressing with our Thanksgiving turkey, and it is simply 'the best.'"

"Aunt Susan's famous pecan pie is always the first to go."

"No family occasion would be complete without Uncle Joe's chicken salad sandwiches."

Well, we heard, we researched, and we captured these bragged-about recipes so that people all over the country . . . and the world . . . could enjoy them.

My co-editor Barbara Moseley and I have been searching for the country's best recipes for three decades, and home cooks everywhere have learned to trust and rely on our cookbooks to bring them fabulous meals their friends and family will love! We always choose recipes based first and foremost on taste. In addition, the ingredients have to be readily available, and the recipes simple, with easy-to-follow instructions and never-fail results.

While touring the country and tasting the local fare, we delight in finding the little secrets that make the big difference. We have eaten buffalo in Wyoming, halibut in Alaska, lobster in Maine, gumbo in Louisiana, each prepared in a variety of creative ways. Finding out about conch in Florida and boysenberries in Oregon and poi in Hawaii . . . . No matter where we venture, this part of our job is always fun, often surprising, and definitely inspiring!

The Southeast region of South Carolina, Georgia, and Florida has so many great recipes, a treasure chest would overflow with them! We loved discovering specialty dishes everywhere we traveled . . . delectable Lowcountry flavors, savory seafood offerings, tempting Key lime pies, enchanting

Charlottes, hearty Hoppin' Johns, satisfying Vidalia onion dishes, and of course, everything peachy. It's a feast for the eyes, the nose, and especially the taste buds. Take a culinary trip with us through this superbly delicious Southeast region of our country . . . a tasty treasure indeed.

Gwen McKee

Gwen McKee and Barbara Moseley, editors of
BEST OF THE BEST STATE COOKBOOK SERIES

BEVERAGES and APPETIZERS

PHOTO © GREATER FORT LAUDERDALE CONVENTION & VISITORS BUREAU.

Flamingo Gardens, located in the Everglades just west of Fort Lauderdale, Florida, includes 60 acres of lush tropical vegetation showcasing rare, exotic, and native plants, along with sparkling waterfalls. It is a haven for flamingos and other wildlife.

Southern Fresh Fruit Tea

5 family-size tea bags
1½ quarts water
1 (46-ounce) can pineapple
  juice
1 (6-ounce) can frozen
  orange juice concentrate

1 (6-ounce) can frozen
  lemonade concentrate
Sweetener of choice to taste

Boil tea bags in water for 5 minutes; let steep. Mix pineapple juice, orange juice, and lemonade in a gallon jug. Carefully pour in the tea; mix well. Add cold water to fill jug. Sweeten to taste; mix well. Serve cold.

VARIATION:
6–8 large lemons
4–6 large oranges
2 quarts water

1½ cups sugar
8 regular-size tea bags
1 cup diced, fresh pineapple

Peel lemons and oranges; carefully remove and discard the pith, reserving the rinds. Squeeze juice from lemons to measure 1½ cups juice; squeeze oranges to measure 2 cups juice. Set juice aside.

   Bring water and sugar to a boil in large saucepan, stirring often; boil 1 minute. Pour over tea bags and rinds; cover and steep for 20 minutes. Discard tea bags and rinds, squeezing tea bags gently to remove all liquid. Be careful not to break the tea bags. Stir in juices and pineapple. Cover and chill at least 2 hours. Serve over ice. Garnish with lemon and orange slices. Makes about 3 quarts.

Tried & True Recipes from Covington, Georgia (Georgia)

Hot Cranberry Tea

3 quarts water, divided
2 cups sugar
1 (2-ounce) box red hot candies
1 (32-ounce) bottle cranberry
  juice cocktail

1 (6-ounce) can frozen orange
  juice concentrate
1 (6-ounce) can frozen
  lemonade concentrate

Boil 2 quarts water, sugar, and red hots until sugar and red hots are dissolved. Add cranberry juice cocktail and orange and lemonade concentrate; and remaining 1 quart water. Serve hot. Makes 1 gallon.

Canopy Roads (Florida)

Lime Luscious

4 cups milk, divided
¼ cup brown sugar
1 (3¾-ounce) package instant
  vanilla pudding mix

¼ cup lime juice
4 scoops lime sherbet
Mint sprigs (optional)

In bowl of electric mixer, blender, or food processor, combine ¼ cup milk with sugar; blend in remaining milk. Add pudding mix and beat smooth. Blend in lime juice and pour into glasses. Float scoop of lime sherbet on top. Mint sprigs make pretty garnish. Makes 4½ cups.

The Orange Bowl Cookbook (Florida)

Daufuskie Freeze

This drink is named after a beautiful and untouched island near Hilton Head Island. The drink itself has become probably the most popular drink I serve at Hilton Head. It is seemingly a perfect combination of ingredients that compliment each other extremely well. Be careful, you too may become a Daufuskie Island addict.

3–4 medium strawberries,
  hulled
3 or 4 ice cubes

1½ ounces light rum
2 ounces orange juice
1½ ounces coconut cream

Place strawberries, then ice into blender. Add remainder of ingredients and blend until smooth and creamy. Garnish with fresh strawberry, if desired. Makes 1 (12-ounce) serving.

Note: To prepare this drink using frozen strawberries, substitute 2 ounces of frozen strawberries for the fresh strawberries. Equally excellent without alcohol.

Pool Bar Jim's Famous Frozen Drinks (South Carolina)

Slushy Strawberry Daiquiris

7 (6-ounce) cans frozen
 lemonade
6 (10-ounce) packages frozen
 strawberries

2½ (2-liter) bottles 7-Up
½ gallon rum
Fresh strawberries for garnish

Thaw and mix lemonade and berries. Add 7-Up and rum. Put in freezer for 3 days. Will be slushy. Scoop into pretty glasses and top each with a strawberry. Makes a 5-gallon bucket of daiquiris.

Country Club Cooks (Florida)

Mango Colada

A piña colada with mango. What could be more refreshing?

6 ounces coconut cream
6 ounces pineapple juice
4 ounces mango purée

4 ounces spiced white rum
8 ice cubes

Place all ingredients, except ice, in a blender and add ice cubes one at a time. Blend until smooth. Makes 4 servings.

The Mongo Mango Cookbook (Florida)

Mulled Wine

1 (1.75-liter) bottle dry
 red wine
4 cups apple cider
½ cup sugar
28 whole cloves
1 orange, cut into 6 wedges

2 lemons, cut into 4 wedges
 each
2 cinnamon sticks
Thin lemon slices, pierced with
 whole cloves for garnish

Pour wine, apple cider, and sugar into a 6-quart pot. Bring to a gentle simmer. Insert 2 cloves into each wedge of citrus fruit, and add to simmering wine. Add cinnamon sticks. Simmer at least 45 minutes. Serve hot in mugs and garnish with lemon slices pierced with cloves. Serves 8–12.

Gracious Goodness: Christmas in Charleston (South Carolina)

Kahlúa

Serve as an after-dinner liqueur, or over vanilla ice cream with whipped cream, nuts, and shaved chocolate.

2 rounded tablespoons instant
  coffee
1 cup water

3 cups white sugar
1 vanilla bean, finely chopped
1 fifth vodka

Boil coffee, water, and sugar. Stir until completely dissolved. Cool completely. Add finely chopped vanilla bean. Add vodka. Cork in airtight vessel. Store in a cool place for 30 days.

Puttin' on the Peachtree... (Georgia)

It's Almost Bailey's

1 cup Irish whiskey
1 (14-ounce) can sweetened
  condensed milk
4 eggs
2 tablespoons vanilla

2 tablespoons chocolate extract
1 tablespoon coconut extract
1½ tablespoons powdered
  instant coffee or espresso

Mix all ingredients in blender at LOW speed until thoroughly blended. Transfer to a bottle with a tight cover or good cork. Refrigerate 8 hours or until ready to serve. Shake well; serve very cold or over ice. Serves 6.

Peachtree Bouquet (Georgia)

Streets with "Peachtree" in the name are common in Georgia. As a matter of fact, there are about fifty-five streets that include the word. Peachtree in Atlanta is one of America's best-known streets. It winds north from downtown Atlanta through the heart of Buckhead, closely following the Chattahoochee Ridge route of the Indian-era Peachtree Trail. Downtown, it's Peachtree *Street*, but after it merges with West Peachtree and heads north, it becomes Peachtree *Road*.

Coffee Punch

An early morning eye-opener.

1½ cups sugar
1 cup hot coffee
1 gallon very strong coffee,
  chilled
1 quart milk
1½ tablespoons vanilla

1 quart vanilla ice cream,
  softened
1 quart chocolate ice cream,
  softened
2 cups whipping cream,
  whipped

Dissolve sugar in hot coffee; add to chilled coffee. Chill until ready to serve. At serving time, add milk and vanilla to chilled coffee. Stir in softened ice creams. Immediately before serving, fold in whipped cream. If using only a portion of recipe, keep extra punch well chilled. Makes 2+ gallons.

Culinary Memories of Merridun, Volume 1 (South Carolina)

Planter's Punch

2 ounces light rum
1 ounce Myers dark rum
6 ounces orange juice
6 ounces pineapple juice
½ ounce grenadine

Ice
1 ounce banana liqueur, divided
2 orange slices, lime slices,
  maraschino cherries, and
  pineapple spears for garnish

Combine rums, orange juice, pineapple juice, and grenadine in a shaker with ice; shake well and strain into 2 hurricane glasses. Top each glass with ½ ounce banana liqueur and garnish with orange slice, lime slice, pineapple spear, and maraschino cherry.

Recipes from the Olde Pink House (Georgia)

More hurricanes hit the Florida peninsula than any other part of the United States. Hurricane Andrew, which hit Florida in 1992, was the third fiercest hurricane ever recorded on mainland America at the time. Gusts reached 145 miles an hour and the cost of the damage was estimated at about $25 billion, making Andrew the most expensive natural disaster in U.S. history until Hurricane Katrina devastated the Gulf Coast in 2005. The fiercest hurricane was an unnamed storm that struck the Florida Keys in 1935.

Guacamole

2 ripe avocados
Juice of 1 lime
½ teaspoon salt
½ teaspoon chili powder
2 teaspoons fresh onion juice

4 drops red hot sauce
½ (3-ounce) package cream
   cheese, softened
1 tablespoon minced pimento
   (optional)

Peel avocados, remove pits, and mash with silver fork to prevent darkening. Add lime juice, then blend in seasonings and cream cheese. If pimento is used, stir it in last. Use as a dip with potato chips or stuff tomatoes for salad. If guacamole must stand for some time, place in refrigerator with avocado pit placed in center and it will not darken.

Famous Florida Recipes (Florida)

Peachy Lime Guacamole

1 medium Georgia peach
5 medium ripe avocados
1 cup chopped fresh cilantro
Salt and black pepper to taste

Garlic salt to taste
Cayenne pepper to taste
Juice of 1 lime

Peel peach and halve, removing pit. Chop into very small pieces. Peel avocados and halve, removing pits. Place avocado halves cut side down and slice thinly; rotate and slice into small pieces. Combine peach, avocados, cilantro, and seasonings in a large glass bowl. Add lime juice gradually, tossing gently. Chill 1 hour or longer. Toss before serving. Serve with blue corn tortilla chips or your favorite chips.

True Grits (Georgia)

Sunchaser Salsa

1 (28-ounce) can whole
  tomatoes
1 large Spanish or Vidalia
  onion

4–10 jalapeño peppers
Salt to taste

Squish tomatoes with fingers; remove any remaining cores. Dice the onion fine; seed and dice jalapeño peppers. Mix all well. Serve with chips, Tostitos, or Doritos.

Variations: Add mashed, ripe avocado to make guacamole. Add sour cream or melted cheese for chile con queso. Add chopped fresh cilantro for flavor.

Cooking in Paradise (Florida)

Sun-Dried Tomato Dip with Roasted Red Peppers

8 sun-dried tomato halves
2 (7-ounce) jars roasted red
  bell peppers, drained
1 clove garlic, minced
1 tablespoon fresh lemon juice
2 tablespoons chopped fresh
  flat-leaf parsley

4 ounces cream cheese, softened
$\frac{1}{2}$ cup sour cream
$\frac{1}{8}$ teaspoon salt
Pepper to taste
Pita chips

Combine sun-dried tomatoes with enough hot water to cover in a bowl. Let stand 5 minutes; drain and pat dry. Pat the red peppers dry with a paper towel. Combine sun-dried tomatoes, red peppers, garlic, lemon juice, and parsley in a food processor container. Process until smooth. Add cream cheese, sour cream, salt, and pepper. Process until blended. Spoon into serving bowl. Chill, covered, until serving time. Garnish with additional chopped fresh parsley. Serve with pita chips. Makes about 2 cups.

Down by the Water (South Carolina)

Curry Dip

2 cups mayonnaise
2 cups sour cream
¼ teaspoon turmeric
2 tablespoons curry powder
4 teaspoons sugar
½–2 teaspoons garlic powder
2 teaspoons salt
2 tablespoons lemon juice
½ cup freshly chopped parsley

Mix together and use fresh vegetables as dippers. Should be made several days in advance. Keeps well.

Lost Tree Cook Book (Florida)

Pizza Dip

1 (8-ounce) package cream cheese, softened
1 (14-ounce) jar pizza sauce
⅓ cup chopped onion
1½ cups grated mozzarella cheese
1 (6-ounce) can ripe olives, drained, chopped
2 ounces sliced pepperoni, chopped
Light corn chips

Preheat oven to 350°. Press cream cheese into bottom of 9-inch glass pie pan. Spread pizza sauce over cream cheese and layer remaining ingredients in order listed. Bake at 350° for 25 minutes. Serve with light corn chips. Yields 8–10 servings.

Georgia On My Menu (Georgia)

Smoked Oyster Dip

2 (6-ounce) cans smoked oysters
1 tablespoon Worcestershire
1 teaspoon Tabasco, or to taste
1 pint sour cream

Mash oysters with fork; stir in Worcestershire and Tabasco. Stir into sour cream. Mix well and let stand overnight. Serve with Fritos corn chips or Ritz Crackers.

Variation: Use 1 can oysters and 1 can smoked clams.

Sawgrass and Pines (Florida)

Hot Crabmeat Dip

1 (8-ounce) package cream
  cheese, softened
1 tablespoon milk
1 (6½-ounce) can Alaskan
  King crabmeat, well drained
2 tablespoons finely chopped
  onion

½ teaspoon cream-style
  horseradish
¼ teaspoon salt
Dash of pepper
Dash of Worcestershire
½ cup slivered almonds

Combine cream cheese and milk. Add crabmeat with onion and horseradish, salt, pepper, and Worcestershire. Blend well. Spoon into oven-proof dish, and sprinkle slivered almonds on top. Bake 15 minutes at 375°. Serve hot with sesame seed wafers.

Foresters' Favorite Foods (Georgia)

Island Crab Dip

1 (8-ounce) package cream
  cheese, softened
1 (8-ounce) container sour
  cream
¼ cup mayonnaise
1 tablespoon Worcestershire
½ teaspoon fresh lemon juice
1 teaspoon dry mustard

¼ teaspoon garlic powder
¼ teaspoon salt
⅛ teaspoon coarsely ground
  black pepper
½ cup grated Cheddar cheese
1 pound fresh lump crabmeat
2 tablespoons cream sherry
Cream or milk

Combine cream cheese, sour cream, mayonnaise, Worcestershire, lemon juice, mustard, garlic powder, salt, pepper, and Cheddar cheese in a double boiler. Slowly heat mixture, stirring while heating. When hot, add crabmeat and sherry. Add cream to reach desired consistency. Serve in a silver chafing dish with bland crackers.

Faithfully Charleston (South Carolina)

There are 882 islands (or "keys") in the Florida Keys that are large enough to be shown on maps. Florida is home to an additional 4,510 islands 10 acres or larger, second only to Alaska's total island acreage. The Florida reef tract, extending 200 miles from Key Biscayne to the Dry Tortugas, contains approximately 6,000 coral reefs.

Baked Crock of Artichoke, Brie and Lump Crab

1 leek, chopped
1 ounce minced garlic
1 Vidalia onion, diced
2 tablespoons olive oil
½ cup chopped spinach
½ cup chopped artichoke hearts
¼ cup Riesling wine
1 bunch mixed fresh tarragon, parsley, and dill, chopped
⅔ cup heavy cream
8 ounces Brie cheese, cut into cubes
1 pound fresh jumbo lump crabmeat
¼ cup Grey Poupon Dijon Mustard
2 tablespoons Tabasco sauce
Salt and pepper to taste

Preheat oven to 425°. Sauté leeks, garlic, and onion in oil in a large skillet until light brown. Add spinach and artichokes to skillet. Deglaze with wine and cook until spinach is soft. Add cream, tarragon, parsley, and dill. Bring to a slight simmer. Stir in cheese until blended. Remove from heat, and pour into a mixing bowl; cool.

In a separate bowl, combine crabmeat, mustard, and Tabasco sauce. Season with salt and pepper. Add to cheese mixture. Transfer mixture to a large casserole dish or individual ramekins. Bake 10 minutes or until slightly browned. Yields 6–8 servings.

Treasures of the Tropics (Florida)

Crab Pie

This goes far because it is so rich.

1 pound backfin crabmeat
½ bottle of capers
2 cups mayonnaise
½ cup grated sharp Cheddar cheese
Crackers

Combine crab, capers, and mayonnaise. Put in pie plate and cover with grated cheese. Bake at 350° until cheese is melted, about 10 minutes. Serve hot on crackers. Yields 15 very generous servings.

The Enlightened Gourmet (South Carolina)

Layered Crab or Shrimp Cocktail Spread

Guests gather around this . . . it's a winner.

12 ounces cream cheese, softened	Pinch garlic salt
1 tablespoon Worcestershire	6 ounces chili sauce
1 tablespoon fresh lemon juice	8 ounces fresh crabmeat or shrimp, cut up
1 tablespoon grated onion	Dried parsley flakes

Blend together cheese, Worcestershire, lemon juice, onion, and garlic salt. Spread mixture evenly in an 8-inch quiche dish or shallow serving dish. Spread chili sauce evenly over first layer. Spread crabmeat or cut up shrimp over chili sauce. Sprinkle generously with dried parsley flakes. Cover with Saran Wrap and refrigerate a minimum of 12 hours. Serve with crackers. Serves 10–12.

Cook and Deal (Florida)

Marinated Shrimp

3 pounds cooked, peeled shrimp	1 tablespoon Worcestershire
1 cup ketchup	Dash of Tabasco
1 cup vinegar	2 bell peppers, cut in rings
½ cup Wesson oil	1 onion, cut in rings
1 tablespoon sugar	1 teaspoon celery seed
Salt and pepper to taste	2 bay leaves
Several sliced carrot sticks	1 clove garlic, chopped
	2 tablespoons mustard

Place shrimp in large bowl with cover. Mix remaining ingredients and pour over shrimp; cover and marinate in refrigerator at least 24 hours.

The McClellanville Coast Cookbook (South Carolina)

Shrimp Mousse

Out of this world! Good served with crackers as an hors d'oeuvre or as a luncheon salad.

2 cups sour cream
1 pound cream cheese, softened
1 cup mayonnaise
½ cup finely minced green bell pepper
¼ cup finely minced pimento
½ cup chili sauce
1 teaspoon salt
⅛ teaspoon Tabasco
1 tablespoon Worcestershire
2 tablespoons gelatin
Juice of 2 lemons
¼ cup cold water
6 cups finely chopped cooked shrimp

Cream together sour cream, cream cheese, and mayonnaise. Add all seasonings and vegetables. Dissolve gelatin in water and lemon juice. Heat in a double boiler 5–10 minutes. Gradually fold this into cheese mixture. Add shrimp and blend very well. Pour into well-chilled (spray with nonstick product) ring mold and chill overnight.

Frederica Fare (Georgia)

Shrimp and Corn Fritters

1 pound shrimp
1 cup corn
½ cup diced onion
½ cup diced red bell pepper
½ cup chopped scallion
½ cup chopped fresh cilantro
½ cup diced fresh jalapeño peppers
1½ cups buttermilk pancake mix
½ cup all-purpose flour
1 teaspoon salt
1 teaspoon black pepper
Juice of 1 lime
1 cup beer
Oil for frying

Cook shrimp. Chill, peel, and devein. Coarsely chop shrimp. Cook corn and drain. Combine shrimp, corn, and remaining ingredients, except oil. Refrigerate for at least 60 minutes. Using a small ice cream scoop or a soup spoon, drop batter into 350° oil. Fry 2–3 minutes or until golden brown. Place fritters on a paper towel to drain. Serve hot with cocktail or mustard sauce. Yields 6–10 servings.

Calypso Café (Florida)

Teriyaki Scallops

16 (30- to 40-count) sea
  scallops
8 bacon strips
6 tablespoons teriyaki sauce

2 tablespoons pineapple juice
Pinch of granulated garlic
Dash ground ginger

Wrap each scallop tightly with half a bacon strip, and secure with a toothpick. Place in a baking pan and pour mixture of teriyaki, pineapple juice, garlic, and ginger over scallops. Bake in 350° oven for 10–12 minutes until scallops are just done and bacon is medium. Arrange scallops on dishes and pour hot sauce over. Garnish dish with fresh fruit and tomato rose. Serves 2 as an appetizer.

Recipe from The Courtyard on Grove, Merritt Island
Intracoastal Waterway Restaurant Guide & Recipe Book
(Florida)

Sesame Chicken Fingers with Honey Dip

½ cup Hellmann's mayonnaise
1 teaspoon dry mustard
1 teaspoon chopped onion
¼ cup sesame seeds

½ cup fine dry bread crumbs
2 cups thinly sliced chicken
  breast

Mix mayonnaise, dry mustard, and onion together and set aside. Mix sesame seeds and bread crumbs together and set aside. Coat chicken first with mayonnaise mixture, then crumb mixture. Place on greased baking sheet and bake 12 minutes at 425°. Serve hot with Honey Dip.

HONEY DIP:

1 cup mayonnaise

2 tablespoons honey

Mix mayonnaise and honey.

Note: Use half the recipe if only a few people.

Cooking in Paradise (Florida)

Gingerbread House Boursin

2 (8-ounce) packages cream
  cheese, softened
¼ cup butter, softened
¼ cup sour cream
2 tablespoons chopped chives

1 tablespoon chopped parsley
1 clove garlic, chopped
Salt and freshly ground black
  pepper to taste

Mix cream cheese and butter together until smooth in food processor; add sour cream and pulse a few seconds to blend. Add remaining ingredients and stir to mix. Use as a spread on crackers or as stuffing for celery or cherry tomatoes. Mixture may also be put in a decorative mold, chilled 4–5 hours, and served with crackers. Makes 2 cups.

The Gingerbread House Cookbook (Georgia)

The Gingerbread House in Savannah, Georgia, is considered one of the most outstanding examples of Steamboat Gothic gingerbread carpentry in the United States. When the home was built by the Asendorf family in 1899, people soon began calling it the Gingerbread House, because of the elaborate gingerbread arches and spindles adorning the front porches and side balcony of the house. Today, "Savannah's most photographed house" is a favorite site for weddings, receptions, parties, corporate functions, tour group dinners, and other events.

Luscious Pimento Cheese

Great for sandwiches or on crackers!

1½ pounds extra sharp white Cheddar cheese, grated
1 (10-ounce) jar stuffed green olives, drained, chopped
1 (12-ounce) jar roasted red peppers, drained, chopped
½ cup freshly grated Parmesan cheese
½ cup mayonnaise
2 tablespoons chopped parsley
½ teaspoon freshly ground black pepper
¼ teaspoon cayenne pepper
1 tablespoon minced onion
½ cup sliced almonds, toasted

Combine all ingredients. Refrigerate several hours before serving.

Faithfully Charleston (South Carolina)

Plains Cheese Ring

Former First Lady Rosalyn Carter is given credit for making this addictive spread popular. It's said that it was one of Jimmy's favorites and was always on the Carter family's holiday table. It can be served with a meal, but also makes a great addition to an appetizer table. You will be pleasantly surprised at the way the unlikely ingredients interact.

1 pound sharp Cheddar cheese, grated, then allow to soften
1 cup chopped pecans
1 cup mayonnaise
1 small onion, grated
Black pepper to taste
Dash of cayenne
Strawberry preserves

Combine all ingredients except preserves. (A food processor works well and eliminates the need to chop ingredients.) Place in ring mold, greased with a little mayonnaise. Chill. When ready to serve, un-mold. Fill center with preserves. Serve with buttery crackers. Serves 8–12.

Savannah Collection (Georgia)

WWW. WIKIPEDIA.COM

Jimmy Carter was born October 1, 1924, in Plains, Georgia. In 1975, when Jimmy Carter began his race for the presidency, the rural town of Plains had a population of only 653. Many Americans marveled at how a man from such a small-town upbringing came to broaden his horizons to eventually become the 39th president of the United States (1977–1981). In 2002, Carter won the Nobel Peace Prize for his efforts to find peaceful solutions to international conflicts, to advance democracy and human rights, and to promote economic and social development.

Firecracker Chile Cheese Pie

Light up your taste buds with this festive appetizer.

1 cup crushed tortilla chips
3 tablespoons melted butter
16 ounces cream cheese,
  softened
2 eggs
1 (4-ounce) can chopped green
  chiles
2 fresh jalapeños, minced

4 ounces shredded Colby cheese
4 ounces shredded Monterey
  Jack cheese
¼ cup sour cream
Chopped green onions, chopped
  tomatoes, and sliced black
  olives for garnish

Mix crushed tortilla chips and melted butter in a bowl. Press over bottom of a 9-inch springform pan. Bake at 325° for 15 minutes.

Beat cream cheese and eggs in a mixing bowl. Mix in green chiles, jalapeños, Colby cheese, and Monterey Jack cheese. Pour over baked layer. Bake at 325° for exactly 30 minutes. Cool for 5 minutes.

Place on a serving plate. Loosen side of pan with a knife and remove. Spread sour cream over pie. Garnish with green onions, tomatoes, and olives. Serve with additional chips. Serves 8–10.

Savor the Moment (Florida)

Spinach Cheese Squares

4 tablespoons butter
3 eggs
1 cup all-purpose flour
1 cup milk
1 teaspoon salt
1 teaspoon baking powder

1 pound Monterey Jack cheese
  or any other mild white
  cheese, grated
2 (10-ounce) packages frozen
  chopped spinach, thawed,
  drained

Preheat oven too 350°. In a 9x13 inch baking pan melt butter in oven. Remove from oven. In a large mixing bowl, beat eggs, then add flour, milk, salt, and baking powder. Mix ingredients well. Add cheese and spinach. Pour all ingredients into baking pan and bake for 35 minutes. Remove from oven, cool 45 minutes in order to set. Cut into bite-size squares.

To freeze: Place squares on a cookie sheet and allow to freeze, then transfer into plastic bags. Before serving, remove from bags, place on cookie sheet, and heat in oven at 325° for 12 minutes. Yields 25 appetizers.

Palm Beach Entertains (Florida)

Hot Artichoke Cheese

1 (8½-ounce) can artichokes, drained, cut in bite-size pieces

1 cup grated Parmesan cheese
1 cup Hellmann's mayonnaise

Mix ingredients together and bake in flat baking dish 20 minutes at 350°, until brown on top. Serve hot on crackers. Triple for large casserole.

Note: Hellmann's mayonnaise is a must; it does not make the casserole greasy.

Carolina Cuisine Encore! (South Carolina)

Aunt Margaret's Blue Cheese Pull Aparts

Everyone loves these, especially men.

1 (12-ounce) package refrigerator biscuits
½ cup butter or margarine, melted

1 (4-ounce) package crumbled blue cheese

Cut each biscuit into quarters; place in quiche dish. Combine butter and blue cheese; mix well and spoon over biscuits. Bake at 350° for 20 minutes. Serve with cocktail forks to pull apart. Yields 40 bite-size pieces.

'Pon Top Edisto (South Carolina)

Bacon and Tomato Tarts

3 tomatoes, chopped and drained
1 pound bacon, cooked crisp and crumbled
1 cup mayonnaise
1 tablespoon Italian seasoning

1½ cups shredded Swiss cheese
1 Vidalia onion, chopped
2 (15-count) packages miniature phyllo shells

Mix tomatoes, bacon, mayonnaise, seasoning, cheese, and onion in a bowl. Spoon into phyllo shells. Arrange on a baking sheet. Bake at 350° for 15 minutes or until golden brown. Serves 30.

Par 3: Tea-Time at the Masters® (Georgia)

Sandpipers Onion Tart

SHELL:

1 cup flour
½ cup butter, melted

1 cup grated sharp Cheddar
cheese

Preheat oven to 350°. Mix Shell ingredients to form a soft dough and press into pie plate or quiche pan.

FILLING:

3 large or 4 medium onions,
chopped
¼ cup butter
¼ cup flour
1 cup milk, divided

1 egg, beaten
¼ cup grated sharp Cheddar
cheese
Dashes sea salt, pepper, and
paprika

In a nonstick skillet, sauté onions in butter till translucent; sprinkle with flour to give a coated look. Add a little milk to the beaten egg, then the remaining milk to the onions. Slowly cook to make a white sauce; stir often.

Add egg and milk mixture to onions and cook for 1 minute on low heat. Add cheese, salt, and pepper, and mix well. Remove from heat and pour into prepared pie shell. Sprinkle with paprika, bake for 30 minutes. Serve warm. Serves 4–6.

Variation: Add a topping of ½ cup chopped broccoli or cauliflower florets just before baking.

The Cruising K.I.S.S. Cookbook II (Florida)

Vidalia Sweet Onion Appetizer

1 cup finely chopped Vidalia
sweet onions

1 cup shredded Swiss cheese
1 cup mayonnaise

Mix all ingredients together and pour into pie plate. Bake 20–30 minutes at 375°–400° until brown and bubbly on top. Remove from oven and serve with your favorite crackers or bread thins.

Note: This recipe can be halved or doubled. Just keep the proportions equal.

Vidalia Sweet Onion Lovers Cookbook (Georgia)

Fried Pickles

1 cup all-purpose flour
¼ teaspoon salt
Black pepper to taste
1 egg

¼ cup milk
1½ cups sliced dill pickles,
   drained

Mix flour, salt, and pepper in a bowl. Lightly whip egg and milk in a separate bowl. Heat oil (about 2 inches) to 325°. Dip pickle slices first into flour mixture, then egg mixture, and finally back into flour. Carefully place pickles into hot oil. Do not overcrowd. Fry until golden brown, about 8 minutes, turning once. Drain on paper towels. Serve warm with ranch dressing.

Best Kept Secrets (South Carolina)

Pickled Okra

1 or 2 small hot red peppers*
1 cup vinegar
1 cup water

1 clove garlic, cut in two
1 pound small okra
Salt

Combine all ingredients except okra in saucepan and bring to a boil. Wash okra. Don't cut below the stem line, as they get slippery. Drop about a quarter of the okra at a time in the hot liquid and blanch 4–5 minutes. Remove and blanch next portion. Pack blanched okra, standing up, in 2 sterile pint jars. Put 1½ teaspoons salt in each jar on top of okra.

Bring liquid back to a boil and pour over okra. Be sure ½ clove of garlic gets in each jar. Seal jars. Let age several days. Yields 2 pints.

*Use peppers about the size of a small cherry tomato; otherwise use a 1-inch piece of a long skinny hot pepper. These peppers are HOT, so adjust to your own personal taste. (Dispose of some seeds.)

Cypress Gardens Cookbook (Florida)

The nation's original celebration of okra began in Irmo, South Carolina, in 1973 with the annual Okra Strut Festival, a two-day event featuring okra-eating and okra-growing contests, a street dance, parade, arts and crafts, rides and amusements, and more.

Bollin Party Sandwiches

1 (8-ounce) package cream
  cheese, softened
1 (4-ounce) can pitted, sliced
  black olives, drained
6 or 7 slices crisp bacon,
  crumbled
1 cup finely chopped toasted
  pecans
1 cup chopped fresh parsley
1 small onion, grated
2 teaspoons lemon juice
Salt and pepper to taste
Mayonnaise for desired
  consistency
Sandwich bread

Combine all ingredients, except bread; mix well. Spread filling generously on bread to make sandwiches. Trim crusts and cut into triangles. Yields 7 dozen small sandwiches.

Putting on the Grits (South Carolina)

Carolina Sunshine Sandwiches

CHEESE FILLING:

1 cup shredded sharp Cheddar
  cheese
1–2 ounces crumbled blue
  cheese
¼ cup chopped toasted pecans
¼ cup mayonnaise (more, if
  needed)
Dash of Tabasco

Mix all ingredients together. Add more mayonnaise, if needed, to make desired spreading consistency.

PEACH FILLING:

2 ounces cream cheese,
  softened
¼ cup peach preserves

Mix cream cheese and preserves until well blended.

12–16 slices white bread   6–8 slices wheat bread

Remove crust from bread. Spread 2–3 teaspoons Cheese Filling on white bread. Place a piece of wheat bread on top; spread with 1–2 teaspoons Peach Filling. Top with white bread. Complete other sandwiches. Cut each sandwich into 4 triangles. Makes about 6–8 whole sandwiches.

Culinary Memories of Merridun, Volume 2 (South Carolina)

Cheese Planks

4 slices bacon, fried crisp,
  drained
4 ounces shredded Cheddar
  cheese
1 small onion, chopped
1 (2½-ounce) package slivered
  almonds
½ cup mayonnaise
1 teaspoon Worcestershire
Salt and pepper to taste
18 or more slices thin sliced
  white bread

Put bacon, cheese, onion, and almonds in food processor and chop until fine. Remove from processor and mix with mayonnaise, Worcestershire, salt and pepper. Trim crust from bread slices and spread with cheese mixture. Slice each piece of bread into 4 strips. Place on baking pan and bake at 350° for 15 minutes or until crisp. Yields 24 servings.

Prescriptions for Good Eating (South Carolina)

Cheese Caraway Nips

These keep well in a tin for drop-in company.

1 cup sifted all-purpose flour
2 teaspoons dry mustard
  (or more to taste)
1 teaspoon salt
¾ cup grated sharp Cheddar
  cheese
2 teaspoons caraway seeds
⅓ cup shortening
4 tablespoons water

Preheat oven to 450°. Combine flour, mustard, salt, cheese, and caraway seeds. Mix in shortening. Sprinkle with water. Form into 2 balls. Sprinkle with additional flour and refrigerate until firm. Roll out as thinly as possible. Work quickly to keep dough cold. Cut into strips and place on ungreased cookie sheet. Bake 7–9 minutes. Yields 4 dozen.

Temptations (Georgia)

Cosmopolitan Cheddar Crisps

½ cup grated Parmesan
  cheese
1 pound extra sharp Cheddar
  cheese, shredded
1 stick salted butter, softened

½ teaspoon cayenne pepper
½ teaspoon water (optional)
2 cups flour
Kosher salt

Combine Parmesan cheese, Cheddar cheese, butter, and cayenne in mixing bowl; mix well. Add ½ teaspoonful of water, if needed, to moisten (some cheeses are wetter than others). Add flour, mixing until mixture forms a ball. Roll or press out by hand on a lightly floured surface. Cut into strips and place on a baking sheet. Bake at 350° for 15–20 minutes or until the edges begin to brown. Press in kosher salt crystals while hot.

These will last a week when stored in glass or metal—less in plastic.

Some Assembly Required (Georgia)

Sugared Nuts

2 cups pecan halves
1 cup sugar
5 tablespoons water

1 teaspoon cinnamon
½ teaspoon salt
1 teaspoon vanilla

Toast nuts at 350° about 8 minutes. Cook other ingredients, except vanilla, until soft-ball stage (234°). Remove from heat and add vanilla. Add nuts and stir until sugar coats nuts and becomes sugary. The nuts will have a frosty appearance. Lift out and place on rack to cool. Separate.

Southern Cooking (South Carolina)

Munchies

An easy gift.

6 cups popped popcorn
1 (6-ounce) bag corn chips
2 cups bite-size pretzels
1 (3-ounce) can Chinese
 noodles

1 stick margarine
2 teaspoons Worcestershire
¼ teaspoon Tabasco
⅛ teaspoon garlic powder

Combine popcorn, chips, pretzels, and noodles. Melt margarine; stir in sauces and garlic. Pour over popcorn; toss to coat. Bake at 250° for 1 hour. Stir every 15 minutes. Cool and store in airtight containers. Yields 12 cups.

Best of the Holidays (Georgia)

White Trash

1 (12-ounce) box Golden
 Graham cereal
1 (12-ounce) box raisins
3 cups roasted peanuts, or
 1 (24-ounce) jar peanuts
2 cups peanut butter

1 (12-ounce) package semisweet
 chocolate morsels
1 stick butter
1 (16-ounce) box confectioners'
 sugar

Mix cereal, raisins, and peanuts in large container. Over low heat, melt peanut butter, chocolate morsels, and butter; stir well. Let cool and pour over cereal mixture; mix well. After cooling, place mixture in large paper bag. Pour in box of confectioners' sugar and shake until mixture is coated. Keep in airtight container. Great snack for a crowd, especially teenagers.

Note: This makes a large amount and it is easier to handle if you divide it into two batches when you do the shaking.

Southern Manna (Georgia)

BREAD and BREAKFAST

PHOTO © GEORGIA DEPARTMENT OF ECONOMIC DEVELOPMENT.

A relaxing view of moss-draped magnolias from an inviting front porch is just one of the amenities at Sutlive House Bed and Breakfast, which was built in 1820. Guests enjoy true southern elegance and hospitality in this charming historic home located in Fort Gaines, Georgia.

Seasoned Pull-Apart Rolls

1 tablespoon Morton Nature's
   Seasons Seasoning Blend
1 tablespoon dried, crushed
   oregano
1 tablespoon dried basil

1 (36-count) bag frozen dinner
   rolls, thawed, but still cold
¼ cup butter, melted
¼ cup grated Parmesan cheese

Mix together seasoning blend, oregano, and basil. Arrange 12 rolls in bottom of 10-inch tube pan coated with nonstick cooking spray. Brush rolls with butter and sprinkle with ⅓ herb blend and cheese. Repeat layers of rolls, butter, herbs, and cheese twice. Cover with plastic wrap and allow to rise until nearly doubled in size. Bake at 375° for 35 minutes. Cover with foil during the last 15 minutes of baking.

Cooking Carley Style (South Carolina)

Southern Popovers

1½ cups all-purpose flour
1½ cups milk

3 eggs, slightly beaten
½ teaspoon salt

Combine all ingredients in blender and blend until smooth. Place well-buttered muffin tins in oven at 450° for 3 minutes, or until a drop of water sizzles when dropped in them. Remove tins from oven; fill ⅔ full with batter. Bake at 450° for 30 minutes; reduce heat to 300° and bake an additional 10–15 minutes. Serve immediately. Yields 1 dozen.

A Taste of South Carolina (South Carolina)

Dr. John Gorrie of Apalachicola, Florida, invented a machine that produced ice. This machine lay the groundwork for modern refrigeration and air-conditioning. On May 6, 1851, he was granted Patent No. 8080. The original model of his machine and the scientific articles he wrote are now at the Smithsonian Institution.

Onion Herb Bread

Absolutely delicious!

1 package dry yeast
¼ cup warm water
1 cup cottage cheese, heated
  to lukewarm
2 tablespoons sugar
1 tablespoon dry onion
2 teaspoons dill seeds
1 tablespoon butter, softened

¼ teaspoon baking soda
1 teaspoon salt
1 egg
2¼–2½ cups all-purpose
  flour, sifted
½ cup butter, melted
1½ teaspoons celery seeds

Preheat oven to 350°. Dissolve yeast in warm water. In large bowl, combine cottage cheese, sugar, onion, dill seeds, butter, soda, salt, and egg. Add yeast. Gradually add flour, enough to make a stiff dough. Mix well. Cover and let rise until double. Punch down. Turn dough into greased 9x5-inch loaf pan. Let rise until double. Bake 40–50 minutes. When bread is removed from oven, pour mixture of melted butter and celery seeds over top. Yields 1 loaf.

Fare by the Sea (Florida)

Cheese Biscuits

1 cup all-purpose flour
½ cup margarine, softened
⅛ teaspoon salt

2 cups grated sharp Cheddar
  cheese

In large bowl, combine flour, margarine, and salt. Add cheese, and roll into balls. Place balls on ungreased baking sheet. Bake at 350° for 10 minutes. Makes 3 dozen.

Recipe submitted by The Bed & Breakfast of Sumter
Palmetto Hospitality Inn Style (South Carolina)

Cream Cheese Biscuits

1 (3-ounce) package cream
cheese, softened
1 stick butter, softened

1 cup all-purpose flour
½ teaspoon salt

Mix all ingredients and roll out to ¼-inch or less thickness. Cut with small cookie cutter. Place on ungreased baking sheet and bake at 350° for 20 minutes or 400° for 10 minutes. Makes about 40 small biscuits.

Flavored with Tradition (South Carolina)

Sweet Potato Biscuits

The next time you prepare sweet potatoes, fix a little extra so you can make these moist, delicious biscuits.

2 cups all-purpose flour
2 teaspoons baking powder
1 teaspoon salt
¾ cup mashed, cooked
sweet potatoes

½ cup margarine, melted
2 tablespoons brown sugar
½ teaspoon baking soda
¾ cup buttermilk

Sift together flour, baking powder, and salt. Combine mashed sweet potatoes, margarine, and sugar in a small bowl. Beat together with a wire whisk. Stir baking soda into the buttermilk. Combine all ingredients, and stir to form a soft dough. If the dough is too sticky, add a little more flour. Place on a floured surface and knead dough for a few minutes. Roll dough ½ inch thick, and cut with a floured biscuit cutter. Bake at 400° for 20 minutes or until lightly browned. Butter and serve hot with jelly. Makes 10 biscuits.

Southern Bread Winners (Georgia)

The Constitution of the Confederate States of America was the supreme law of the Confederate States of America. It was adopted on March 11, 1861, and in effect through the conclusion of the American Civil War. The original, hand-written document is currently located in the University of Georgia archives in Athens, Georgia. It is on display annually on April 26th, Confederate Memorial Day.

Kitty's Biscuits

2 cups sifted self-rising flour
1 tablespoon sugar
½ cup plus 1 rounded
  tablespoon Crisco
¾ cup very cold milk
  (buttermilk may be
  substituted, adding ⅛
  teaspoon baking soda)

Sift flour and sugar into bowl and work Crisco into flour using hand. Pour milk into mixture, enough to make a soft dough. Handle lightly, using upward motions instead of pressing down. Toss onto floured board and lightly roll out with floured rolling pin to about ½ inch in thickness, for fluffy biscuits, ¼ inch for crusty biscuits. Cut out with a small biscuit cutter. Dip cutter in flour often for easy cutting. Place on greased cookie sheet and bake on top rack in preheated 450° oven 5–7 minutes until golden brown.

To freeze, place pan of unbaked biscuits in freezer until firm, then package in plastic bags. They will keep as long as two weeks. Take out as many as needed and place on greased tin pan and thaw. Follow same baking instructions. Makes approximately 2½ dozen.

Gator Country Cooks (Florida)

Cornmeal Supper Biscuits

1½ cups self-rising flour
½ cup self-rising cornmeal
  mix
1 teaspoon sugar
⅓ cup shortening
¾ cup plus 2 tablespoons
  buttermilk

Heat oven to 450°. Lightly grease a cookie sheet. In medium bowl, combine flour, cornmeal mix, and sugar; mix well. With pastry blender or fork, cut in shortening until mixture resembles coarse crumbs. Add buttermilk, stir with fork until soft dough forms and begins to pull away from sides of bowl. On lightly floured surface, knead dough just until smooth. Roll out dough to ½-inch thickness. Cut with floured 2-inch round cutter. Place on greased cookie sheet. Bake at 450° for 10–12 minutes or until golden brown. Serve warm.

Georgia National Fair Blue Ribbon Cookbook (Georgia)

Sweet Onion Cornbread

2 cups self-rising cornmeal
1 tablespoon sugar
1 teaspoon baking powder
2 cups milk
1 egg

4 tablespoons vegetable oil, divided
2 cups finely chopped sweet onions

Preheat oven to 350°. In a large mixing bowl, combine the cornmeal, sugar, and baking powder. Add the milk, egg, and 2 tablespoons of oil, mixing well (the batter will be quite thin). Stir in the onions and mix well. Grease a 10-inch iron skillet with the remaining oil, pour in the batter, and bake for 30–35 minutes or until light brown. Let cool 10 minutes before serving. Makes 8 servings.

Breads and Spreads (Georgia)

Cornbread Dressing with Sausage and Giblets

¼ pound pork sausage, browned and crumbled
1 package cornbread mix, prepared according to directions
1 large onion, chopped
1 rib celery, chopped

1½ ounces turkey giblets
½ onion, whole
½ rib celery, whole
¾ cup water
½ cup milk
2 large eggs, slightly beaten
7½ ounces chicken broth

Preheat oven to 350°. Butter a 9x13-inch baking dish. Brown sausage in a heavy skillet. Remove sausage from pan and crumble into a large bowl. Discard the fat from skillet but do not wipe out pan. Crumble cornbread and add to sausage. In same pan, sauté chopped onion and chopped celery until onion is transparent. Add to sausage mixture in large bowl.

Simmer the turkey giblets, ½ onion, and ½ rib celery in water. Cover and cook until tender, about 20 minutes. Discard onion and celery. Remove giblets, chop, and add to sausage and vegetables. Add giblet water. Stir in milk and eggs until well blended. Add chicken broth and stir until evenly moist. Pour into baking dish. Bake approximately 45 minutes until dressing is set and browned.

Bread of Life–Chef Curtis Watkins (Georgia)

Eva's Hush Puppies

2 cups self-rising meal
1 cup self-rising flour
2 small onions, diced
1 small bell pepper, diced
3 eggs

1 (16-ounce) can whole-kernel
  yellow corn
1 tablespoon sugar
2½ tablespoons vegetable oil

Mix meal, flour, onions, and bell pepper in a large mixing bowl, then add corn, eggs, sugar, and oil. The batter should be fairly stiff, not soupy like cornbread. Drop by tablespoonful into hot, deep oil. As it cooks and browns on one side, it will flip over and brown on the other side. Check with a fork on the first 2 or 3 to time the amount of time needed for each batch.

Feeding the Flock (Florida)

Squashpuppies

Squash
1–2 eggs, depending on
  amount of squash
1 onion, chopped

Cornmeal/flour mixture
Salt and pepper or other
  seasonings

Cook as many squash as you desire. Add eggs and chopped onion to mixture, then add enough cornmeal/flour mixture to thicken the squash. Season to taste. Cook in deep hot oil as you would hushpuppies. These will not be as round as hushpuppies, but make a delicious dish to eat with fish or anything.

Southeastern Wildlife Cookbook (South Carolina)

Augusta's Best Strawberry Bread

3 cups all-purpose flour
2 cups sugar
1 teaspoon baking soda
1 teaspoon salt
1 teaspoon cinnamon

4 eggs, beaten
1¼ cups vegetable oil
2 (10-ounce) packages frozen
　strawberries, thawed, chopped
1 cup chopped pecans

Sift flour, sugar, baking soda, salt, and cinnamon into large mixing bowl. Make well in center. Combine eggs, oil, strawberries, and pecans. Add to sifted ingredients, stirring until well combined. Spoon batter into 2 greased and floured 9x5-inch loaf pans. Bake at 350° for 1 hour. Cool bread in pans 10 minutes. Remove bread from pans. Cool completely on wire racks. Yields 2 loaves.

Second Round, Tea Time at the Masters® (Georgia)

Lemon Tea Bread with Blueberries

¼ cup plus 2 tablespoons
　butter or margarine, softened
1 cup sugar
2 eggs
1½ cups all-purpose flour
1 teaspoon baking powder

Pinch of salt
½ cup milk
1 heaping tablespoon grated
　lemon rind
1 cup blueberries (fresh or
　frozen)

Cream butter. Add sugar until well blended, then add eggs. Begin adding flour, baking powder, and salt. Add some milk, then rest of flour. Stir in lemon rind and blueberries. Bake in greased loaf pan for 55 minutes at 350°.

GLAZE:

⅓ cup sugar
3 tablespoons lemon juice

2 teaspoons grated lemon rind

Combine sugar, lemon juice, and lemon rind in saucepan, and heat until sugar dissolves. (Works well in microwave also). Punch holes in top of baked loaf and pour mixture over warm bread. Makes 1 loaf, but it is so good you might as well go ahead and make 2 and freeze one.

One Course at a Time (South Carolina)

Sunshine Muffins

Laden with fruit and nuts, these muffins will bring a touch of tropical sunshine to any brunch or breakfast, and really don't need any additional spread.

½ cup milk
¼ cup vegetable oil
2 eggs
½ cup raisins
1½ cups rolled oats
2 cups baking mix
½ cup sugar

½ cup packed brown sugar
1 teaspoon cinnamon
½ cup shredded carrot
1 cup shredded apple
1 (12-ounce) can crushed
   pineapple, drained
¼ cup chopped walnuts

Combine milk, oil, and eggs in a medium bowl, and beat lightly. Stir in raisins and oats. Let stand for several minutes. Add baking mix, sugar, brown sugar, cinnamon, carrot, apple, pineapple, and walnuts, and mix just until moistened. Spoon into greased muffin cups, filling ½ full. Bake at 400° for 20 minutes or until golden brown. Serves 12.

Tropical Settings (Florida)

Peach Muffins

Perfect for ripe Georgia peaches; a summertime treat.

⅓ cup butter, softened
1 cup sugar, divided
1 egg
1½ cups all-purpose flour
1½ teaspoons baking powder
½ teaspoon salt

¼ teaspoon ground nutmeg
½ cup milk
½ cup chopped peaches
1 teaspoon ground cinnamon
½ cup butter, melted

Preheat oven to 350°. Cream butter and ½ cup sugar. Add egg; mix. Combine flour, baking powder, salt, and nutmeg; stir flour mixture into butter mixture alternately with milk. Stir in peaches. Fill greased muffin cups ⅔ full. Bake 20–25 minutes. Mix remaining ½ cup sugar with cinnamon. When muffins are done, immediately dip tops into melted butter, then into cinnamon-sugar mixture.

Peachtree Bouquet (Georgia)

Bran Muffins

We place Bran Muffins at the top of the list. They are so good for us and yet easy to make.

1 egg	1 teaspoon baking soda
2 tablespoons safflower oil	¼ teaspoon sea salt
2 tablespoons honey	1 cup bran
2 tablespoons molasses	¾ cup whole-wheat flour
¾ cup yogurt	¼ cup water

Mix first 5 ingredients together. Add remaining ingredients; mix well. Butter and flour a muffin tin or use paper muffin holders. Bake 30 minutes at 350°. Cool before serving.

Variations: Add ½ cup raisins or sunflower seeds: Bake in 8x10-inch glass pan, cut into squares: Add 1 cup mashed ripe banana; Add 1 cup fresh or frozen blueberries: Add 1 cup finely chopped apples: Add ¼ teaspoon nutmeg, ½ teaspoon cinnamon, and ½ cup chopped apples.

Step-by-Step to Natural Food (Florida)

Baby Broccoli Muffins

1 (10-ounce) package frozen chopped broccoli	4 eggs, beaten
1 (7½-ounce) box corn muffin mix	1 stick margarine, melted
	¾ cup cottage cheese
	1 large onion, chopped

Preheat oven to 425°. Grease miniature muffin tins. Cook broccoli according to package directions. Drain well. Mix corn muffin mix, eggs, melted margarine, cottage cheese, onion, and drained broccoli until blended. Put in miniature muffin tins and bake 10–12 minutes. Yields about 5–6 dozen muffins.

Bear Flair: Dollop with sour cream and tiny fresh broccoli florets. Marvelous! These freeze very nicely.

Unbearably Good! (Georgia)

Florida Blueberry Streusel Coffee Cake

Florida's blueberries are the first to ripen in North America and are large and flavorfully sweet. Blueberries contain vitamins A and C, are a good source of fiber, iron, and potassium, and are high in antioxidants.

TOPPING:

½ cup packed brown sugar

3 tablespoons flour

2 teaspoons cinnamon

2 tablespoons butter, softened

¾ cup chopped walnuts

In a small bowl, combine all ingredients for Topping, except nuts, and stir until mixture resembles fine crumbs. Stir in the nuts, and set aside.

BATTER:

½ cup butter, softened

1 cup sugar

2 teaspoons grated lemon rind

3 eggs

2 cups flour

1 teaspoon baking powder

1 teaspoon baking soda

½ teaspoon salt

1 cup sour cream

2 cups blueberries

In a large mixing bowl, cream butter until fluffy; add sugar and grated lemon rind, and beat well. Add eggs, one at a time, beating well after each addition. In a bowl, combine dry ingredients. Add flour mixture to the creamed mixture alternately with sour cream, blending well after each addition. Spread batter into a greased 9x13-inch baking pan. Sprinkle blueberries and then topping over the batter. Bake at 350° for 30–35 minutes. Serve warm.

Florida Cook Book (Florida)

Eggnog Custard French Toast

2 eggs
1 egg white
2 cups low-fat eggnog
3 teaspoons rum extract

½ teaspoon nutmeg, divided
16 (1-inch-thick) slices French
 bread
2 tablespoons powdered sugar

In medium bowl, combine eggs and egg white. Beat until well combined. Add eggnog, rum extract, and ¼ teaspoon nutmeg. Mix well. Dip bread slices into eggnog mixture, coating both sides. Place in 2 (9x13-inch) ungreased baking dishes in a single layer. Pour remaining eggnog over bread slices. Cover and refrigerate overnight.

When ready to serve, preheat oven to 425°. Spray cookie sheet with nonstick cooking spray. Place bread on cookie sheet. Bake 12–15 minutes or until golden, turning once during baking. To serve, sprinkle French toast with powdered sugar and remaining nutmeg. Spoon Berry Sauce on top. Serves 8.

BERRY SAUCE:
1 cup frozen raspberry blend
 juice concentrate, thawed

1 cup jellied cranberry sauce
3 tablespoons sugar

Combine frozen concentrate, cranberry sauce, and sugar over low heat. Heat until sugar is melted. Serve over French toast.

Gracious Goodness: Christmas in Charleston (South Carolina)

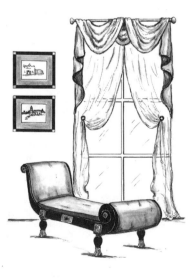

Overnight French Toast

This is a terrific breakfast recipe when you have house guests. Combine ingredients in the evening and bake the next morning.

1 loaf French bread	1½ teaspoons ground
8 eggs, beaten	cinnamon
2 cups milk	⅛ teaspoon salt
1 teaspoon vanilla	

Slice French bread into 16 pieces, discard ends. Beat remaining ingredients until frothy. Place bread slices in 2 (9x13-inch) pans. Pour egg mixture over bread. Turn slices over to coat evenly on both sides. Cover pans with foil or plastic wrap and refrigerate overnight. Next morning place bread on lightly greased cookie sheet and bake in preheated 450° oven 5 minutes or until golden, turning once. Serve hot with honey or syrup. Serves 8.

Encore (Georgia)

Popover Pancake

It's fun to watch it pop and it's mighty good, too!

½ cup all-purpose flour	2 tablespoons confectioners'
½ cup milk	sugar
2 eggs, slightly beaten	Juice of ½ lemon
¼ cup butter	

Preheat oven to 425°. In mixing bowl combine flour, milk, and eggs. Beat lightly. The batter will be slightly lumpy. Put butter into a 12-inch round frying pan with heat-proof handle. Place in oven until very hot. Pour in batter, return to oven, and bake 20 minutes or until pancake is puffed all around sides of pan and golden brown. Remove from oven and sprinkle with confectioners' sugar and lemon juice. Serve immediately. Serves 2 or 3.

Cook and Deal (Florida)

Cheese-Whiz Grits

2 cups milk
2 cups water
½ teaspoon salt
1 cup quick cooking grits
1 stick butter or margarine

½ cup half-and-half
1 (5-ounce) container Cheese
   Whiz
Garlic powder to taste (optional)

Bring combined water and milk to a boil, and add salt and grits, stirring constantly with a wire whisk. Lower heat to medium-low and cover loosely. Watch mixture carefully as it thickens quickly. Stir occasionally with whisk to prevent lumps. Lower heat to low and continue cooking. When mixture is very thick, remove from heat, and stir in butter, half-and-half, Cheese Whiz, and garlic powder. Combine well and return to low heat (simmer), or place in preheated pan of water over low heat. Continue heating until piping hot. Careful not to scorch bottom. Serve with pat of butter or sprinkle with black pepper. Serves 10.

Cooking with Class (Florida)

Crustless Ham and Grits Pie

⅓ cup quick-cooking grits
1 cup water
1 cup evaporated milk
¾ cup shredded Cheddar
   cheese
¾ cup chopped cooked
   lean ham

3 eggs, beaten
1 tablespoon chopped fresh
   parsley
½ teaspoon dry mustard
½ teaspoon hot pepper sauce
¼ teaspoon salt

Cook grits in water using package directions, omitting the salt. Mix grits, evaporated milk, cheese, ham, eggs, and seasonings in a bowl. Spoon into a greased 9-inch pie plate. Bake at 350° for 35 minutes. Let stand 10 minutes before serving. Serves 6.

True Grits (Georgia)

Roasted Garlic Grits "Fries"

2 cups chicken broth
½ cup heavy cream
½ stick unsalted butter
1 tablespoon roasted or
 minced garlic
½ cup stone-ground grits
Salt and pepper to taste
2 tablespoons grated Parmesan
 cheese

3 eggs, plus ¼ cup water
1 cup all-purpose flour,
 seasoned with salt and pepper
2 cups panko (Japanese) bread
 crumbs
Canola oil for deep-frying

Bring first 4 ingredients to a boil. Whisk in grits, turn down heat to low, and simmer approximately 45 minutes, stirring every few minutes. Taste, and adjust seasoning with salt and pepper; stir in Parmesan cheese. Coat a shallow 7x10-inch pan with nonstick spray, and pour grits into pan. Refrigerate and allow grits to set (at least 4 hours, but preferably overnight).

Once thoroughly chilled, dump the solid block of grits onto counter, and cut into thin sticks, about ½ x ½ x 4 inches. In a bowl, whisk eggs together with water and a pinch of salt and pepper.

Put flour in another bowl, and season lightly with salt and pepper. Place bread crumbs into a third bowl; season with salt and pepper. To bread the "fries," roll them in flour; be sure to coat each one evenly. Dip each "fry" into egg wash and then into crumbs; press crumbs onto "fries" so each is completely covered. Repeat. Store breaded "fries" in refrigerator until ready to cook. Fry in canola oil at 365° until crisp and lightly golden brown. Drain, and serve hot. Yields 4 servings.

Recipe from Bateaux Restaurant, Lady's Island
Lowcountry Delights III (South Carolina)

In 1985, the broker of a large grits company did some research, and discovered that St. George, South Carolina, eats more grits per capita than any other place in the world. They were the grits-eating champions; thus the World Grits Festival was born. The weekend-long festival is held each April. It has been estimated that the crowds during the three-day festival sometimes exceed 45,000!

Made by grinding corn or hominy into bits, grits were first produced by Native Americans many centuries ago.

Charleston Cheese Soufflé

3 cups fresh, untoasted white bread cubes

1 cup fresh or frozen chopped onion

Salt and pepper to taste

1 (12-ounce) package grated Cheddar cheese (3 cups), divided

1½ cups milk

4 eggs, beaten

1 tablespoon Worcestershire

2 tablespoons yellow mustard

3 tomatoes, thinly sliced

3 tablespoons butter, sliced

Spray an 8½x11-inch glass baking dish with baking spray (or grease with butter). Combine bread cubes, onion, salt, pepper, and 2 cups grated cheese. Spread into baking dish. Combine milk with next 3 ingredients; mix well. Pour egg mixture over ingredients in baking dish, and sprinkle with remaining cheese. Arrange tomato slices on top, and dot with sliced butter. Bake in a 325° oven for 1 hour. Yields 6 servings.

Note: An egg substitute may be used instead of eggs, and the soufflé may be prepared in advance and refrigerated overnight. Delicious served with cured ham!

Recipe from Long Point Inn, Mount Pleasant
Lowcountry Delights (South Carolina)

WWW.OCONEECOUNTRY.COM

Started in 1852 by Blue Ridge Railroad, the Stumphouse Mountain Tunnel is bored for more than a mile into the granite heart of Stumphouse Mountain. Due to the beginning of the Civil War, work to tunnel through the mountain was halted, and eventually altogether abandoned. The tunnel lay idle for nearly eighty years, until the early 1940s when, because of its cool dampness, the tunnel was successfully used by Clemson University to make blue cheese for the first time ever in the South. Stumphouse Mountain Tunnel is now used as a tourist attraction by the city of Walhalla.

Country Breakfast Pie

1 pound bulk sausage, cooked, crumbled, and drained
1½ cups grated Swiss cheese
1 (9-inch) deep-dish pie crust
4 eggs
¼ cup chopped red bell pepper
¼ cup chopped green bell pepper
2 tablespoons chopped onion
1 cup light cream
1 tomato, sliced (optional)

Preheat oven to 375°. Mix sausage and cheese and sprinkle in pie crust. Lightly beat eggs in a mixing bowl. Add bell peppers, onion, and cream to eggs. Pour mixture into pie crust. Top with tomato slices, if using. Bake 40–45 minutes. Cool on a rack 10 minutes. Serves 6–8.

First Come, First Served...In Savannah (Georgia)

Carolina Gentleman's Breakfast Casserole

Good hearty casserole—men love it! Use mild pork sausage for a tamer-flavored casserole; try hot pork sausage to pump up the flavor.

4 English muffins, halved
1 pound sausage, cooked, drained
3 eggs
1 (10¾-ounce) can cream of mushroom soup
1½ cups milk
1¼ cups shredded Swiss cheese, divided

Line a 9x13-inch baking dish with halved English muffins. Add sausage. Mix eggs, soup, and milk together with 1 cup cheese, and pour over sausage. Sprinkle with remaining ¼ cup cheese. Cover and bake in a preheated 350° oven 20 minutes or until warmed through. Serves 8.

Dining Under the Carolina Moon (South Carolina)

Pepperoni Bread

1 (16-ounce) box hot roll mix
1¼ cups hot water
2 tablespoons vegetable oil
2 teaspoons dried oregano
1 egg white, lightly beaten
½ cup grated Parmesan
  cheese

7 ounces sliced turkey
  pepperoni
½ cup shredded reduced-fat
  mozzarella cheese
½ cup shredded reduced-fat
  Cheddar cheese

Preheat oven to 375°. In a large bowl, combine roll mix and yeast packet from box. Pour in water and oil. Mix well, and knead 5 minutes. Cover dough, and let it sit in a warm place until it rises to double in size. (It'll be twice as big as it was when you started.)

Divide dough, and roll into 2 balls. Sprinkle each round with 1 teaspoon oregano. Combine egg white and Parmesan cheese in a medium-size bowl. Spread half the egg mixture on each round of dough. Top with pepperoni slices. Sprinkle with mozzarella and Cheddar cheeses.

Roll each round into a fat stick and turn under the ends. Place on an ungreased baking sheet, and put into oven. Bake until tops are light brown, about 30 minutes. Let bread cool, and cut into slices. Makes 15 servings.

I Love to Cook Book (South Carolina)

Overnight Strawberry Jam

3 cups sugar   3 cups strawberries

Add sugar to strawberries and let set overnight. Next morning, boil 20 minutes, then let mixture set all day and seal cold in jars. The berries stay whole, and jam is a nice color.

Note: Never cook more than 3 cups at a time.

Golden Isles Cuisine (Georgia)

SOUPS, CHILIS, and STEWS

PHOTO © SOUTH CAROLINA DEPARTMENT OF PARKS, RECREATION, AND TOURISM, WWW.DISCOVERSOUTHCAROLINA.COM.

One of South Carolina's most recognized natural landmarks, Table Rock Mountain was named by the Cherokees, who imagined the Great Spirit sitting on nearby Stool Mountain and dining at the "table." The scenery in Table Rock State Park is some of the best in the Upcountry, with lakes and waterfalls, trails and forests.

Broccoli-Cream Cheese Soup

1 cup chopped green onions
4 tablespoons butter
4 (8-ounce) packages cream
  cheese, cubed
4 cups half-and-half
4 cups chicken broth
6 (10-ounce) packages frozen
  chopped broccoli

2 teaspoons lemon juice
2 teaspoons salt
1 teaspoon pepper
Slivered almonds
Fresh parsley

Sauté green onions in butter in large saucepan or Dutch oven. Add cubed cheese and half-and-half to onions, and stir over low heat until cheese is melted. Stir in chicken broth; set aside. Cook broccoli according to package directions; drain. Blend half of broccoli mixture in food processor or blender until smooth. Add processed broccoli and remaining chopped broccoli to soup mixture. Stir in lemon juice and seasonings. Heat thoroughly. Toast almonds and serve with a sprig of parsley. Serves 16.

Uptown Down South (South Carolina)

Frosty Tomato Cream

Wonderful!

1 small onion, peeled, chopped
1 small cucumber, peeled,
  chopped
8 sprigs parsley
1 cup yogurt or sour cream

1 ($10\frac{3}{4}$-ounce) can tomato
  soup
1 ($10\frac{3}{4}$-ounce) can chicken
  broth

In a blender, purée onion, cucumber, and parsley. Blend in yogurt or sour cream and tomato soup. Skim fat from broth and blend broth with other ingredients. Chill. Yields approximately 6 ($\frac{2}{3}$-cup) servings.

The Enlightened Gourmet (South Carolina)

Gazpacho

A Florida favorite.

1 cucumber, peeled, cut in
  chunks
½ green bell pepper, seeded,
  cut in chunks
1 small onion, cut in chunks
2 tomatoes, peeled, cubed

½ ripe avocado, peeled, cubed
4 cups tomato juice
3 tablespoons olive oil
2 tablespoons wine vinegar
½ teaspoon oregano
Salt to taste

Using steel blade of food processor, coarsely chop cucumber. Transfer to bowl. Process green pepper and onion until finely chopped. Add to cucumber. Add tomatoes and avocado to cucumber along with remaining ingredients. Chill at least 2 hours.

Fare by the Sea (Florida)

Red Pepper Soup

Just a wonderful soup, and such a pretty color.

4 tablespoons olive oil
1 medium onion, chopped
5 red peppers, seeded and
  chopped
2 medium potatoes, diced

1 clove garlic, minced
5 cups chicken broth
1 cup evaporated milk
Chopped green onion and sour
  cream for garnish

Heat oil, then add onion, and cook until transparent. Add red peppers; cook until soft. Add potatoes, garlic, and chicken broth. Cook for 1 hour, then put in blender and mix; add milk. Serve with chopped onion and a dot of sour cream. Serves 8.

Les Soups Fantastiques (Florida)

The 327-foot former Coast Guard cutter *Duane* was intentionally sunk in 120 feet of water off Key Largo, Florida, in 1987 to create an "artificial reef." There are several artificial reefs in the Florida Keys. The sites are usually composed of bridge spans, concrete rubble, steel pipes, barges, and steel boats. Artificial reefs are an important part of the marine environment in the Keys, providing essential habitats for marine life, as well as recreational opportunities for divers and fishermen.

Quick Onion Soup

½ stick butter
3 large onions, sliced thin
3 (10-ounce) cans consommé
¼ cup red wine

1 cup grated Swiss or Parmesan
  cheese
1 cup croutons

Melt butter and sauté onions until clear. Add consommé and wine. Pour into oven casserole, sprinkle with cheese and bake in a pre-heated 350° for 30 minutes. To brown cheese, broil for a minute after cooking. Pass croutons. Serves 4.

Cooking on the Go (South Carolina)

Hoppin' John Soup

2 teaspoons oil
3 strips bacon, chopped
2 cups collard greens, cleaned,
  chopped
½ cup diced onion
¼ cup diced carrot
¼ cup diced celery
1 ham hock
¼ teaspoon minced garlic

2 quarts chicken stock*
1 cup black-eyed peas, cooked**
1 cup cooked rice
1 medium green bell pepper,
  diced
1 medium red bell pepper, diced
Salt, pepper, Tabasco, and white
  vinegar to taste

In a large 1-gallon pot, heat oil; add chopped bacon, and cook until crisp, stirring occasionally. Add collard greens, onion, carrot, celery, ham hock, and garlic. Cook until onion is translucent, then carefully add chicken stock. Bring to a boil, then simmer 1–1½ hours, or until ham hock is soft.

Remove ham hock; set aside to cool. Add black-eyed peas, rice, and green and red peppers. Season with salt, pepper, Tabasco, and white vinegar to desired flavor. Remove meat from ham hock, dice, and place into soup. Serves 6–8.

*May substitute canned broth, bouillon, or water for chicken stock.

**May substitute 1 (15-ounce) can black-eyed peas for cooked peas.

Recipe by Chef Eric Sayers, C.Q.'s, Hilton Head Island
Soups, Stews, Gumbos, Chilis, Chowders, and Bisques
(South Carolina)

White Chili Soup

On a diet? Try this!

1 medium onion, chopped
1 cup chopped green pepper
1 cup chopped red pepper
1 cup chopped celery
1 or 2 jalapeño peppers,
3 medium cloves garlic,
  chopped
4 tablespoons olive oil
1 pound ground turkey meat,
  browned
2 tablespoons cumin powder
½ cup chopped fresh basil, or
  1 tablespoon dry basil

1 tablespoon thyme
2 tablespoons chopped parsley
  chopped
3 cups cooked navy beans, or
  canned
1½ cups cooked barley
6 cups chicken broth
2 cups shredded Cheddar cheese
Chopped green onions for
  garnish

Cook the first 6 ingredients in olive oil until transparent. Add turkey and mix well. Add cumin, basil, thyme, and parsley. Mix again and add beans, barley, and chicken broth. Cook 15 minutes. Stir in cheese until thoroughly blended. Serve with chopped green onions. Serves 8.

Les Soups Fantastiques (Florida)

Hearty Tortellini Soup

2 cloves garlic, crushed
1 tablespoon margarine
2 (14½-ounce) cans chicken
  broth
1 (8-ounce) package fresh or
  frozen cheese tortellini

1 (10-ounce) package frozen,
  chopped spinach, thawed
1 (16-ounce) can stewed
  tomatoes, undrained and
  coarsely chopped
Grated Parmesan cheese

In a large saucepan over medium heat, cook garlic in margarine for 2–3 minutes. Add broth and tortellini; heat to a boil. Reduce heat and simmer for 10 minutes. Add spinach and tomatoes; simmer 5 minutes more. Serve topped with cheese. Delicious. Serves 6.

Heaven in a Pot (Florida)

Georgia Peanut Soup

1 shallot, chopped
2 stalks celery, chopped
2 teaspoons butter or
   margarine
1 tablespoon flour
1 cup chicken stock,
   divided

3 tablespoons smooth, salt-free
   peanut butter, made from
   freshly ground peanuts
½ cup low-fat milk
½ cup water
2 tablespoons crushed, salt-free
   Georgia peanuts

Sauté shallot and celery in melted butter in a medium skillet for 5 minutes. Add flour, tossing to coat well. Stir in half the chicken stock; simmer 5 minutes. Add remaining chicken stock; simmer 5 minutes longer. Strain, separating liquid from vegetables. Blend peanut butter into reserved liquid in a saucepan. Stir in milk.

Combine ¾ cup peanut butter and stock mixture with reserved vegetables in a blender or food processor; process until smooth; stir into saucepan. Cook until heated through, adding water as needed for desired consistency. Serve hot or cold, topped with crushed peanuts. Serves 4.

True Grits (Georgia)

The official state crop of Georgia is the peanut. Georgia is the number-one peanut-producing state in the country, accounting for almost half of the total U.S. peanut crop. More than 50% of the crop goes to peanut butter production. In 2005 Georgia farmers harvested 755,000 acres of peanuts for a yield of 2.2 billion pounds.

Mama Tucker Soup

This is even better the next day.

1 large or 3 small ham hocks
3 (16-ounce) cans tomatoes, mashed
1–2 stalks celery, chopped
1–2 (12-ounce) packages frozen carrots
2–3 onions, chopped fine
2 (12-ounce) packages frozen peas (optional)
2 (12-ounce) packages frozen butter beans
2 (17-ounce) cans whole-kernel corn
1–2 (12-ounce) packages frozen okra
1 bell pepper, chopped
Salt and pepper

Cook ham hocks 4–5 hours in 8–9 quarts water. Add tomatoes, celery, carrots, and onions; cook 2 hours longer. Add peas and butter beans; cook 30 minutes. Add corn and okra; cook 30 more minutes. Add bell pepper 30 minutes before serving. Season with salt and pepper to taste. Serve with crackers or cornbread.

Main Street Winder (Georgia)

After Thanksgiving Turkey-Vegetable Soup

2 tablespoons vegetable oil
1 cup diced cooked ham
1 medium onion, chopped
1 cup sliced mushrooms (optional)
1 large white potato, cubed
1 cup diced celery
1 cup sliced carrots
½ green bell pepper, diced
2 tablespoons parsley
1 bay leaf
1 roast turkey carcass, broken in pieces
4 cups hot water
1 large tomato (may use canned)
Salt and pepper to taste

Heat pressure cooker. Add oil, and lightly sauté ham, onion, and mushrooms. Add potato, celery, carrots, green pepper, parsley, bay leaf, turkey carcass, and water. Do not fill pressure cooker over ⅔ full. Put lid on and cook at high pressure 15 minutes. Let pressure drop at its own accord. Remove pieces of turkey carcass, and separate bits of meat from bone. Return meat to soup. Stir in tomato, salt and pepper. Reheat without cover. Makes 6 servings.

Ridge Recipes (South Carolina)

Cheeca Lodge's Jamaican Seafood Soup

SOUP BASE:

2 ounces apple-smoked bacon, chopped
⅓ cup diced yellow onion
½ cup diced celery
½ cup diced leek
2 tablespoons packed dark brown sugar
Pinch of cayenne pepper

1 ounce Jamaican jerk seasoning
2 cups fish broth
5 fresh plum tomatoes, diced
½ bunch fresh tarragon, chopped
Salt to taste
Croutons, sliced scallions, or yogurt for garnish

Cook bacon in a saucepan. Add onion, celery, and leek. Cook over low heat for 15 minutes or until vegetables are translucent. Add sugar and cook 3 minutes over low heat. Add cayenne pepper and jerk seasoning. Cook 1 minute. Stir in broth and tomatoes. Simmer 30 minutes. Add tarragon and salt.

SEAFOOD:

3 ounces shrimp, coarsely chopped
3 ounces snapper, dolphin, or grouper, coarsely chopped

3 ounces stone crabmeat, coarsely chopped
6 tablespoons butter

Cook shrimp, snapper, and crabmeat in butter over low heat until done. Place in soup bowls. Top with hot Soup Base. Garnish with croutons, sliced scallions, or yogurt. Yields 4 servings.

Calypso Café (Florida)

She-Crab Soup

"She-crab" is much more of a delicacy than "he-crab," as the eggs add a special flavor to the soup. The street vendors make a point of calling "she-crab" loudly and of charging extra for them.

1 tablespoon butter	Few drops onion juice
1 teaspoon flour	1/8 teaspoon mace
1 quart milk	1/8 teaspoon pepper
2 cups white crabmeat and	1/2 teaspoon Worcestershire
crab eggs	4 tablespoons dry sherry
1/2 teaspoon salt	1/4 pint cream, whipped

Melt butter in top of double boiler and blend with flour until smooth. Add milk gradually, stirring constantly. To this add crabmeat and eggs and all seasonings except sherry. Cook slowly over hot water for 20 minutes. To serve, place one tablespoon of warmed sherry in individual soup bowls, then add soup and top with whipped cream. Sprinkle with paprika or finely chopped parsley. Serves 4–6.

Secret: If unable to obtain "she-crabs," crumble yolk of hard-boiled eggs in bottom of soup plates.

Charleston Receipts (South Carolina)

Crab Island Bisque

1 pound Florida blue crabmeat	3 tablespoons all-purpose flour
2 tablespoons finely chopped	1 teaspoon salt
onion	1/4 teaspoon paprika
2 tablespoons finely chopped	1/8 teaspoon white pepper
celery	1 quart milk
1/4 cup margarine or butter,	1/4 cup chopped parsley
melted	

Remove any remaining shell or cartilage from crabmeat. Cook onion and celery in margarine until tender, but not brown. Blend in flour and seasonings. Add milk gradually, stirring constantly; cook until thickened. Add crabmeat and heat. Just before serving, sprinkle with parsley. Yields 6 servings.

Crab Island Cookbook (Florida)

Savannah Shrimp Bisque

A luscious, light and elegant beginning for any dinner.

1 tablespoon unsalted butter
1 tablespoon vegetable oil
½ cup finely chopped yellow
  onion
½ cup finely chopped celery
⅓ cup finely chopped carrot
2 tablespoons all-purpose flour
3 cups chicken broth
1 (14½-ounce) can whole
  tomatoes, drained and
  chopped
½ cup dry white wine or
  fish stock

1 bay leaf
1 teaspoon dried marjoram
⅛ teaspoon nutmeg
1 pound medium shrimp,
  peeled and deveined, cut
  into ½-inch pieces
1 cup whipping cream
½ teaspoon salt
2 tablespoons fresh lemon juice
Fresh marjoram sprigs for
  garnish

Heat butter and oil in a large saucepan over medium-high heat. Stir in onion, celery, and carrot; sauté 5 minutes, or until tender. Add flour and cook and stir until bubbly. Stir in broth, tomatoes, wine, bay leaf, marjoram, and nutmeg. Bring to a boil; reduce heat and simmer, covered, for 15 minutes. Discard bay leaf and let mixture cool.

Purée soup in batches in a food processor or blender until smooth. Return soup to saucepan. Add shrimp and cook, uncovered, over medium heat 1 minute. Blend in cream; cook 2 minutes longer, or until soup is heated through and shrimp are firm and pink. Remove from heat and season with salt and lemon juice. Garnish with marjoram sprigs. Makes 6 (1-cup) servings.

For a lighter version, use 1 cup low-fat milk and 2 tablespoons whipping cream instead of 1 cup whipping cream.

First Come, First Served...In Savannah (Georgia)

Sherman's March to the Sea is the name commonly given to the Savannah Campaign conducted in late 1864 by Major General William Tecumseh Sherman of the Union Army during the American Civil War. The campaign began with Sherman's troops leaving the captured city of Atlanta, Georgia, on November 15th, and ended with the capture of the port of Savannah on December 22nd. Savannah was spared, and Sherman gave it as a "Christmas present" to President Lincoln.

Creamy-Rich Seafood Chowder

This makes a delightful main dish with crusty French bread and tossed salad or served in mugs as an appetizer before dinner with company. Add a good cold California Chablis wine and put anchovies on top of the salad and you have a festive and almost instant company meal.

1½ pounds raw, chopped
  shrimp
1 pint chicken stock
1 pound crabmeat
½ cup heavy cream
1 quart milk

White pepper
¼–½ teaspoon thyme (to
  taste)
½ stick butter
Salt to taste

Simmer raw, chopped shrimp in chicken stock till pink. Add remainder of ingredients and heat till hot, but be very careful not to let boil, as it will curdle. Serve right away or allow to stand up to 45 minutes or an hour, but don't leave heat on. Serves 4–6.

Frederica Fare (Georgia)

Vidalia Onion Chowder

2 tablespoons oil
4 pounds or 4 medium Vidalia
  onions, chopped coarsely
1 (20-ounce) package frozen
  mashed potatoes
1 tablespoon minced garlic
2 (14-ounce) cans chicken
  broth

2 cups frozen kernel corn
2 bay leaves
¼ teaspoon dried thyme
⅛ teaspoon pepper
½ cup sour cream
4 slices bacon, cooked, crumbled
  (or bacon bits)

Heat oil in heavy deep skillet; add onions, and cook over medium heat until tender, about 10 minutes. Heat potatoes in microwave per package directions. Add garlic to onions; mix well. Add broth, potatoes, corn, herbs, and pepper; bring to a boil, stirring often. Remove bay leaves; stir in sour cream. Sprinkle crumbled bacon on top and serve.

A Collection from Summerville Kitchens (South Carolina)

Okra Gumbo Soup

1 pound smoked sausage, cut in half lengthwise, then crosswise in ½-inch slices
1 onion, chopped
1 green bell pepper, chopped
4 cups water
1 (14½-ounce) can stewed tomatoes
1 (16-ounce) package frozen okra
1 teaspoon garlic powder
1 tablespoon Worcestershire
1 teaspoon dried basil
1 teaspoon dry mustard
1 teaspoon thyme
2 teaspoons chili powder
2–3 bay leaves
Salt and pepper to taste

Lightly sauté sausage in iron frying pan. Remove and set aside. In same pan, lightly sauté onion and green pepper. Transfer sausage and sautéed vegetables to large soup pot. Add water and next 2 ingredients. Bring to a slow boil, then reduce heat and add remaining ingredients. Simmer slowly 30–45 minutes. Yields 6–8 servings.

Great Cooks Rise...with the May River Tide (South Carolina)

Seafood Gumbo

½ pound bacon, diced
½ cup diced onion
½ cup diced celery
½ cup diced green bell pepper
2 cloves garlic, crushed
1 teaspoon basil
1 teaspoon oregano
2 teaspoons salt
1 teaspoon pepper
2 cups clam juice
2 cups water
1 (2-pound) can tomatoes, chopped
2 (10-ounce) packages frozen okra
2 pounds shrimp, cleaned
1 pound fish (flounder or haddock), diced
1 pound scallops, cooked
1 cup white wine
1 cup sherry

In large soup pot, sauté bacon until cooked. Add onion, celery, green pepper, garlic, and spices. Cook 10 minutes, until vegetables are tender. Add clam juice, water, tomatoes, and okra; cook 15 minutes. Add remaining ingredients and simmer 30 minutes.

Secrets from the Galley (Florida)

Mr. Frank's Chili

2 pounds ground beef
1 medium onion, chopped
1 green bell pepper, seeded,
  chopped
1 (12-ounce) can tomato paste
1 teaspoon salt
Freshly ground pepper to taste
1 tablespoon brown sugar
½ teaspoon thyme
1 tablespoon cumin

2 tablespoons garlic powder
1 teaspoon cayenne pepper
1 teaspoon oregano
2 bay leaves
1 tablespoon BBQ sauce
2 tablespoons Worcestershire
2 cups water
2 beef bouillon cubes
1 cup red wine

In a skillet, sauté ground beef, onion, and green pepper until meat is no longer pink; stir often. Pour meat mixture into large pot, then add tomato paste, salt, pepper, brown sugar, thyme, cumin, garlic powder, cayenne pepper, oregano, bay leaves, BBQ sauce, Worcestershire, water, bouillon cubes, and wine; bring to a boil. Reduce heat, and simmer several hours on low heat, stirring periodically.

A Taste Through Time (South Carolina)

40-Minute Chili

2 tablespoons oil
1 onion, chopped
1 or 2 cloves garlic, minced
1 pound ground meat
2 (10¾-ounce) cans
  condensed tomato soup

2 (16-ounce) cans kidney beans
2 teaspoons chili powder
½ teaspoon salt
⅛–¼ teaspoon red pepper
  (optional)
Dash of black pepper

In oil, sauté onion and garlic. Brown meat; stir in soup, beans, chili powder, salt, and peppers. Cover and simmer 30 minutes, stirring occasionally.

Chilimania! (Florida)

The Lady & Sons Crab Stew

4 tablespoons butter
3 tablespoons all-purpose flour
1 tablespoon minced garlic
2 cups heavy cream
2 cups half-and-half
2 fish-flavor bouillon cubes
1 pound crabmeat, picked free
   of any broken shells

¼ cup sherry
½ teaspoon white pepper
1 (8-ounce) bottle clam juice
   (optional)
Grated Parmesan for garnish
Snipped chives for garnish

Heat butter in a large saucepan over medium heat. Add flour, stirring to blend in; add garlic. Gradually add cream and half-and-half, stirring constantly. Add bouillon cubes and stir well. As the mixture begins to thicken, add crabmeat, sherry, and pepper. If the stew seems too thick, thin it with clam juice, which will also add a lot of flavor. Serve in a mug, garnished with grated Parmesan and snipped chives. Serves 10–12.

The Lady & Sons, Too! (Georgia)

Creamy Oyster Broccoli Stew

3 cups milk
2 (10¾-ounce) cans
   condensed Cheddar cheese
   soup
1 (10-ounce) package frozen
   chopped broccoli

1 cup frozen loose-pack hash
   brown potatoes
1 small onion, chopped
1 tablespoon butter
1 pint shucked oysters or 2
   (8-ounce) cans whole oysters

In 3-quart saucepan combine milk and soup. Stir in broccoli, potatoes, and onion. Cook, stirring occasionally, over medium heat until bubbly, breaking up broccoli with fork till thawed. Simmer, covered, for 10 minutes. Remove from heat; cool. Cover and chill.

At serving time, in 3-quart saucepan, reheat soup. In separate pan, sauté fresh drained oysters in butter; cook over medium heat till edges curl. Add to broccoli mixture; heat through. (If using canned oysters, just add undrained oysters directly to soup; heat through.) Serves 4–6.

Island Events Cookbook (South Carolina)

Frogmore Stew

Frogmore is the name of a fishing community on St. Helena Island, South Carolina. According to legend, a fisherman could not find any fish for his stew, so he came up with a concoction of leftovers that became known as Frogmore Stew. A political stump rally favorite.

3 quarts water
2 tablespoons seafood
  seasoning
½ cup salt
2 lemons, cut in half
4 (12-ounce) cans beer
10 ears corn, cut into 2-inch
  pieces
3 pounds smoked or kielbasa
  sausage, cut into 1-inch
  pieces

Small red potatoes (optional)
8–10 medium onions, peeled,
  not cut
2 heads cauliflower, cut into
  florets
5 pounds medium shrimp,
  headed

Use a large pot, 32–40 quarts. Add 3 quarts of water, bring to a boil, and add seasoning, salt, lemons, and beer. After pot is boiling, add corn, sausage, and potatoes, if desired, and cook 5 minutes. Add onions and cauliflower, and cook 5 minutes. Add shrimp, and cook 3–5 minutes, until shrimp is pink or barely separated from the shell at the head end. (Overcooking shrimp will make them tough or mushy.) When ready, spread on table covered with newspaper, and serve with containers of melted butter and seafood cocktail sauce. Serve with green salad and garlic toast.

A Collection from Summerville Kitchens (South Carolina)

Richard Gay of Gay Seafood Company claimed to have invented Frogmore Stew in the early 1960s. The story goes that while he was on National Guard duty in Beaufort, South Carolina, he was preparing some leftovers for his fellow guardsmen. He brought the recipe home with him, and it soon became popular in his area. According to Gay, the Steamer Restaurant on Lady's Island was the first establishment to offer Frogmore Stew commercially.

Brunswick Stew

2 pounds pork or chicken, chopped
½ teaspoon black pepper
1 teaspoon hot sauce
2 tablespoons Worcestershire
⅓ cup drippings (pork or bacon)

½ cup barbecue sauce
1½ cups ketchup
2 cups diced potatoes, cooked
3 (20-ounce) cans cream-style corn

Place all ingredients in saucepan, cover and heat slowly. Salt and more hot sauce may be needed according to taste. Makes about 2 quarts.

Famous Recipes from Mrs. Wilkes' Boarding House (Georgia)

Crockpot Barbecued Beef Stew

2 pounds stew beef
2 tablespoons oil
1 cup sliced onions
1 large clove garlic
½ cup chopped green bell pepper
⅛ teaspoon pepper

1 (8-ounce) can tomatoes
⅓ cup barbecue sauce
2 cups beef stock
½ teaspoon salt
1 (4-ounce) can mushrooms
3 tablespoons cornstarch
¼ cup cold water

Brown beef in oil. Put onions, garlic, and pepper in bottom of crockpot. Add beef and remaining ingredients except cornstarch and water. Cook on LOW 8–10 hours. Dissolve cornstarch in water; add to crockpot, and simmer until thick. Serve over rice.

Carolina Cuisine Encore! (South Carolina)

SALADS

PHOTO © VISIT FLORIDA.

Tucked at the edge of the Atlantic Ocean in Daytona Beach, Florida, the Daytona Beach Bandshell is one of the area's most recognizable landmarks. Constructed in 1936, the 48x114-foot bandshell is made of coquina rock, Florida's native stone.

Spinach Salad
& Honey-Sesame Seed Dressing

HONEY-SESAME SEED DRESSING:

1 clove garlic, minced	2 tablespoons honey
2 tablespoons Dijon mustard	Freshly ground pepper
2 tablespoons orange juice	⅓ cup olive oil
3 tablespoons white wine vinegar	1 tablespoon sesame seeds

Place garlic, mustard, orange juice, vinegar, honey, and pepper in blender; slowly add olive oil, blending until emulsified. Transfer to a jar and stir in sesame seeds. Chill. Take from refrigerator 30 minutes before dressing salad.

SALAD:

2 large oranges	1 pound bacon, fried crisp, crumbled
2 packages fresh spinach, washed	
4 thin green onions, thinly sliced	

Cut ½-inch slice from tops and bottoms of oranges. Sit oranges on cutting board on cut end. With a sharp knife, cut away peel and white pith. Cut between membranes to remove sections. Refrigerate oranges. Put spinach in a bowl, and cover with paper towels. Refrigerate. Just before serving, add orange sections and green onions, then dressing. Top with crumbled bacon. Toss. Serve immediately.

Jefferies Relay Team: Generating a Cure (South Carolina)

With more than 43 million visitors annually, Orlando attracts more visitors than any other amusement park destination in the United States. People from all over the world plan repeated vacations here. Major parks include Disney World's Magic Kingdom®, Epcot®, MGM Studios®, Animal Kingdom®, Blizzard Beach®, and Typhoon Lagoon®. In the same area is SeaWorld Orlando®. Universal Orlando® has two theme parks: Universal Studios Florida® and Universal's Islands of Adventure®.

Avocado Spinach Salad

Fresh spinach, washed,
  drained, snipped to pieces
  with kitchen shears
½ cup water chestnuts, sliced
2 cups fresh bean sprouts
2 hard-boiled eggs, diced

5 slices bacon, fried crisp,
  crumbled
1 red onion, sliced thin,
  separated into rings
1 avocado, sliced, sprinkled with
  lime juice

Toss all ingredients with Papaya Seed Dressing

PAPAYA SEED DRESSING:
Intriguing—you'll learn to always keep a jar of it in the fridge!

1 cup red wine vinegar
½ cup superfine sugar
1 teaspoon dry mustard
1 tablespoon Pickapeppa sauce

1 teaspoon seasoned salt
2 tablespoons grated onion
2 cups oil
3 tablespoons papaya seeds

Combine first 6 ingredients in electric blender. Add oil with blender on HIGH, in infinitely fine stream. It is the little bit at a time that thickens dressing. Add and blend papaya seeds for a short time, or only until dressing looks as if it contained coarsely ground pepper.

Maurice's Tropical Fruit Cook Book (Florida)

The Best Salad

2 heads romaine lettuce
1 pint fresh strawberries,
  sliced

½ cup walnuts, lightly toasted
1 cup shredded Monterey Jack
  cheese

Tear lettuce into bite-size pieces. Combine lettuce, strawberries, walnuts, and cheese in a salad bowl, and toss to combine. Drizzle Red Wine Vinaigrette over salad; toss to coat.

RED WINE VINAIGRETTE:

1 cup vegetable oil
½ cup red wine vinegar
¾ cup sugar
2 cloves garlic, minced

½ teaspoon paprika
½ teaspoon salt
½ teaspoon white pepper

Combine oil, vinegar, sugar, garlic, paprika, salt, and white pepper in a bowl, and whisk to mix.

Meet Me at the Garden Gate (South Carolina)

Make Ahead Lettuce Salad

1 head lettuce, shredded
½ cup chopped celery
¼ cup chopped green bell
  pepper
½ cup chopped onion
2 cups chopped fresh spinach

1 (10-ounce) package frozen
  peas, cooked slightly, cooled
1 pint Hellmann's mayonnaise
2 tablespoons sugar
1 cup grated Parmesan cheese
½ cup crumbled crisp bacon

Grease 9x13-inch pan. Arrange first 6 ingredients in order given. Do not stir. Spread mayonnaise evenly over all. Add next 3 ingredients in order. Cover tightly and refrigerate 24 hours. Cut in squares. Serves 16.

The Stuffed Griffin (Georgia)

Seven Day Slaw

This slaw is called 'Seven Day Slaw' because without any mayonnaise, it will easily last for seven days.

1 head cabbage
2 red onions
⅓ cup plus 2 tablespoons
  sugar, divided
1 cup oil

1 cup vinegar
½ tablespoon dry mustard
¼ tablespoon salt
¼ tablespoon black pepper

Slice cabbage and onions thinly or shred them. Toss with ⅓ cup sugar. Mix remaining ingredients and bring to a boil. Pour boiling mixture over cabbage, let set, and in 5 minutes, mix. Chill in refrigerator and serve on leaves of romaine. Serves 4.

Hudson's Cookbook (South Carolina)

Duke's Mayonnaise was created by Eugenia Duke of Greenville, South Carolina, in 1917. Since its creation, Duke's, which is the only major label mayonnaise made without sugar, has never changed the original recipe.

Greek Cole Slaw

1 medium head cabbage	1 carrot

Shred cabbage and carrot as thin as possible.

DRESSING:

½ cup olive oil	1 teaspoon oregano
¼ cup chopped fresh parsley	2 lemons, seeds removed
1 clove garlic, chopped	Salt and pepper to taste

Put oil, parsley, garlic, oregano, lemons, salt and pepper in a food processor or small chopper. Blend to a fine dressing. Add to cabbage and carrot mixture, and mix well.

The Lazy Cook's Cookbook: A Greek Odyssey (South Carolina)

Southern-Style Potato Salad

4 pounds potatoes (about 4 large potatoes)	1 tablespoon mustard
3 hard-cooked eggs, grated	1 tablespoon salt
1 cup mayonnaise	½ teaspoon freshly ground pepper
½ cup sour cream	½ pound bacon, cooked, crumbled
¼ cup finely chopped celery	
2 tablespoons finely chopped onion	Chopped fresh parsley for garnish
2 tablespoons sweet pickle relish	Grape tomatoes for garnish

Cook potatoes in boiling water 40 minutes or until tender; drain and cool. Peel potatoes; cut into 1-inch cubes. Stir together potatoes and eggs. Stir together mayonnaise and next 7 ingredients; gently stir into potato mixture. Cover and chill.

Sprinkle with bacon just before serving. Garnish with parsley and tomatoes, if desired.

Best Kept Secrets (South Carolina)

Sour Cream Potato Salad

There is none better.

5 cups diced, boiled potatoes
1 tablespoon grated onion
½ cup diced cucumber
¾ teaspoon celery seeds
1½ teaspoons salt
½ teaspoon freshly ground
  pepper

1 tablespoon chopped parsley
3 hard-cooked eggs, whites
  diced, yolks mashed
1½ cups sour cream
½ cup Hellmann's mayonnaise
¼ cup vinegar
1 teaspoon prepared mustard

Potato salad is best made from red waxy potatoes, cooked in their jackets and peeled and marinated while still warm. Combine potatoes, onion, cucumber, celery seeds, salt, pepper, and parsley, and mix together lightly. Add diced whites to potato mixture. Combine mashed yolks with sour cream, mayonnaise, vinegar, and mustard; add to potatoes and gently blend together. Refrigerate several hours. Taste; some like a little more salt and pepper. Serves 10.

Cook and Deal (Florida)

Corn, Tomato, and Vidalia Sweet Onion Salad

1½ cups diced ripe tomatoes
⅓ cup chopped Vidalia sweet
  onion
2 medium ears fresh corn,
  cooked and cooled
⅛ teaspoon salt

1 tablespoon plus 1 teaspoon
  balsamic vinegar
1 tablespoon olive oil
15 fresh basil leaves
Salt and ground pepper to taste

Combine tomatoes and onion. Scrape corn and juice off cobs; this should equal about 1 cup. Add corn to tomatoes and onions. Whisk together salt and vinegar. Add oil and whisk. Stack basil leaves and slice into shreds. Add to tomato mixture. Combine vinegar mixture with vegetables and toss to coat. Season with salt and pepper. Cover and refrigerate 1 hour to 2 days. Serves 4.

Note: This salad is good with grilled fish.

Vidalia Sweet Onion Lovers Cookbook (Georgia)

Vegetable Rainbow Platter

This is a very attractive dish that can be used as a salad or a vegetable with dinner.

2 (10-ounce) packages baby lima beans
½ teaspoon dill
Wishbone Italian Dressing
3–4 slices tomatoes
Tomato French Dressing
8 small zucchini squash
½ cup grated Parmesan cheese
2 (10-ounce) packages frozen sugar-glazed carrots
½ cup wine vinegar
2 (10-ounce) packages frozen asparagus spears
½ cup capers and liquid

Cook lima beans as directed; drain. Cover with dill and Italian dressing; cover and refrigerate overnight. Place sliced tomatoes in bowl and cover with French dressing. Cover and refrigerate overnight. Slice zucchini thin and cook 5 minutes in salted water. Drain and toss with Parmesan cheese. Cover and refrigerate overnight. Cook carrots as directed; drain. Toss with wine vinegar. Cover and refrigerate overnight. Cook asparagus as directed; drain. Sprinkle with capers and liquid. Cover and refrigerate overnight.

SAUCE:

1 cup sour cream
1 cup mayonnaise
2 tablespoons lemon juice
Salt and pepper to taste
Lots of chopped parsley

Arrange vegetables on large platter and place bowl of sauce in center.

Cypress Gardens Cookbook (Florida)

Anything-Goes Marinated Salad

You can choose vegetables according to what's in season or to your own personal preference. It's important to blanche the broccoli and cauliflower before putting this recipe together. Note that this recipe requires 8–24 hours of marinating in the refrigerator, so make it about a day before you need it.

1 head broccoli	8 ounces commercially prepared
1 head cauliflower	oil and vinegar (Greek or
1 bowl ice water	Italian salad dressing)
10–12 radishes	Salt and pepper to taste
1–2 medium zucchini, sliced	1–2 ripe tomatoes, chopped
1–2 medium yellow squash,	(optional)
sliced	Fresh parsley or basil, chopped
1 large red, yellow, or Vidalia	(optional)
onion, chopped, or 5–7 green	
onions, sliced	

Chop broccoli and cauliflower into bite-size pieces. Bring a large pot of water to a boil. Prepare a bowl of ice and water. Blanche broccoli and cauliflower in boiling water for 1–2 minutes. Put immediately into ice water. Drain well.

Mix all vegetables in a large bowl. Pour 6–8 ounces of prepared dressing over vegetables. Any oil-and-vinegar-based, non-creamy dressing will do.

Cover vegetables tightly and refrigerate for 8–24 hours. Invert container several times so all vegetables are covered by dressing. Taste before serving. Add salt and pepper to taste. Add ripe tomatoes and fresh parsley or basil as garnish, if desired. Serves 6–8.

The Essential Catfish Cookbook (Florida)

On April 18, 1998, Athens, Georgia, hosted the largest compact disc release party in history: local band Widespread Panic gave a free concert that attracted almost 100,000 music fans. Athens is world-renowned for its music scene, and nurtured such bands as REM, the B-52s, Widespread Panic, Drivin' and Cryin', and Pylon, just to name a few.

Perkie's Salad

1 (16-ounce) can French-style
   green beans, drained
1 (17-ounce) can tiny peas,
   drained
1 teaspoon garlic powder
10 tablespoons mayonnaise

1 medium onion, thinly sliced
2 teaspoons sugar
2 teaspoons seasoned salt
½ teaspoon pepper
5 bacon slices, cooked, crumbled

Spread half the green beans and half the peas on a shallow 1½-quart dish. Sprinkle with garlic powder. Spread 5 tablespoons mayonnaise evenly over peas. Place half of sliced onion over mixture. Sprinkle with 1 teaspoon sugar, 1 teaspoon salt, and ¼ teaspoon pepper. Repeat layers, omitting garlic.

Cover and leave at room temperature 1 hour. Refrigerate at least 2 hours. Toss gently before serving. Garnish with bacon. Serves 6.

Heart of the Palms (Florida)

Tropical Carrot-Raisin Salad

1½ cups coarsely shredded
   carrots
¼ cup raisins
1 (8-ounce) can unsweetened
   crushed pineapple, drained
   well

¼ cup plain nonfat yogurt
1 tablespoon reduced-calorie
   mayonnaise
1½ teaspoons peanut butter
⅛ teaspoon ground cinnamon

Combine carrots, raisins, and pineapple in a bowl. Toss gently. Combine yogurt and remaining ingredients in a separate bowl. Stir well. Mix all together, stirring well. Cover and chill. Yields 3 servings.

The Best of Living in South Carolina (South Carolina)

Olive Macaroni Salad

1 (8-ounce) box macaroni, boiled
2 tomatoes, peeled and diced
1 (4-ounce) can sliced black olives
2 stalks celery, cut small
Garlic salt to taste
Salt and pepper to taste
Chopped pimentos, enough for color
¼ pound sharp cheese, grated
Onion, grated
Mayonnaise

Drain macaroni and dry on a towel. Mix with all other ingredients, adding onion and mayonnaise to taste. Let it sit overnight or from morning until night. Makes a large bowl.

Sherman Didn't Burn Our Recipes, Bartow's Still Cooking (Georgia)

Pasta Salad

3 small yellow squash, washed, cubed
2 small zucchini squash, washed, cubed
1 (12-ounce) package garden-style swirl macaroni (or elbow)
4–6 green onions, sliced thin
15–20 salad tomatoes, washed, stem end sliced, quartered
½ sweet bell pepper, chopped

Put squash and zucchini in microwave-safe bowl. Cover with plastic wrap. Microwave on HIGH 2 minutes, stir, and microwave 2 minutes more; add to macaroni that has been cooked in salted water, rinsed, and drained. When macaroni is cool, add remaining ingredients and toss.

DRESSING:
¼ cup extra light olive oil
¼ cup tarragon white wine vinegar
1 package Sweet 'n Low
½ teaspoon garlic powder with parsley
1 tablespoon Salad Supreme Seasoning

Mix ingredients well; pour over salad and mix. Best if made several hours before serving, allowing flavors to blend. Keeps in refrigerator for days.

A Carolina Country Collection (South Carolina)

Paella Salad

The flavors blend nicely when this salad is made 4–5 hours before serving. Try adding a few shakes of red pepper flakes for added zip. For a striking visual effect, alternate spinach leaves and quartered tomatoes in a circular pattern and mound salad in the center.

1 (10-ounce) package yellow rice
2 boneless chicken breasts, cooked, cut into 1-inch pieces
⅓ pound shrimp, cooked, peeled
½ red pepper, chopped
½ green pepper, chopped

3 scallions (including stems), chopped
2 medium tomatoes, seeded and chopped
⅓ cup olive oil
1 garlic clove, minced
2 tablespoons tarragon vinegar
⅛ teaspoon dry mustard

Cook yellow rice according to instructions on package. Add chicken, shrimp, peppers, scallions, and tomatoes; set aside.

In a jar, combine olive oil, garlic, tarragon vinegar, and dry mustard; shake until well mixed. Pour over rice mixture. Serve at room temperature or warm. Yields 5–6 servings.

A Slice of Paradise (Florida)

Dixie Cornbread Salad

1 (6-ounce) box cornbread mix
1 (12-ounce) package bacon
3 large tomatoes, diced
1 large Vidalia onion, diced

1 large bell pepper, diced
½ cup sweet pickle relish
½ cup sweet pickle juice
1 cup mayonnaise (or to taste)

Prepare cornbread according to package directions. Cool; crumble into very small pieces. Cook bacon, drain and crumble or chop. In large glass bowl, layer ½ cornbread, ½ tomatoes, ½ onion, ½ pepper, ½ bacon, ½ sweet pickles, and sweet pickle juice. Top with a thin layer of mayonnaise. Repeat layering until remaining ingredients are used. To make salad more attractive, save a little of each ingredient (except mayonnaise) to garnish the top.

Bread of Life–Salem Baptist Church (Georgia)

Crunchy Chicken Salad

An unexpected combination of flavors and textures.

DRESSING:

2 (3-ounce) packages chicken-flavored ramen noodles
¾ cup vegetable oil

⅓ cup white vinegar
¼ cup sugar

Combine contents of seasoning packets from ramen noodles, oil, vinegar, and sugar in a bowl and mix well.

SALAD:

1 (12-ounce) package broccoli slaw
1 Red Delicious apple, cored and sliced
1 cup sunflower kernels
1 cup sweetened dried cranberries or raisins

1 bunch green onions, chopped
1 red bell pepper, chopped
1 cup slivered almonds
1 rotisserie chicken, boned and chopped

Combine broccoli slaw, apple, sunflower kernels, dried cranberries, green onions, bell pepper, almonds, and chicken in a large bowl. Add dressing and toss to coat. Crumble ramen noodles and add just before serving. Toss to mix. Serves 8.

Par 3: Tea-Time at the Masters® (Georgia)

Gourmet Chicken Salad with Fresh Peaches

A delicious luncheon main course.

2 cups cubed cooked chicken
¾ cup chopped celery
¾ cup cut white seedless grapes
¾ cup cubed fresh peeled peaches

½ cup mayonnaise
½ cup sour cream
Seasoning salt to taste
Fresh peach sliced for garnish
Parsley for garnish

Lightly toss chicken, celery, grapes, and peaches together. Mix mayonnaise and sour cream and pour over salad. Add seasoning salt and mix gently. Store in refrigerator until ready to use. Garnish with fresh peach slices and parsley. Makes 6 servings.

The Peach Sampler (South Carolina)

Grilled Chicken Salad

2 boneless, skinless chicken
    breast halves
Garlic powder
Greek seasoning (optional)
Fat-free Italian dressing
4 cups torn salad greens

2 plum tomatoes, sliced
2 thin slices Bermuda onion
½ cup fat-free Cheddar or feta
    cheese
Italian dressing or vinaigrette

Preheat grill. Pound chicken to ¼-inch thickness with a mallet. Cut into 1-inch slices, but leave about ½ inch uncut at one end, so strips stay together. Sprinkle with garlic powder and Greek seasoning, if desired. Place on grill. Cook about 5 minutes on each side, until no longer pink. Baste both sides with fat-free dressing, and cook about 30 seconds on each side.

Meanwhile, divide and pile greens onto 2 plates. Spread one tomato over each pile, then separate onion slices into rings and add. Sprinkle cheese on top, and drizzle with vinaigrette to taste. Remove chicken from grill. Cut slices completely apart and lay on top of salad. Serve hot or cold. Makes 2 servings.

Cooking for Two, No Nonsense Cookbook (Florida)

PHOTO © ANDY NEWMAN / FLORIDA KEYS TCC.

WWW.WIKIPEDIA.COM

A registered National Historic Landmark, the Hemingway Home and Museum offers guided tours of Ernest Hemingway's home, writing studio and Key West, Florida's first swimming pool. Hemingway was given a six-toed cat named Snowball in 1935 by a ship's captain. Descendants of that cat still remain on the museum grounds. Of the 60 cats that roam the grounds, over half are also polydactyl like their ancestor.

Chicken and New Potato Salad

15–18 small new potatoes, unpeeled, cut into bite-size chunks

2 cups cooked chicken, cut into small pieces

1 cup finely chopped fresh broccoli or spinach

1 cup grated carrots

½ cup chopped green onion

Cook potatoes until just tender. In a large bowl, combine chicken, potatoes, and vegetables and mix well.

DRESSING:

1 cup plain yogurt

2 tablespoons mayonnaise

1 teaspoon prepared mustard

2 medium cloves garlic, crushed

1 teaspoon fresh, finely chopped basil or ½ teaspoon dried

1 teaspoon fresh, finely chopped oregano or ½ teaspoon dried

¼ teaspoon freshly ground black pepper

In small bowl, combine all ingredients and blend well. Pour Dressing over salad and toss. Chill at least 2 hours. Serves 8.

Cross Creek Kitchens (Florida)

Crab-Potato Salad

4 cups cooked stone crabmeat, cartilage removed, lightly flaked with a fork

6 medium potatoes, boiled, chilled, peeled and cubed

4 eggs, hard-cooked, chilled, peeled and diced

½ medium green bell pepper, stem and seeds removed, finely diced

1 medium onion, finely diced

2 ribs celery, finely diced

2 cups mayonnaise

¼ cup sweet pickle relish

1 tablespoon salt

½ teaspoon freshly ground black pepper

Lettuce (optional)

Combine all ingredients except lettuce, and chill for several hours. Serve as is, or in crisp lettuce cups.

Variation: Substitute crawfish (Florida lobster), cut into bite-size pieces.

Cookin' in the Keys (Florida)

Seaside Crab and Avocado Salad

2 cups flaked crabmeat
2 avocados, peeled, diced
1½ teaspoons lime juice
2 hard-cooked eggs, chopped
2 tablespoons minced onion
1 tablespoon capers
½ cup chopped celery

½ teaspoon salt
Dash of pepper
½ cup mayonnaise
1 clove garlic, pressed
3 tablespoons chili sauce
Lettuce leaves

Combine crabmeat and avocados in a bowl and sprinkle with lime juice. Add eggs, onion, capers, celery, salt, and pepper. Blend mayonnaise, garlic, and chili sauce. Pour over salad and toss lightly. Serve on lettuce leaves. Yields 6 servings.

Educated Taste (Georgia)

Black Bart's Seafood Ambrosia

This is also good served as a dip with crackers or stuffed into jalapeño or banana pepper halves for a fire-breathing surprise!

1–1½ cups white meat fish,
 cooked, flaked
1 medium red onion, chopped
4 stalks celery, chopped
½ green bell pepper, chopped
1 large dill pickle, chopped
2 tablespoons oil

2 tablespoons lemon juice
1 tablespoon parsley flakes
1 teaspoon salt
1 cup mayonnaise
Lettuce leaves
Tomato wedges

Mix thoroughly all but lettuce and tomatoes. Refrigerate in airtight container until ready to use. Serve on lettuce leaves with tomato garnish.

Note: To cook fish, fillet, leaving skin on, cut into bite-size pieces, then boil in water seasoned with crab boil.

Thyme Waves (Florida)

Lowcountry Shrimp Salad

1½ pounds popcorn-size
  shrimp, peeled, tail removed,
  cooked, drained
2 stalks celery, diced into
  ⅛-inch pieces
1 rounded teaspoon Lawry's
  Garlic Salt

½ teaspoon dry dill weed
4–5 tablespoons Hellmann's
  mayonnaise
¾ teaspoon lemon juice,
  freshly squeezed with seeds
  removed

Mix together first 5 ingredients. Stir in lemon juice, and chill until ready to serve. Serve on lettuce. Yields 4–6 servings.

Recipe from Plum's Waterfront Cafe, Beaufort
Lowcountry Delights III (South Carolina)

Grapefruit Shrimp Salad

1½ cups fresh grapefruit
  sections
2 cups cooked, cleaned shrimp
1 cup diced celery
1 tablespoon fresh lemon juice

1 tablespoon heavy cream
½ cup mayonnaise
¼ teaspoon salt
¼ teaspoon white pepper
Salad greens

Combine grapefruit, shrimp, and celery. Mix together lemon juice, cream, mayonnaise, salt, and pepper. Add to first mixture and toss. Serve on bed of salad greens. Serves 4.

Secrets from the Galley (Florida)

Over 200 years ago, Charleston, South Carolina, was the site of America's first golf course and golf club. In 1786 the South Carolina Golf Club was formed and established "Charleston Green" in what is now downtown Charleston. In fact, the term "green fee" is thought to have evolved from the membership fees paid by club members to maintain their course. While Charleston Green is a long-gone memory, it established a heritage and tradition of golfing excellence.

Avocado Shrimp Salad

2 ripe avocados, peeled, halved
Lemon juice
1 pound raw, headless, peeled
  shrimp
1 (8-ounce) can crushed
  pineapple, drained
½ cup finely chopped green
  bell pepper

½ cup finely chopped celery
⅔ cup firm sour cream
1 teaspoon onion salt
1 cup shredded Swiss cheese
Red tip lettuce, picked, washed,
  drained, for garnish

Coat avocado halves with lemon juice; chill. Cook shrimp in large quantity salted water 3 minutes. Drain and cool in refrigerator. Combine pineapple, bell pepper, celery, sour cream, onion salt, and shrimp. Refrigerate 30–45 minutes.

    Scoop out hollow of avocado to allow room for mixture. Mound mixture on halves and cover with shredded cheese. Refrigerate until ready to serve on bed of lettuce.

Charleston Receipts Repeats (South Carolina)

Tomato Aspic Ring

2 tablespoons gelatin	½ cup Rhine wine
½ cup cold water	½ teaspoon salt
2 (8-ounce) cans tomato sauce	1 tablespoon minced onion
2 tablespoons lemon juice	2 tablespoons parsley
1 cup sour cream	1 cup chopped celery

Soften gelatin in water. Heat tomato sauce to boiling, add gelatin, stir until dissolved. Add lemon juice, sour cream, wine, and salt. Mix in onion, parsley, and celery. Chill until slightly thickened, then top with Avocado Mixture.

AVOCADO MIXTURE:

4 cups mashed avocados	½ teaspoon sugar
4 tablespoons lemon juice	⅛ teaspoon red pepper
3 tablespoons gelatin softened in ½ cup cold water	3 tablespoons onion juice
	¾ cup mayonnaise
1 teaspoon salt	

Mix all together except mayonnaise. Set in refrigerator until partly congealed. Beat with beater and add mayonnaise. Serve on tomato ring with the following shrimp sauce.

SOUR CREAM SHRIMP SAUCE:

Garlic, cut	½ cup ketchup
½ pound cooked, chopped shrimp	2 tablespoons Worcestershire
	1½ tablespoons grated onion
1 pint sour cream	1 teaspoon salt

Rub bowl with garlic and mix in remaining ingredients.

The Colonel's Inn Caterers'—Tallahassee Historical Cookbook (Florida)

WWW. WIKIPEDIA.COM

Savannah, Georgia (left), known as America's first planned city (wide streets arranged in a grid pattern), was built in the mid-1700s. The downtown district is a National Historic Landmark and is considered one of America's most beautiful cities. Established as the capital of South Carolina in 1786, Columbia (right) was South Carolina's first planned city and the second planned city in the United States.

Congealed Coca-Cola Cranberry Salad

A Georgia Thanksgiving classic.

1 (3-ounce) package orange
  gelatin
1 cup boiling water
1 (16-ounce) can whole
  cranberry sauce
1 envelope gelatin, softened
  in ½ cup cold water

1 (20-ounce) can crushed
  pineapple, undrained
1 tablespoon lemon juice
1 tablespoon grated orange rind
1 cup chopped pecans or
  walnuts
6 ounces Coca-Cola Classic

Dissolve orange gelatin in boiling water; add cranberry sauce and blend well. Add plain gelatin. Add remaining ingredients and stir just to blend. Spray an 8-cup mold with nonstick cooking spray. Pour mixture into mold. Chill. When mixture begins to gel, stir to distribute nuts evenly. Continue to chill until firm. Yields 8 servings.

Georgia On My Menu (Georgia)

Easy Strawberry Salad

1 (6-ounce) package strawberry
  Jell-O
1 envelope plain gelatin
2 cups boiling water
1 (16-ounce) package frozen
  strawberries
1 (15-ounce) can crushed
  pineapple, drained

1 cup chopped nuts
½ (6-ounce) package mini
  marshmallows
1 cup sour cream
1 (8-ounce) package cream
  cheese, softened
½ cup sugar

Combine dry Jell-O and plain gelatin. Add 2 cups boiling water and stir well. Add strawberries, drained pineapple, nuts, and marshmallows. Pour into long casserole and congeal. Mix sour cream, cream cheese, and sugar with mixer. Spread on top of salad; chill.

Seasoned with Light (South Carolina)

Blueberry Salad

1 (15-ounce) can crushed
  pineapple, drained, save juice
1 (6-ounce) package black
  cherry or blackberry Jell-O
1 cup cold water
1 (21-ounce) can blueberry pie
  filling

Add enough water to pineapple juice to make 2 cups. Bring to a boil and add to gelatin. Stir until dissolved. Add cold water. Add pineapple and blueberry pie filling and let congeal. Cover with Topping.

TOPPING:
1 (8-ounce) package cream
  cheese, softened
½ cup sour cream
½ cup sugar
1 cup chopped nuts

Mix ingredients together and spread over congealed gelatin mixture.

Feeding the Faithful (South Carolina)

Florida Sunshine Salad

This is good with fowl, pork or ham. It may also be used at holiday time in place of cranberry sauce.

1 (12-ounce) can apricot nectar
1 (3-ounce) package lemon
  gelatin
1 (6-ounce) can frozen orange
  juice concentrate, thawed,
  undiluted
1 (3-ounce) package cream
  cheese, softened
½ cup chopped pecans

Heat apricot nectar to boiling point. Dissolve lemon gelatin in this. Add undiluted orange juice concentrate. Make small balls of cream cheese to which pecans have been added and place 3 balls in each individual mold. Fill mold with juice mixture and refrigerate until jelled. Makes 1 large or 6 individual molds.

Seminole Savorings (Florida)

Mozart's Magic Fruit
(Marinated Fruit)

This is very attractive served in small, stemmed dessert dishes for brunch or dinner.

1½ cups cantaloupe balls
1½ cups honeydew balls
1½ cups fresh pineapple
  chunks
1 (11-ounce) can Mandarin
  oranges, drained
1 cup fresh strawberries,
  stemmed

1 (6-ounce) can frozen
  lemonade, thawed, undiluted
¼ cup orange marmalade
2 tablespoons orange-flavored
  liqueur
Mint leaves

Combine cantaloupe, honeydew, pineapple chunks, Mandarin oranges, and strawberries in a large serving bowl. In a small bowl, combine lemonade, marmalade, and liqueur. Stir well. Pour over fruit and toss gently. Cover and chill 2 hours before serving. Garnish with mint leaves. Serves 6–8.

Music, Menus & Magnolias (South Carolina)

Golden Glow Ambrosia

1 (16-ounce) can peaches
  (halves or slices), drained
1 (16-ounce) can pears (halves
  or slices), drained
1 (20-ounce) can pineapple
  chunks, drained (reserve
  ¼ cup juice)
1 teaspoon lemon juice

1 apple, peeled and sliced
1 (6-ounce) jar maraschino
  cherries, drained
½ cup pecan halves
⅓ cup butter
¾ cup light brown sugar
2 teaspoons curry powder

Preheat oven to 325°. Arrange peaches and pears in bottom of baking dish sprayed with nonstick spray. Scatter pineapple chunks over peaches and pears. Arrange lemon juice-coated apples in dish. Blot cherries and scatter over other fruit along with pecans. Melt butter; stir in sugar, curry, and reserved pineapple juice. Heat and stir until sugar is dissolved. Pour over fruit and bake, uncovered, basting occasionally, for 45–60 minutes. Makes 12 servings.

Grandma Mamie Jones' Family Favorites (Georgia)

Street Party Grape Salad

1 (8-ounce) package cream
cheese, softened
1 (8-ounce) container sour
cream
¼ cup sugar

1 tablespoon vanilla
4 pounds seedless grapes, mixed
colors
½ cup brown sugar
½ cup crushed pecans

Cream together cream cheese, sour cream, sugar, and vanilla. Fold grapes into cream cheese mixture. Sprinkle brown sugar and crushed pecans on top just before serving; toss.

Cooking Carley Style (South Carolina)

Hudson's House Dressing

½ quart mayonnaise
2 dashes Tabasco
3 tablespoons crushed black
pepper
¼ cup grated Parmesan
cheese

½ ounce lemon juice
⅛ teaspoon garlic powder
¼ cup water
2 dashes Worcestershire
Croutons

Mix all ingredients well and serve over a tossed green salad. Top with croutons. Yields approximately ¾ quart.

Hudson's Cookbook (South Carolina)

Lemon Mayonnaise

Easy to make. This is delicious in potato salads or spread on ham sandwiches with sliced ripe tomatoes.

2 egg yolks
2 tablespoons lemon juice,
freshly squeezed
1 heaping teaspoon dry
mustard

Dash of cayenne pepper
Dash of salt
1 cup vegetable or olive oil

In electric blender or food processor, blend all ingredients, except oil. With machine still running slowly add oil in steady stream just until mixture thickens, about a minute. Makes 1¼ cups.

Cooking in the New South (Georgia)

VEGETABLES

PHOTO © GEORGIA DEPARTMENT OF ECONOMIC DEVELOPMENT.

Known as the sweetest onion in the world, the Vidalia onion is the official state vegetable of Georgia. Its sweet taste is attributed to the low amount of sulfur in the soil in which the onions are grown.

Creamy Potato Sticks

¼ cup all-purpose flour
½ teaspoon salt
1½ cups milk
1 (10¾-ounce) can condensed
 cream of celery soup,
 undiluted

½ pound American cheese,
 cubed
5–6 baking potatoes, peeled
1 cup chopped onion
Paprika

In a saucepan, combine flour and salt; gradually whisk in milk until smooth. Bring to a boil; cook and stir for 2 minutes. Remove from heat. Whisk in soup and cheese until smooth. Set aside. Cut potatoes into 4x½x½-inch sticks; place in a greased 9x13x2-inch baking dish. Sprinkle with onion. Top with cheese sauce. Bake uncovered at 350° for 55–60 minutes or until potatoes are tender. Sprinkle with paprika. Yield 6 servings.

Good Cooking (Florida)

Garlic Gruyère Mashed Potatoes

6 medium potatoes, peeled and
 cut into 1-inch pieces
¾ cup milk, heated
½ cup sour cream
¼ cup (½ stick) butter or
 margarine, softened
½ teaspoon salt
⅛ teaspoon red pepper

1 garlic clove, minced
¼ cup shredded Gruyère
 cheese
2 green onions, thinly sliced
⅓ cup chopped baked ham
 (optional)
Sliced green onions (optional)

Combine the potatoes with enough water to cover in a saucepan. Bring to a boil. Boil for 15 minutes or until tender; drain. Mash potatoes in a bowl with a potato masher. Stir in the hot milk, sour cream, butter, salt, red pepper, and garlic.

Add the cheese, 2 thinly sliced green onions and ham to the potato mixture and mix well. Spoon into a serving bowl and sprinkle with sliced green onions, if desired. Serves 6–8.

Bay Fêtes (Florida)

Mander's Reunion Hash Browns

1 (32-ounce) package frozen
    hash browns
1 (10¾-ounce) can cream of
    chicken soup
Lots of grated Cheddar
    cheese

1 cup diced onion
½ cup sour cream
1 cup milk
½ stick margarine, melted,
    divided
Cornflakes

Mix everything together, except ½ the melted margarine and the cornflakes. Put into greased casserole dish. Top with cornflakes and remaining margarine. Bake at 350° for 45 minutes.

My Best to You (Georgia)

Potato Patties

Leftover mashed potatoes
1 onion, finely chopped
1 egg, beaten

Salt and pepper to taste
2 tablespoons flour
Cooking oil

Mix potatoes, onion, egg, seasoning, and flour. Heat cooking oil in skillet on high heat. Make patties, and cook in hot oil; reduce to medium heat, and brown on both sides. Eat for breakfast, lunch, or dinner. Good with syrup, toast, bacon, etc.

Cooking with Miracle Deliverance (South Carolina)

Smiling Joe Fries

3 potatoes, peeled, cut for
    French fries
¼ pound Cheddar cheese

¼ pound bacon, cooked,
    crumbled
¼ cup chopped green onions

Fry potatoes in oil. Remove from oil to microwave dish and add cheese, bacon, and onions on top of fries. Pop into microwave to melt cheese.

The Lazy Cook's Cookbook: A Greek Odyssey (South Carolina)

Dilled New Potatoes

16 small new potatoes,
   washed but not peeled
½ cup butter, melted

3 tablespoons fresh dill weed
Salt and pepper to taste

In a large saucepan cover potatoes with cold water. Place on high heat and boil 20 minutes or until fork tender. Drain. Place in a serving bowl, toss in butter, dill, salt and pepper. Elegant, simple, and delicious. Serves 8.

Please Don't Feed the Alligators (South Carolina)

Shrimp Stuffed Baked Potatoes

6 medium baking potatoes
1 stick butter or margarine
½ cup half-and-half
⅜ cup finely chopped green
   onions

1½ cups shredded Cheddar
   cheese
1 teaspoon salt
1½ pounds shrimp, peeled,
   cooked

Wash potatoes; bake at 425° for 60 minutes or until done. When cool to touch, cut potatoes in half lengthwise. Carefully scoop out pulp, leaving a shell about ¼-inch thickness.

In a large bowl, mix potato pulp, butter, half-and-half, onion, cheese, and salt. Whip until smooth. By hand, stir in shrimp. Stuff shell with potato mixture. Bake at 425° for 15 minutes. Garnish with 1 or 2 whole shrimp.

One Course at a Time (South Carolina)

Sliced Candied Potatoes

4 large sweet potatoes, peeled,
  thinly sliced
1 cup light brown sugar
1 cup granulated sugar

2½ tablespoons flour
Dash of salt
4 tablespoons butter, melted
1 teaspoon lemon flavoring

Place sliced potatoes in a buttered baking dish. Mix brown sugar and granulated sugar with flour and salt. Sprinkle over sliced potatoes; mix melted butter and lemon flavoring, and drizzle over top. Add enough hot water to allow potatoes to cook (start with ½ cup). Bake in 350° oven 30 minutes, until tender and candied. Serves 6.

Go-o-od Goodies from Good Hope's Good Cooks
(South Carolina)

Mandarin Orange and Sweet Potatoes

10 medium-size sweet potatoes,
  scrubbed, dried
¼ cup butter or margarine,
  divided
6 tablespoons dark brown
  sugar, divided

3 tablespoons rum
½ teaspoon salt
2 (11-ounce) cans Mandarin
  orange slices, divided
2 tablespoons chopped pecans

Place potatoes on paper towels and bake on HIGH in microwave oven, 16–18 minutes. Remove and wrap in foil for 5 minutes. Mix mashed sweet potatoes with 2 tablespoons butter, 4 tablespoons sugar, rum, salt, and 1 can Mandarin orange slices. Combine remaining butter, sugar, and nuts with other can of Mandarin orange slices. Put on top of potato mixture, which you have placed in a casserole. Bake uncovered at 7 Power, for 7–8 minutes or until warmed through. Let stand 5 minutes, covered. You may use canned sweet potatoes if in a real hurry.

Lost Tree Cook Book (Florida)

Sweet Potato Snowballs

This is GREAT for the holiday season!

2 cups mashed sweet potatoes
¼ cup margarine, melted
2 eggs
½ cup evaporated milk
¾ cup sugar

Dash of cinnamon
Dash of nutmeg
Dash of allspice
1 (10-ounce) bag marshmallows
1 (3½-ounce) can coconut

Combine sweet potatoes, margarine, eggs, milk, sugar, and spices. Beat until smooth. Halve marshmallows and cover each half with potato mixture. Roll potato balls in coconut. Place on greased baking dish; bake at 350° until marshmallow is melted. Remove from baking dish with spatula.

Southern Manna (Georgia)

Orange-Banana Yams

1 (23-ounce) can whole sweet
  potatoes in heavy syrup
1 tablespoon cornstarch
⅓ cup firmly packed light
  brown sugar

1 cup orange juice
1 tablespoon butter
1 tablespoon grated orange rind
3 medium bananas

Drain sweet potatoes and save syrup for other use. Slice potatoes in half, lengthwise. Place in a single layer in an oblong, 1½-quart glass baking dish.

Stir together cornstarch and brown sugar in small saucepan. Gradually stir in orange juice, keeping smooth. Stir constantly over moderate heat until clear and thickened. Remove from heat. Stir in butter and orange rind.

Peel bananas. Score by drawing a fork lengthwise down sides. Slice crosswise about ¼-inch thick. Arrange bananas over sweet potatoes. Spoon orange sauce evenly over top so yams, and especially bananas, are covered with it.

Bake in preheated 400° oven until bubbling hot, 15–20 minutes. Serve at once. Serves 6.

Citrus Lovers Cook Book (Florida)

Collard Greens

Do not season collards until they have cooked down, as it is very easy to have a heavy hand with the salt and pepper.

3 pounds collard greens, washed, chopped

2 cups water

½ pound side meat or ham bone or 1 ham hock

1 tablespoon white vinegar

Put ingredients into large pot, cover, bring to a boil, reduce heat to simmer and cook 45 minutes, or until tender. Serve to 4 with homemade Cornbread.

CORNBREAD:

1 egg

1½ cups whole milk

3 tablespoons vegetable oil or bacon drippings

2 cups plain yellow cornmeal

3 teaspoons baking powder

1 teaspoon salt

Combine egg, milk, and oil in bowl. Add remaining ingredients and stir until smooth. Dot muffin pan with oil or bacon drippings. Preheat pan in oven about 3 minutes; remove and pour in batter—about ⅔ full. Place in oven preheated to 425° and bake 20–25 minutes.

Southern Vegetable Cooking (South Carolina)

Old-Time Fried Okra

Truly southern.

½ cup all-purpose flour

½ cup cornmeal

½ teaspoon salt

⅛ teaspoon pepper

1 egg, beaten

1 quart sliced okra (slice crosswise ¼-inch or less)

1 cup shortening

Combine flour, cornmeal, salt, and pepper; mix well. In separate bowl, stir beaten egg into okra. Dredge in flour mixture. Heat shortening in large skillet until hot. Add okra and fry until brown and crisp. Remove from pan and drain well on paper towels.

Editor's Extra: Can use egg white only to coat okra.

Encore (Georgia)

Easy Italian Vegetables

1 small onion, sliced
2 medium zucchini, sliced
  lengthwise in 4 pieces
2 medium yellow squash, sliced
  lengthwise in 4 pieces

1 medium tomato, cut in
  into 8 wedges
½ cup Italian dressing

Preheat oven to 450°. Center onion on a sheet of heavy-duty aluminum foil. Layer zucchini, squash, and tomato over onion. Spoon salad dressing over vegetables. Bring up foil sides. Double-fold top and ends to form a packet, leaving room for heat circulation inside. Place on a cookie sheet and bake for 35–40 minutes.

A Collection of Favorite Recipes (Florida)

Impossible Garden Pie

Easy, light meal.

2 cups quartered and sliced
  zucchini
1½ cups diced tomatoes
½ cup chopped onion
½ cup grated Parmesan
  cheese

¼ teaspoon pepper
1½ cups skim milk
¾ cup Bisquick
3 eggs

Place layer of zucchini, tomatoes, and onion in a lightly greased 7x11-inch casserole. Sprinkle with Parmesan and pepper. Combine milk, Bisquick, and eggs. Beat until smooth, about 1 minute, and pour over vegetables. Bake at 400° for 30 minutes. Allow to sit 5 minutes before cutting. Makes 6 servings.

A Taste of Georgia, Another Serving (Georgia)

Athens, Georgia, is the birthplace of America's first garden club, the Ladies Garden Club of Athens, founded in 1891 with twelve members. The primary aims of this newly established organization were: "To promote a love of gardening for the amateur and the professional; to protect our native trees, wild flowers and birds; and to encourage a regard for civic beauty in our various communities." Founders Memorial Garden, on the University of Georgia's North Campus, was established to honor the club. The project was begun in 1939 and completed in 1946.

Tomatoes Stuffed with Summer Squash

1 pound yellow squash, grated
1 pound zucchini, grated
2 teaspoons salt
8 small tomatoes
Salt and pepper to taste
Olive oil as needed
1 onion, chopped

2 tablespoons butter
2 tablespoons olive oil
1 cup heavy cream
Salt and pepper to taste
½ cup grated Swiss cheese
¼ cup plus 4 tablespoons grated
   Parmesan cheese, divided

Spread squash and zucchini in a large colander. Sprinkle with salt, toss and let drain 30 minutes. Transfer vegetables to a tea towel and squeeze out remaining moisture.

Preheat oven to 325°. Slice tops off tomatoes and scoop out seeds. Sprinkle insides with salt and pepper. Brush with olive oil. Bake, cut side up, on a baking sheet 10 minutes. When done, remove tomatoes and invert on a rack to drain 30 minutes.

Sauté onion in butter and olive oil until soft. Add squash and zucchini. Cook 2 minutes. Stir in cream, salt and pepper. Cook until cream is absorbed. Remove pan from heat. Stir in Swiss cheese and ¼ cup Parmesan cheese. Stuff tomatoes with mixture and sprinkle tops with remaining 4 tablespoons Parmesan cheese. Broil 3-4 minutes until tops are bubbly and golden. If prepared ahead and refrigerated, cook, covered, at 300° for 15 minutes before putting under broiler. Makes 8 servings.

Variation: Line bottom of a casserole with sliced tomatoes, cover with squash mixture, sprinkle with Parmesan, and proceed as usual.

Jacksonville & Company (Florida)

Seaside Stuffed Squash

An attractive way to serve squash—and good.

1 pound summer squash
½ cup chopped green bell
  pepper
½ cup grated Cheddar cheese

½ cup sour cream
½ cup minced onion
4 slices bacon, cooked, crumbled

Boil squash 10–12 minutes. Slice lengthwise. Scoop out pulp. Add remaining ingredients to pulp and mix well. Fill squash with mixture, placing each in a baking dish. Bake 20 minutes in at 350° preheated oven. May be prepared ahead of time and refrigerated until ready to bake. Serves 6.

Sugar Beach (Florida)

Crowd Pleasing Casserole

2–3 cups cooked squash
1 onion, chopped
2 carrots, grated
1 egg, slightly beaten
½ stick butter, sliced
½ cup mayonnaise
1 tablespoon sugar

1 cup grated Cheddar cheese,
  divided
1–1½ cups cracker crumbs,
  divided
Dash of cayenne pepper
Salt and pepper to taste
Oregano to taste

Put well-drained, hot squash in large mixing bowl. Add onion, carrots, egg, butter, mayonnaise, sugar, half of cheese, and half of cracker crumbs. Season with cayenne pepper, salt, pepper, and oregano. Mix all ingredients well. Put into buttered 1½-quart casserole dish and top with remaining cheese and crumbs. Bake at 350° for 20 minutes.

Island Events Cookbook (South Carolina)

Fried Green Tomatoes with Rémoulade

2 medium green tomatoes
1 tablespoon salt, divided
1 tablespoon freshly cracked
  black pepper, divided
2 cups panko (Japanese
  bread crumbs)
2 tablespoons paprika
1 cup chopped fresh parsley
4 eggs
2 cups all-purpose flour
2 cups vegetable oil

Slice tomatoes and sprinkle with salt and pepper. Combine panko, paprika, parsley, and remaining salt and pepper. Crack eggs in separate bowl, and put flour in another. Dip tomatoes into flour, shaking off excess—this is very important; dip into egg, letting excess drip off. Press tomatoes into bread crumbs, thoroughly coating both sides. Heat oil in skillet. When oil is hot, add tomatoes, frying on medium heat. Cook until golden on both sides. Drain on paper towels. Drizzle with Rémoulade and serve with a fresh lemon slice. Serves 8.

RÉMOULADE:

¼ cup ketchup
1 cup mayonnaise
¼ cup chopped fresh
  parsley
2 teaspoons hot pepper sauce
1 medium shallot
2 tablespoons capers
2 teaspoons vinegar
1 tablespoon paprika
2 teaspoons lemon juice

Combine all ingredients in food processor. Blend until smooth. Refrigerate for 2 hours.

Fine Dining Georgia Style (Georgia)

The Navy's famous Blue Angels flying squadron is based in Pensacola, Florida, and was established in 1946 to enhance recruiting. Their first air show was held at Craig Field in Jacksonville, Florida, on June 15, 1946. The fastest speed flown during an air show is about 700 mph (just under Mach 1) and the slowest speed is about 120 mph. The squadron's six demonstration pilots fly in more than 70 shows at 34 locations throughout the United States each year from March to November.

Beaufort Tomato Pie

1 (9-inch) deep-dish frozen pie
  shell, baked, cooled
2–3 large ripe tomatoes,
  thickly sliced
Salt and pepper to taste
Dried sweet basil to taste

Chives to taste
3 green onions, chopped
1 cup (scant) Miracle Whip
1 cup shredded sharp Cheddar
  cheese

Fill pie shell with tomato slices. Sprinkle with salt, pepper, basil, chives, and green onions. Mix Miracle Whip and cheese. Spread over tomatoes, sealing to the edges. Bake 35 minutes at 350°. Serves 6–8.

Dining Under the Carolina Moon (South Carolina)

Thunder Pie

2 medium-large Vidalia onions,
  thinly sliced
3 tablespoons butter
1 deep-dish pie crust, unbaked
3 eggs, beaten
½ cup half-and-half

½ cup sour cream
2 dashes Tabasco
1 cup shredded 4-cheese
  Mexican blend
Salt and pepper to taste

Sauté onions in butter over medium heat until limp and transparent. Place in pie crust that has been lightly greased to prevent sogginess. Mix eggs, half-and-half, sour cream, Tabasco, cheese, salt and pepper in a bowl, and pour over onions. Bake at 450° for 20 minutes, then turn oven to 300° and bake for an additional 20–25 minutes.

Cookin' on Island Time (Florida)

Farmer Mose Coleman from Vidalia, Georgia, discovered in 1931 that the onions he planted were not hot, as expected—they were sweet! In the 1940s, word began to spread about the onions from Vidalia. Consumers, then, gave the onions their famous name. Georgia's state legislature passed the Vidalia Onion Act of 1986 which authorized a trademark for Vidalia Onions and limits the production area to Georgia.

Dixie's Vidalia Casserole

3–4 Vidalia onions, sliced thin
Butter for sautéing
1 (10¾-ounce) can cream of
  chicken or cream of
  mushroom soup, undiluted
½ soup can of milk
1 tablespoon soy sauce
Pepper to taste
¼ pound grated Swiss cheese
French bread, sliced, quartered
  and buttered

Heat oven to 350°. Sauté onions in small amount of butter until yellow and soft. Blend and heat soup, soy sauce, milk, and pepper. Place onions in ungreased 1½-quart shallow baking dish. Place grated cheese on top of onions; add soup mixture. Place quartered buttered bread on top. Bake uncovered 30 minutes. Serves 6.

Vidalia Sweet Onion Lovers Cookbook (Georgia)

Baked Stuffed Onions
or What Else Can You Do with Vidalias?

4 large, flat Vidalia onions,
  peeled
Weight Watchers butter-
  flavored spray
1 clove garlic, minced
1 teaspoon canola oil
1 teaspoon lemon juice
1 (10-ounce) package frozen
  chopped spinach, defrosted
  and squeezed dry
¼ teaspoon black pepper
¼ cup bread crumbs
¼ cup feta cheese, crumbled

Spray onions with butter spray. Place onions in microwave casserole and cover; cook on HIGH 10–12 minutes or until onions are tender. Cool; scoop out centers, leaving a 2- to 3-layer shell. Cut a small amount off bottom, if necessary, to keep flat. Chop centers. Toss centers with garlic; cook in microwave with oil for 2 minutes on HIGH. Stir in lemon juice, spinach, and pepper. Cook, uncovered, on HIGH for 3 minutes. Fold in bread crumbs and cheese. Mound spinach mixture into onions; place on plate. Cover with wax paper and microwave on MEDIUM power for 6–8 minutes, until heated through. Turn dish at least once. Let stand, covered, for 5 minutes.

Family Collections (Georgia)

Southern Baked Beans

1 pound dried navy beans
6 cups water
2 minced garlic cloves
2 large onions, sliced
1 small, dried, hot red pepper
1 bay leaf
¾ pound sliced salt pork, or
  4 strips bacon

3 tablespoons molasses
¼ cup catsup
1 teaspoon dry mustard
½ teaspoon ground ginger
1½ teaspoons Worcestershire
½ teaspoon salt
¼ cup firmly packed brown
  sugar

Cover beans with water and bring to a boil; boil for 2 minutes. Cover and let stand 1 hour. Add next 5 ingredients; cook until beans are tender. Drain; save 2 cups liquid. Add remaining ingredients, except sugar, to liquid. Place beans in a shallow 2-quart baking dish. Arrange slices of pork on top and add liquid. Sprinkle with brown sugar. Bake at 400° for 1 hour.

Puttin' on the Peachtree... (Georgia)

Green Beans with Tomatoes and Feta

2 (16-ounce) packages frozen
  French-cut green beans,
  thawed
1 teaspoon olive oil
2 garlic cloves, minced
2 teaspoons Italian seasoning
4 plum tomatoes, chopped

2 tablespoons fresh lemon juice
¼ teaspoon salt
½ teaspoon freshly ground
  pepper
1 (4-ounce) package feta cheese,
  crumbled
¼ cup pine nuts, toasted

Drain green beans, pressing out excess moisture. Heat oil in a large nonstick skillet until hot. Add garlic and Italian seasoning. Cook over medium heat 1 minute. Add green beans. Cook 5–7 minutes. Stir in tomatoes. Cook 2 minutes or until heated through, stirring constantly. Stir in lemon juice, salt, and pepper. Sprinkle with feta cheese and pine nuts. Yields 6 servings.

Tapestry (South Carolina)

Company Beets

Great with pork chops.

1 (8-ounce) can crushed
pineapple, drained, reserve
juice

1 (14-ounce) can sliced beets,
drained
2 tablespoons cornstarch

Mix crushed pineapple with beets in saucepan over medium-low heat. Thicken with cornstarch mixed with a little pineapple juice.

Recipes & Memories (South Carolina)

Broccoli with Hollandaise Sauce

STEAMED BROCCOLI:

1 bunch broccoli, stems
peeled and tied
1 teaspoon salt

1-2 tablespoons butter or
margarine

Place broccoli in pot in upright position. Bring water level to the base of florets. Add salt and bring water to a boil. Cook about 10 minutes, or until stem near head is tender. Remove and drizzle with melted butter or margarine. One bunch normally serves 4.

HOLLANDAISE SAUCE:

2 egg yolks
¼ cup butter or margarine,
melted
¼ cup boiling water

1 tablespoon lemon juice
¼ teaspoon salt
Dash of cayenne

Water in bottom of double boiler should be no more than 1 inch deep. You do not want boiling water to touch the upper pot. Bring water to a boil on high heat; reduce to medium heat. In top pan of double boiler, beat egg yolks lightly with wire whip. Stir in melted butter. Add boiling water slowly, stirring constantly until sauce thickens. Remove immediately, then stir in lemon juice, salt, and cayenne.

Southern Vegetable Cooking (South Carolina)

Broccoli Rice Casserole

1 cup chopped onions
1 teaspoon canola oil
2 cups broccoli florets, fresh
   or frozen
1 (10¾-ounce) can low-sodium
   cream of mushroom soup
¼ cup skim milk
1 cup cooked rice
2 tablespoons grated Parmesan
   cheese

Sauté onions in oil until tender, but not brown. Add broccoli, and cook over medium heat till crisp-tender, but not done. Blend soup and milk together, then add to broccoli mixture. Add rice. Cook and stir over low heat until hot and mixed. Place in 2-quart casserole dish that has been sprayed with nonstick spray. Sprinkle with Parmesan cheese. Bake uncovered at 350° for 35–40 minutes, until casserole is bubbly and broccoli is tender.

A Taste Through Time (South Carolina)

Eggplant Parmigiana

1 large eggplant, unpeeled
Salt and pepper to taste
1 cup dry bread crumbs
2 eggs
Cooking oil for frying (olive oil
   preferred)
1½ cups tomato sauce, heated
   to spread evenly
½ pound cheese of choice
   (sliced mozzarella is the
   classic cheese for this dish)
1 teaspoon crumbled dried basil
½ cup grated Parmesan cheese

Wipe eggplant clean and cut in ¼-inch circular slices. Season with salt and pepper. Dip into bread crumbs, then in lightly beaten eggs, and again into bread crumbs. Place individually on cookie sheet and refrigerate 30 minutes. Heat lightly oiled skillet and fry slices until brown and tender. Drain on absorbent paper towels. Next, lightly butter baking dish; pour in some of the tomato sauce, spreading evenly. Arrange eggplant slices over the sauce. Cover with a layer of cheese, more sauce and a sprinkling of basil. Repeat procedure until dish is filled. Top with Parmesan. Bake in pre-heated 350° oven 25–30 minutes.

Southern Vegetable Cooking (South Carolina)

Spinach Madeline

There's a cute story about this recipe. A friend of mine who grew up in the North was going to use this recipe for entertaining. She called one night and said she had been to two liquor stores to find "vegetable liquor" and it was not available. Of course, Down South we just call it "pot likker," but vegetable liquor is the same thing—any juice that remains after cooking a vegetable. My friend will never live this down!

2 (10-ounce) packages frozen chopped spinach
4 tablespoons butter or margarine
2 tablespoons flour
2 tablespoons chopped onion
½ cup evaporated milk
½ cup vegetable liquor
½ teaspoon pepper
¾ teaspoon celery salt
¾ teaspoon garlic salt
1 teaspoon Worcestershire
6 ounces jalapeño or Monterey Jack cheese
½ cup toasted buttered bread crumbs

Cook frozen spinach in pierced packages for 5–7 minutes on FULL POWER. Press spinach in a colander to remove moisture, but reserve liquid (vegetable liquor). In large glass measuring cup, melt butter or margarine for 45 seconds on FULL POWER. Gradually stir in flour, then add onion and cook 2 minutes on 80% POWER. Add milk and vegetable liquor slowly, stirring until lumps are gone. Cook on FULL POWER for 3–4 minutes, stirring after 2 minutes, until sauce thickens. Add seasonings and cheese, stirring rapidly until cheese melts. Stir in drained spinach. Pour into 6-inch square glass casserole dish. Top with bread crumbs, if desired, then reheat on FULL POWER for 2–3 minutes or until bubbly. Serves 4.

Note: This easy-do microwave spinach dish would be nice used as a filling for tomatoes or whole onions—especially Vidalias.

The Dapper Zapper (Georgia)

Abbeville, South Carolina, is where the first organized meeting to adopt the Ordinance of Secession was held on November 22, 1860. One month later, the state of South Carolina became the first state to secede. It was also in Abbeville, on May 2, 1865, that retreating Confederate President Jefferson Davis officially acknowledged the dissolution of the Confederate government. Those points of interest gained the town the nickname "Birthplace and Deathbed of the Confederacy."

Warm Spinach Squares

½ cup vegetable oil
4 eggs, beaten
1 cup biscuit mix
½ teaspoon salt
½ teaspoon seasoned salt
1 teaspoon dried oregano
½ cup grated Parmesan
  cheese
1 cup shredded Cheddar
  cheese

1 cup shredded Monterey Jack
  cheese
1 clove garlic, minced
½ small onion, chopped
  (sauté, if you wish)
2 (10-ounce) packages frozen
  chopped spinach, thawed,
  well drained

Mix oil and eggs until well blended. Stir in biscuit mix, seasonings, and all cheeses. Stir in garlic, onion, and well-drained spinach. Stir to mix well. Batter will be thick. Spread into greased 9x13-inch pan.

Bake at 350° about 25 minutes until puffed and golden. Let cool slightly, then cut into squares. Serve hot, warm, or at room temperature. Makes 20–24 servings.

Note: These freeze well. May also cut these into bite-size squares for an hors d'oeuvre party.

Culinary Memories of Merridun, Volume 2 (South Carolina)

Spanish Corn

Kernels of corn are cooked in a tomato sauce and seasoned with bacon for a very flavorful dish.

1 dozen ears corn
1 pound bacon
1 (16-ounce) can tomato sauce

3 large onions, chopped
Salt and pepper to taste
1½ teaspoons baking soda

Remove corn kernels from cobs. Fry bacon crisp; save. Add corn and tomato sauce to bacon drippings and cook slowly 45–60 minutes; stir frequently, as it burns easily. Add additional bacon drippings, if necessary. Add salt and pepper and baking soda. Remove from heat. Crumble bacon over top before serving.

Gourmet Cooking II (Florida)

Shoe Peg Casserole

3 (11-ounce) cans shoe peg
  corn
2 (15-ounce) cans French-style
  green beans, chopped slightly
1 (10¾-ounce) can cream of
  celery soup
1 (10¾-ounce) can cream of
  chicken soup
1 large onion, chopped and
  sautéed
1 large green pepper, chopped
  and sautéed
1 sleeve Ritz Crackers
1 stick butter, melted

Combine corn, green beans, both soups, onion, and pepper. Pour into a greased 9x13-inch casserole dish. Crush crackers and crumble on top. Drizzle butter over crackers. Bake at 350° for 30 minutes.

Tastes from Paradise (Florida)

Sunshine Carrots

5 medium carrots, peeled
2 tablespoons water
1 tablespoon sugar
1 teaspoon cornstarch
¼ teaspoon salt
¼ teaspoon ginger
¼ cup orange juice
2 tablespoons butter

Slice carrots diagonally, about 1 inch thick. Place in covered 1½-quart glass casserole with water. Cook on HIGH in microwave for 8 minutes. Stir halfway through cooking time. Drain.

Meanwhile, combine sugar, cornstarch, salt, and ginger in a small saucepan. Add orange juice; cook, stirring constantly, until mixture thickens and bubbles. Boil 1 minute. Stir in butter. Pour over hot carrots, tossing to coat evenly. Serves 4.

Note: To cook without microwave, cook carrots covered in a small amount of boiling salted water until just tender, about 30 minutes. Drain.

Gulfshore Delights (Florida)

Callaway Gardens' Carrot Soufflé

3 pounds carrots, cooked,
 mashed
⅓ cup butter
1 pinch salt
⅓ cup milk
Sugar to taste

Vanilla to taste
½ teaspoon cinnamon
1 pinch nutmeg
2 tablespoons flour
2 eggs, beaten

Blend mashed carrots, butter, salt, milk, sugar, vanilla, cinnamon, and nutmeg. Add flour and blend until smooth. Fold in beaten eggs. Pour mixture into a buttered baking dish. Place in 350° oven for 30–40 minutes, or until browned evenly.

Country Cookin' (Georgia)

Open since 1952, Callaway Gardens in Pine Mountain, Georgia, is a world-famous 13,000-acre resort known for its azaleas. Each spring, the Callaway Gardens landscape explodes with the world's most beautiful display of over 20,000 azaleas, plus mountain laurel, dogwoods, daffodils, and daisies.

Green Peas Atlanta

3 tablespoons butter or
   margarine
2 cups coarsely shredded
   lettuce
1 tablespoon sugar

12 small fresh pearl onions
1 (10-ounce) package frozen
   green peas
4 strips bacon, cooked,
   crumbled

Melt butter for 45 seconds on FULL POWER in glass measuring cup in microwave. Place lettuce, sugar, onions, and peas in a 2-quart microwave-safe casserole dish. Cook bacon on bacon grill covered with a paper towel 3–4 minutes on FULL POWER or until crisp. Allow to cool, then crumble. Sprinkle over other ingredients in casserole. Pour melted butter over casserole, then toss ingredients until mixed evenly. Cover with plastic wrap and cook 6–7 minutes on FULL POWER, stirring after 3 minutes. Serves 4–6.

The Dapper Zapper (Georgia)

Swedish Baked Apples with Vanilla Sauce

1 cup ground almonds
¼ cup sugar
¼ cup water
2 egg whites

6 baking apples
2 tablespoons margarine
½ cup dry bread crumbs

In a blender, combine first 4 ingredients to a smooth paste. Set aside. Peel apples and core almost to bottom. Brush apples with melted butter and roll in bread crumbs. Fill cored apples with almond paste. Place apples with sides just touching in a 9-inch pan. Bake at 350° for 30–40 minutes or until fork tender. Serve with Vanilla Sauce.

VANILLA SAUCE:

3 egg yolks
¼ cup sugar

1½ cups heavy cream, divided
1 teaspoon vanilla

In top of double boiler, combine all ingredients, except ½ cup heavy cream. Cook until thickened, beating constantly. Remove from heat, stirring vigorously until custard is cool. Whip remaining ½ cup cream and fold into the cooled custard. Chill and serve over apples. Serves 6.

Seminole Savorings (Florida)

Holiday Cran-Apples

Delicious with turkey and ham.

3 cups chopped, peeled apples
2 cups fresh cranberries

⅓ cup white sugar
⅓ cup brown sugar

TOPPING:

1 stick margarine, melted
1 cup brown sugar
1 cup oatmeal

⅓ cup all-purpose flour
⅓ cup chopped nuts

Combine apples, cranberries, and sugars; pour into a greased 9x13-inch glass baking dish. Combine Topping ingredients and pour over cranberry-apple mixture. Bake in 350° oven 45 minutes. Serves 8–10.

Seasoned with Sunshine (Florida)

Peppered Apples
(Pommes au Poivrées)

Three kinds of pepper are combined with green onions and butter to sauté apples for an excellent accompaniment to pork or chicken dishes. Unusual and delicious.

6 apples, peeled, cored
4 ounces butter, clarified
6 green onions, chopped
⅛ teaspoon white pepper

⅛ teaspoon black pepper
⅛ teaspoon cayenne pepper
½ teaspoon salt

Cut each apple into 8 slices. Sauté apple slices in butter for 2 minutes. Add green onions. Mix well. Lower heat to simmer. Cook for 5 minutes. Add peppers and salt. Cook 2–3 minutes or until apples are tender.

Gourmet Cooking II (Florida)

Pineapple Soufflé

Terrific with ham or pork.

4 slices white bread, crust
  trimmed
2 teaspoons flour
Pinch of salt
½ cup sugar

3 eggs, beaten
1 (15-ounce) can crushed
  pineapple
1 stick margarine

Break up bread into a greased 1½-quart casserole. Add flour, salt, sugar, eggs, and pineapple. Mix well. Dot with margarine and bake at 350° for 45 minutes. Easy. Do ahead. Serves 6.

Culinary Classics (Georgia)

Spiced Peaches

4 cups sugar
2 cups cider vinegar
1 cup water
1 tablespoon whole allspice

1 tablespoon whole cloves
4 (3-inch) sticks cinnamon
4 pounds (16 medium) peaches

Mix sugar, vinegar, and water in 5-quart pan. Tie allspice and cloves in cheesecloth. Put this and cinnamon into mixture. Cover and boil 5 minutes. Peel peaches; drop into boiling syrup a few at a time. Simmer until tender, about 5 minutes. Pack in sterile jars. Cover with syrup. Seal. Yields 2 quarts.

A Taste of Georgia (Georgia)

Mango Chutney

1 quart sliced green mangoes
2 or 3 green bell peppers, chopped
1 large onion, chopped
2 hot peppers, cut very fine (remove seeds unless very hot flavor is desired)
1 clove garlic, sliced
1 tablespoon salt
1 cup grapefruit juice
1 cup cider vinegar
1 pound brown sugar
1 pound seedless raisins
1 tablespoon white mustard seeds
2 teaspoons each: allspice, cinnamon, and cloves
1 (3-ounce) package sliced almonds (optional)
1 or 2 tablespoons finely chopped crystallized ginger (optional)

Combine first 6 ingredients. Let stand 1 hour; drain. Heat grapefruit juice, vinegar, sugar, raisins, mustard seeds, and spices. Add mango mixture. Boil 30 minutes (if pressure cooker is used, cook 15 minutes). Seal while hot. Yields 4 pints.

The Gasparilla Cookbook (Florida)

PASTA, RICE, ETC.

PHOTO © SOUTH CAROLINA DEPARTMENT OF PARKS, RECREATION, AND TOURISM, WWW.DISCOVERSOUTHCAROLINA.COM.

Matthews Creek plunges an estimated 420 feet off Raven Cliff Mountain near Caesars Head State Park in Greenville County, South Carolina. The spectacular view of Raven Cliff Falls is rewarding and worth the moderately difficult hike.

Hogwild Macaroni and Cheese

This dish is so named because it generally causes the menfolk to lose all control. The addition of herbs to the basic macaroni and cheese makes a new experience out of an old favorite.

2 cups elbow macaroni, preferably whole wheat
2 tablespoons butter
1 medium onion, finely chopped
1 tablespoon flour
1 teaspoon Dijon mustard
1 teaspoon fresh basil or ½ teaspoon dried
1 teaspoon fresh thyme or ½ teaspoon dried
1 teaspoon fresh oregano or ½ teaspoon dried

1 large clove fresh garlic, minced, or ½ teaspoon garlic powder
¼ teaspoon freshly ground black pepper
2 cups milk
8 ounces sharp Cheddar cheese, grated, divided
½ cup butter
1 cup bread crumbs

Cook macaroni until just tender. Do not overcook. Drain and keep warm. Preheat oven to 400° and grease a 2-quart casserole. In a heavy, medium saucepan, melt butter and sauté onion until transparent. Stir in flour, mustard, herbs, garlic, and pepper. Stir in milk and heat, stirring constantly until hot and smooth; do not boil. Remove from heat and stir in ¾ of the cheese until melted.

Turn macaroni into casserole. Pour on the cheese sauce and stir until well coated. Top with rest of cheese. In a small pan, melt butter and add bread crumbs. Stir until crumbs are coated. Sprinkle crumbs over casserole. Bake, uncovered, for 20 minutes or until bubbly and brown. Serves 6–8 as a side dish or 4 as a main dish.

Cross Creek Kitchens (Florida)

Pasghetti Pizza

1 (16-ounce) package spaghetti
  noodles
2 eggs
½ cup milk
4 cups mozzarella cheese,
  divided
¾ teaspoon minced garlic

½ teaspoon salt
1 (32-ounce) jar Ragu spaghetti
  sauce
1½ teaspoons oregano
1 (8-ounce) package pepperoni
  slices

Break spaghetti noodles into 2-inch pieces. Cook, drain, and cool. Beat eggs. Stir in milk, 1 cup mozzarella, garlic, and salt. Add noodles. Grease pan, and place mixture into pan. Bake at 400° for 15 minutes. Spread sauce over noodles. Sprinkle with oregano and remaining mozzarella. Top with pepperoni slices. Bake at 350° for 30 minutes.

What's Cooking? in King's Grant (South Carolina)

Tarragon Shrimp Spaghetti

¼ clove garlic
1½ tablespoons olive oil
½ cup white wine
½ cup chicken broth
½ teaspoon lemon juice

¼ teaspoon tarragon
2 teaspoons butter
1 cup uncooked shrimp
Cooked spaghetti or linguini
  noodles

Sauté garlic in olive oil. Add wine, broth, lemon juice, and tarragon. Blend together, then add butter and shrimp. Cover and cook about 3 minutes or until shrimp have just turned pink. Do not overcook or the delicate flavor will be lost. Serve shrimp sauce over noodles. Serves 2.

Apalachicola Cookbook (Florida)

Chicken Tetrazzini

May be prepared ahead of time and frozen.

1 (3½-pound) stewing
  chicken
2 quarts water
1 stalk celery, cut in chunks
1 small onion, quartered
½ cup chopped parsley
2½ teaspoons salt, divided
⅛ teaspoon pepper
½ pound fine noodles

7 tablespoons butter, divided
½ pound sliced mushrooms
¼ cup all-purpose flour
1 cup light cream
¼ cup sherry or cooking
  sherry
1½ cups grated Cheddar cheese,
  or ⅓ cup Parmesan cheese
Paprika

Simmer chicken in water with celery, onion, parsley, 2 teaspoons salt, and pepper, covered, 3–4 hours. Remove chicken from broth; add noodles, and cook 8 minutes. Drain, reserving broth; boil down to 2 cups; strain. Cut meat into pieces.

Preheat oven to 450°. In 3 tablespoons butter, sauté mushrooms; set aside. Into remaining 4 tablespoons melted butter, stir flour, remaining ½ teaspoon salt, reserved broth, and cream. Cook until thickened. Add chicken, mushrooms, and sherry; heat. Place noodles in greased casserole and pour sauce over them. Top with cheese and paprika. Bake 10 minutes in 450° oven. Serves 8.

The Gasparilla Cookbook (Florida)

Fettuccine Almost Alfredo

1 (8-ounce) package fettuccine
½ tablespoon margarine
¼ cup plain low-fat yogurt
2 tablespoons light cream
3 tablespoons grated Parmesan
  cheese

2 tablespoons grated Romano
  cheese
¼ teaspoon salt
Sprinkle of black pepper

Fill a large pot about half full with water. Bring to a boil. Add fettuccine, and cook 8–10 minutes, until tender but still firm. Use a colander to drain the fettuccine, but save ¼ cup of water you cooked it in; set aside. Put fettuccine in serving bowl. Toss fettuccine with water you set aside, margarine, yogurt, cream, Parmesan cheese, Romano cheese, salt, and as much black pepper as you like. Makes 4 servings.

I Love to Cook Book (South Carolina)

Lowcountry Fettuccine

4 ounces fettuccine
1 tablespoon diced pimentos
¼ pound small bay scallops
¼ pound small shrimp, peeled
¼ pound crabmeat
½ teaspoon salt
½ teaspoon pepper
⅓ stick butter
Sherry or white wine to taste (optional)
½ cup frozen baby green peas
Fresh parsley to garnish

Cook fettuccine according to directions on the box about the same time as starting the Garlic-Dill Cream Sauce. Start the seafood about 5 minutes before the Sauce and fettuccine are done. The peas are best when lightly cooked. They may be placed in a wire mesh strainer or colander in the boiling fettuccine water the last minute or two.

Sauté pimentos, scallops, shrimp, and crabmeat with salt, pepper, and butter in a skillet until almost done (only 2–3 minutes). Stir in sherry or wine and cook until just done (about a minute more). Stir in Garlic-Dill Cream Sauce and peas and ladle over individual plates of fettuccine. Serve immediately. Serves 2–3.

GARLIC-DILL CREAM SAUCE:
⅓ stick butter
1 tablespoon self-rising flour
1 cup half-and-half
½ teaspoon sugar
½ teaspoon dill weed, dried
½ teaspoon garlic powder

Melt butter in top section of double boiler. Add flour and stir well. Cook 2 minutes, stirring often. Slowly stir in half-and-half and add sugar, dill, and garlic powder. Stir almost constantly as the Garlic-Dill Cream Sauce gradually thickens.

Southeastern Wildlife Cookbook (South Carolina)

Three geographic land areas define South Carolina: the Atlantic Coastal Plain (comprising two thirds of the state), the Piedmont, and the Blue Ridge region. South Carolinians refer to the eastern Atlantic Coastal Plain as the Lowcountry and the Piedmont and the Blue Ridge regions as Upcountry.

Lowcountry cuisine is the cooking traditionally associated with the South Carolina Low Country and Georgia coast. While it shares features with Southern cooking, its rich diversity of seafood from the coastal estuaries, its concentration of wealth in Charleston and Savannah, and a vibrant Caribbean cuisine and African cuisine influence, Lowcountry cooking has strong parallels with New Orleans and Cajun cuisines.

Mixed Seafood Lasagna

This variation of Italian lasagna layers broad noodles with shrimp, scallops, crabmeat, ricotta cheese, and a velouté sauce. A welcome variation.

1 cup chopped green onions	1 cup sliced mushrooms
8 tablespoons butter, divided	4 tablespoons flour
½ cup white wine	Salt and pepper to taste
½ pound small shrimp	1 egg
½ pound scallops, cut in small pieces	1 pound ricotta cheese
½ pound crabmeat	1 pound lasagna noodles, boiled as directed

Sauté green onions in 4 tablespoons butter. Add wine. Add shrimp and scallops. Cook 5 minutes. Add crabmeat, mushrooms, salt and pepper. Strain, reserving both liquid and seafood.

Melt remaining 4 tablespoons butter in a saucepan. Add flour and cook 2 minutes. Add reserved poaching liquid. Cook until thickened. Salt and pepper to taste. Set aside.

Mix egg with ricotta cheese. In a buttered baking dish place a layer of lasagna noodles. Cover with a layer of ricotta cheese. Spread some of the seafood mixture over ricotta. Cover with a layer of white sauce. Repeat layers of pasta, ricotta, seafood, and white sauce until all is used. Finish with a layer of lasagna and top with a little white sauce. Bake in a 350° oven 30 minutes.

Gourmet Cooking II (Florida)

Black Beans and Rice

1 pound dried black beans,
   washed and drained
6 cups water
½ cup olive oil
1 large onion, coarsely chopped
1 green bell pepper, stem and
   seeds removed, coarsely
   chopped
1 clove garlic, minced
2 bay leaves

2 teaspoons salt
¼ teaspoon black pepper,
   freshly ground
1 smoked ham bone (optional)
1 slice bacon, minced
¼ cup wine vinegar
Cooked yellow rice
Raw rings of onion or scallions,
   cut into ¼-inch rounds

Cover beans with water. Bring to a boil and boil for 2 minutes. Remove from heat; cover pan and let stand for 1 hour.

Heat olive oil in skillet. Add onion, pepper, and garlic. Sauté for about 5 minutes. Add to beans. Add bay leaves, salt, pepper, ham bone, and bacon. Bring to a boil and simmer, covered, for 2 hours or until tender, adding more water if necessary. Remove bay leaves and add wine vinegar. Serve with yellow rice, and garnish with onion rings. Serves 6–8.

Variation: This dish can be improved through the use of any flavorful stock (chicken, ham, vegetable, dry white wine, etc.), rather than water. Also for added flavor: as dish simmers, consider adding ½ cup sliced, pimento-stuffed olives, 1 teaspoon ground oregano, and/or ¼ teaspoon ground cumin.

Note: To cook yellow rice, just cook rice as you normally do, but add a drop or 2 of yellow food color. In Key West, most cooks use an inexpensive condiment called BIJOL, which gives rice a rich yellow color.

Cookin' in the Keys (Florida)

Florida is home to the largest population (about 3,000) of West Indian manatees. The manatee, which can live up to 60 years, is classified as an endangered species.

Savannah River Red Rice

1 cup tomato juice
1½ cups chicken broth
2 tablespoons tomato paste
⅛ teaspoon cayenne
½ teaspoon salt
¼ teaspoon white pepper

½ cup chopped onion
½ cup finely chopped celery
¼ cup chopped green bell
  pepper
6 tablespoons olive oil
2 cups parboiled rice

Combine juice, broth, tomato paste, cayenne, salt, and pepper in a large oven-proof saucepan. Bring to a simmer. Sauté onion, celery, and green pepper in oil in a skillet until tender. Stir in rice, coating with oil. Add rice mixture to tomato mixture; mix well. Bring to a boil. Bake, covered, at 350°, or simmer, covered, for 20–25 minutes. Yields 6 servings.

Variation: May add 4 ounces hot, cooked sausage before baking.

From Black Tie to Blackeyed Peas (Georgia)

Key West Fried Rice

1 medium onion, minced
4 tablespoons butter, divided
2 cups cooked brown rice, cold
½ teaspoon celery seeds
¼ teaspoon ginger
1 tablespoon brown sugar
½ teaspoon Ac'cent
½ teaspoon allspice
2 tablespoons soy sauce

¾ pound ham, cubed
1 pound shrimp, cooked,
  deveined
½ cup nuts (peanuts or
  almonds)
1 egg, well beaten
Parsley
Pineapple (optional)

Sauté onion in 2 tablespoons butter until limp. Add cold rice and remaining 2 tablespoons butter. Fry gently over low heat. Add seasonings and soy sauce. Add ham, shrimp, nuts, and beaten egg. Stir until warm. Garnish with parsley and pineapple. Serves 6 for main course.

Seasons in the Sun (Florida)

Sausage and Rice Casserole

1 pound hot sausage, browned, drained
1 cup chopped celery
1 cup chopped onion
1 cup chopped green bell pepper

1 cup uncooked rice
1 (14½-ounce) can chicken broth, combined with water to yield 2 cups
Salt and pepper to taste

Combine all ingredients in a 2-quart casserole. Cover and bake at 325° for 1 hour. Serves 6.

Stir Crazy! (South Carolina)

Hoppin' John

A traditional New Year's Day feast; peas for good luck, "greens" for money.

1 cup dried cowpeas or black-eyed peas
1 cup raw rice
½ pound slab bacon, or 1 ham hock

1 quart cold water
1 teaspoon salt
¼ teaspoon pepper
⅛ teaspoon cayenne pepper
Chopped onion

Wash and soak peas according to package directions. Cook rice according to package directions. Cut bacon or ham hock into small pieces and fry. Cook peas in 1 quart cold water, adding a little bacon grease. Add salt, pepper, and cayenne. Cook until peas are tender but firm, about 45 minutes. Approximately 1 cup of liquid should remain. Add cooked rice. Heat 2–3 minutes; serve. Garnish with chopped onion and drained bacon or ham. Serves 4–6.

Atlanta Cooknotes (Georgia)

Fountain Inn, South Carolina, is proud of the town's most famous native son, Clayton "Peg Leg" Bates, who lost his leg in a cotton gin accident at the age of twelve. He overcame this tragedy to become a tap dancer. His signature step was the "Imitation American Jet Plane," in which he would jump five feet in the air and land on his peg leg, with his good leg sticking out straight behind him. During his career, Bates performed more than twenty different times on the *Ed Sullivan Show*—more than any other artist.

Chicken and Yellow Rice Valenciana

An Ybor City specialty.

1 (2½-pound) frying chicken, quartered
½ cup fresh olive oil
2 onions, chopped
1 green pepper, chopped
1 clove garlic, chopped fine
2 tablespoons salt
1 bay leaf
1 (14½-ounce) can tomatoes, drained
¼ teaspoon pepper
2½ cups rice
5 cups water plus 2 chicken bouillon cubes
½ cup sherry wine (optional)
⅛ teaspoon saffron
1 cup green peas
1 dozen green olives
1 (2-ounce) jar pimentos

Brown chicken in olive oil over medium heat. Add onions, green pepper, and garlic. Continue cooking until slightly brown, about 5 minutes. Return chicken to pot and stir in salt, bay leaf, tomatoes, and pepper. Add rice, water (in which 2 chicken bouillon cubes have been dissolved), and wine. Dissolve saffron in small amount of water and add to pot (or use a few drops of yellow food coloring mixed with water). Bring to a boil. Bake in preheated oven at 350° for 20 minutes. Garnish with green peas, olives, and pimentos. Makes 4 servings.

Famous Florida Recipes (Florida)

Pimento-Cheese Bake

2 cups grated Cheddar cheese
1 (4-ounce) jar chopped pimentos
1 tablespoon chopped onion
½ cup mayonnaise
12 slices white bread, trimmed
1 teaspoon oregano

Preheat oven to 350°. Mix cheese, pimentos, onion, and mayonnaise. Spread ¾ mixture on slices of bread, and roll up jelly-roll fashion. Place each roll in a 9x13-inch casserole. Spread remaining mixture over all and sprinkle with oregano. Bake 30 minutes or until melted and browned. Serves 6.

Atlanta Cooknotes (Georgia)

Tiropita
(Greek Cheese Pie)

10 sheets fillo dough
½ cup butter, melted
2 (16-ounce) cartons small-
curd cottage cheese, or
ricotta cheese, drained

1 (8-ounce) package cream
cheese, softened
4 eggs, beaten
¼ pound feta cheese, crumbled

Thaw fillo according to package directions. Layer a 11x15-inch pan, or equivalent, with 5 sheets fillo. Butter between each sheet. Mix remaining ingredients; pour mixture on fillo. Top with remaining 5 sheets of fillo, buttering between sheets and top layer. With a sharp knife, score top layer only into 3-inch squares. Bake at 350° for 30 minutes. Cut into squares; serve at once. Serves 15.

Suncoast Seasons (Florida)

Vegetable Quiche

¾ cup egg substitute
1½ cups skim milk
¼ teaspoon pepper
½ teaspoon salt
Pinch of nutmeg
¾ cup grated reduced-fat
Cheddar, mozzarella, and
Swiss cheese combined
2 teaspoons vegetable oil

1½ cups chopped spinach or
broccoli
¼ cup diced onion
¼ cup sliced mushrooms
2 low-fat pie crusts
2 tablespoons chopped parsley
Sprinkle of grated Parmesan
cheese

Preheat oven to 375°. In a mixing bowl, beat eggs. Stir in milk, pepper, salt, nutmeg, and cheese. Put vegetable oil in a small skillet or pan. Add spinach or broccoli, onion, and mushrooms to skillet, and sauté about 10 minutes. Stir sautéed vegetables into egg mixture. Pour equal amounts of quiche mixture into pie crusts. Top with parsley and a sprinkle of Parmesan cheese. Bake 30–35 minutes. Let stand 15–30 minutes before serving. Makes 2 pies with 8 slices each.

I Love to Cook Book (South Carolina)

Vidalia Onion Quiche

3 tablespoons margarine
¼ cup sliced Vidalia onion
½ cup diced ham (or minced clams)
1 pie crust, unbaked, pricked
1½ cups grated Cheddar cheese
1 cup grated Swiss cheese
1 cup grated caraway seed cheese
¼ cup evaporated milk
3 eggs
½ cup sour cream
½ cup crumbled bacon

Melt margarine in a skillet and sauté onions and ham until done. Place in bottom of unbaked pie crust. Mix cheeses, milk, eggs, and sour cream, and pour atop onion and ham mixture. Bake at 350° for 30 minutes and garnish with crumbled bacon.

Island Events Cookbook (South Carolina)

Exceptional Quiche

3 (9-inch) pie shells
1 pound hot bulk sausage
1 cup chopped green bell pepper
1 cup chopped green onions, tops included
2 packages frozen chopped spinach or frozen chopped broccoli
12 ounces grated Monterey Jack cheese
12 eggs, beaten
2 tablespoons seasoned salt
1 teaspoon white pepper
½ cup half-and-half
1 teaspoon cumin
1 teaspoon summer savory

Prick pie shells and bake 5 minutes. Sauté sausage, green pepper, and onions; drain well. In same pan, cook spinach until water is gone. Layer each ingredient, ending with eggs and half-and-half mixed with seasonings poured over it all. These freeze well after baking. Bake 30–40 minutes at 425°.

Sawgrass and Pines (Florida)

MEATS

PHOTO COURTESY OF NASA

Cape Canaveral, Florida, is America's launch pad for space flights. The first U.S. satellite (1958), the first U.S. manned space flight (1961), and the first U.S. moon landing flight (1969), were all launched from Cape Canaveral. Space Shuttle Columbia, *launched on April 12, 1981, was the first space shuttle launched at Cape Canaveral's Kennedy Space Center.*

Tea Marinated Florida Beef Roast

1 (3- to 5-pound) Florida
chuck or shoulder-cut beef
roast

2–3 tablespoons bacon drippings
Pitcher of strong tea
Sauce

Brown roast well in Dutch oven on top of stove in bacon drippings. Make enough very strong tea to cover roast ¾ way. Simmer 3–5 hours, until meat is fork tender. Drain off tea and place meat in baking dish. Pour half of Sauce over meat and baste several times during baking.

SAUCE:

1 cup chili sauce
3 tablespoons brown sugar
Juice of 2 lemons
1 tablespoon Worcestershire
¼ teaspoon celery salt
⅓ cup grated onion

2 tablespoons bacon drippings
1 cup water
1 teaspoon paprika
3 tablespoons vinegar
1 teaspoon salt

Combine all ingredients, and stir to blend. Pour half over meat; save half. Bake uncovered at 325° for 45 minutes. Serve hot Sauce with meat.

Famous Florida Recipes (Florida)

Russian Roast

1 (1¼-ounce) envelope onion
soup mix
2 (8-ounce) bottles Russian
salad dressing
Fresh baby carrots

2 onions, cut in wedges
1 (4-pound) chuck beef roast
1 (14½-ounce) can whole
potatoes, drained

Heat electric slow cooker to HIGH. Pour in soup mix and dressing; mix well. Add carrots and onions. Place meat on top. Add potatoes. Cook on HIGH about 1 hour, then turn to MEDIUM and cook 7–8 hours or until meat is tender. Yields 8 servings.

NeNa's Garden (South Carolina)

Bachelor's Roast

1 (4-pound) beef roast
½ teaspoon each: salt,
  pepper, garlic salt

3 tablespoons cooking oil
1 (8-ounce) bottle Coca-Cola
1 (14-ounce) bottle ketchup

Score roast in several places, fill each slit with seasonings. Sear roast on all sides in oil. Remove from pan; pour off excess fat. Place roast in foil-lined roasting pan. Pour Coca-Cola and ketchup over roast. Cover loosely with foil and bake 3 hours at 325°.

Cooking...Done the Baptist Way (South Carolina)

Pan-Seared Filet Mignon Medallions

4 (4-ounce) tenderloin filets
Salt and pepper to taste
2 ounces olive oil
2 tablespoons chopped
  scallions
2 teaspoons prepared mustard

½ teaspoon tarragon
½ cup dry white wine
1 cup brown sauce
½ cup heavy cream
4 artichoke hearts
2 tablespoons butter

Season filets with salt and pepper, and sauté in hot olive oil until desired doneness. Remove and set aside. Add scallions, mustard, tarragon, and white wine to pan and reduce slightly. Add brown sauce and cream, and simmer one minute.

Quarter artichokes, add to sauce, and simmer 2 minutes. Check seasoning; return filets to warm and stir in butter. Arrange filets on plates and spoon sauce over. Serve with hot vegetable medley. Serves 2.

Intracoastal Waterway Restaurant Guide & Recipe Book
(Florida)

Braciole

1 pound top round steak
4–6 mozzarella slices
4–6 teaspoons butter
⅓ cup Parmesan cheese
2 garlic cloves, chopped or
  garlic powder
¼ cup raisins
Salt and pepper
Olive oil
Tomato sauce

Cut steak into 4–6 pieces, and pound each piece to flatten very thin. Place mozzarella and butter on each piece, then sprinkle with Parmesan, garlic, raisins, salt and pepper. Roll each piece, and tie securely with string.

Sauté in olive oil with salt and pepper until steak rolls are browned on all sides. Drop into your favorite tomato sauce and simmer 1½ hours or until fork tender. Remove from sauce, let cool slightly, then carefully remove string and serve with your favorite pasta.

Preserving Our Italian Heritage (Florida)

Aunt Tency's Spanish Steak

1 large full-cut, round
  beefsteak (1–1½ inches
  thick)
Flour to dredge
Salt and pepper to taste
3 tablespoons bacon drippings
1 large onion, sliced in rounds
1 (14½-ounce) can diced
  tomatoes
Flour to thicken

Wipe meat with a damp cloth and slash fat to keep edges from curling up. Dredge steak in flour mixed with salt and pepper. In a large lidded iron skillet or Dutch oven, heat drippings; brown meat well on both sides. Pour off excess fat, leaving meat and browned bits in the pan.

Place onion rounds on top of meat. Pour tomatoes over all. Cover; cook in a 350° oven for an hour. If too soupy, remove meat to a warm platter and boil down the sauce, or thicken with 1–2 tablespoons flour stirred into a paste with cold water.

Mountain Folk, Mountain Food (Georgia)

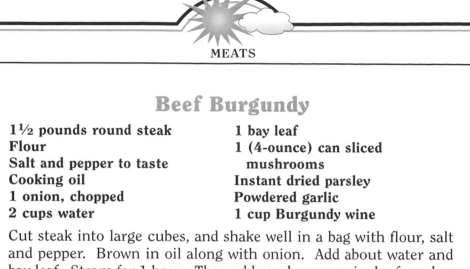

Beef Burgundy

1½ pounds round steak
Flour
Salt and pepper to taste
Cooking oil
1 onion, chopped
2 cups water

1 bay leaf
1 (4-ounce) can sliced
  mushrooms
Instant dried parsley
Powdered garlic
1 cup Burgundy wine

Cut steak into large cubes, and shake well in a bag with flour, salt and pepper. Brown in oil along with onion. Add about water and bay leaf. Steam for 1 hour. Then add mushrooms, pinch of parsley, pinch of garlic, and a cup of Burgundy wine. Simmer until mushrooms are tender; remove bay leaf. Serve over hot rice. Serves 6.

The Sandlapper Cookbook (South Carolina)

Father's Day Steak

½ cup sherry
½ cup soy sauce
¼ cup oil
¼ cup lemon juice
2 tablespoons brown sugar

½ teaspoon ginger
1 garlic clove, minced
⅛ teaspoon hot sauce
1 (3- to 4-pound) London broil
  or top round steak

In saucepan, mix together all ingredients except steak. Cook 10 minutes; cool. Place steak in plastic bag. Add marinade; tie securely; refrigerate 24 hours. Remove steak, reserving marinade to make sauce. Place meat over hot coals or on broiling rack in oven with meat 4–5 inches from heat. Broil 25–40 minutes for rare to medium steak. Brush with marinade; turn occasionally. Carve thin slices diagonally across grain. Serve with sauce.

STEAK SAUCE:

4 teaspoons cornstarch
Reserved marinade

½ pound sliced mushrooms
¼ cup sliced scallions

Stir cornstarch into small amount of water. Add to remaining marinade; bring to a boil. Add mushrooms and scallions. Cook slowly until thickened. Dilute with water until sauce is desired consistency. Serves 6–8.

Sunny Side Up (Florida)

Cabbage and Beef Casserole

2 pounds lean ground beef
1 large onion, chopped
2 tablespoons brown sugar
Salt and pepper to taste

2 (14-ounce) cans tomatoes,
  cut up
1 medium cabbage, chopped
Parmesan cheese

In a large skillet, brown ground beef with onion, brown sugar, and salt and pepper to taste. Add tomatoes. Add chopped cabbage. Bring to a boil, and simmer for 30 minutes. Sprinkle with Parmesan cheese. Serves 6–8.

Cooking with 257 (Florida)

Juicy Meatballs and Gravy

Delicious over rice or creamed potatoes.

1 pound ground beef
¼ cup chopped green bell
  pepper
2 tablespoons chopped onion
1 egg
1 (5-ounce) can evaporated
  milk

1 teaspoon salt
¼ teaspoon pepper
½ cup fine bread or cracker
  crumbs or oatmeal
½ cup flour
½ cup shortening

In large bowl, combine beef with pepper, onion, egg, milk, salt, and pepper. Stir in crumbs or oatmeal. Blend well. Roll into ½-inch balls; roll in flour. Brown in hot shortening on all sides. Remove from pan and make gravy.

CREAM GRAVY:

2 tablespoons flour
2 tablespoons meat drippings
  from pan

1 cup evaporated milk
1 cup water
Salt and pepper to taste

Brown flour in drippings; add milk, water, and seasonings. Stir constantly until it comes to a boil. Add meatballs. As soon as they begin to boil, turn heat down and simmer, covered, about 30 minutes. If gravy gets too thick, add a little extra water. Serves 4.

Bountiful Blessings from the Bauknight Table
(South Carolina)

Barbecue Burger Casserole

This is a great casserole for kids—actually, for the kid in all of us. A dill pickle garnish makes the dish!

2 pounds ground sirloin
1 medium sweet onion, chopped
¾ cup barbecue sauce
¾ cup ketchup
1 tablespoon Dijon mustard
½ teaspoon salt
½ teaspoon pepper
1 (8-ounce) package cream cheese, softened

1 (8-ounce) container sour cream
¾ cup chopped green onions
1 (8-ounce) package wide egg noodles, cooked, drained
2 cups shredded Colby-Jack cheese, divided
Chopped dill pickle

Cook ground sirloin and onion in a large skillet over medium heat, stirring until beef crumbles and is no longer pink. Drain and return to skillet. Add barbecue sauce and next 4 ingredients to beef mixture. Simmer until mixture is warmed through, stirring often.

Combine cream cheese and sour cream, stirring until smooth. Stir in green onions and hot cooked noodles. Layer half of noodle mixture in a greased 2-quart baking dish. Top with half of beef mixture. Sprinkle with 1 cup cheese. Top with remaining noodle mixture and remaining beef mixture. If desired, cover and chill overnight. If chilled, let stand at room temperature 30 minutes before baking.

Cover and bake at 350° for 30 minutes, or until thoroughly heated. Uncover and sprinkle with remaining 1 cup cheese. Bake 5 more minutes. Garnish with chopped dill pickle. Serves 8.

Dining Under the Carolina Moon (South Carolina)

Cheeseburger Pie

2 pounds hamburger meat
1 cup chopped onions
3 eggs
1½ cups milk

1 cup Bisquick
1 pint pizza sauce
2 cups shredded mozzarella
   cheese

In a saucepan, brown meat and onions. Season slightly. Drain and pour into a loaf pan. Mix eggs, milk, and Bisquick, and pour over hamburger mixture. Pour pizza sauce on and top with cheese. Bake at 350° for 30–40 minutes.

500 Favorite Recipes (South Carolina)

Popover Mushroom Pizza Bake

BASE:

1 pound ground beef
1 pound fresh mushrooms or
  1 (8-ounce) can mushrooms
½ cup chopped green bell
  pepper

½ cup chopped onion
1 (10½-ounce) can or jar pizza
  sauce with cheese
1 teaspoon oregano
1 teaspoon garlic salt

Preheat oven to 400°. In large skillet or Dutch oven, cook and stir ground beef, mushrooms, green pepper, and onion until meat is browned. Thoroughly drain fat. Stir in pizza sauce, oregano, and garlic salt. Simmer 10 minutes.

POPOVER TOP:

2 eggs
1 cup milk
1 tablespoon vegetable oil
1 cup all-purpose flour

Salt to taste
1½ cups shredded mozzarella
  cheese
½ cup grated Parmesan cheese

In small bowl of electric mixer, blend together eggs, milk, and oil. Add flour and salt. Beat at MEDIUM speed about 1½ minutes or until smooth. Spoon hot beef mixture into shallow 2-quart baking dish. Sprinkle with mozzarella cheese. Pour topping evenly over base. Sprinkle with Parmesan cheese. Bake about 30 minutes or until puffy and golden brown. Makes 6–8 servings.

Bethel Food Bazaar II (South Carolina)

Lucy's Spaghetti Meat Sauce

None better . . . makes a lot . . . freeze some.

3 large onions, chopped
2 cloves garlic, minced
¼ stick butter
¼ cup oil
3 pounds ground chuck
1 pound fresh mushrooms,
  sliced, use stems, too
2 (28-ounce) cans Italian
  tomatoes

1 (12-ounce) can tomato paste
1 tablespoon chili powder
1 tablespoon sugar
¼ teaspoon each: marjoram,
  oregano, basil, thyme
3 bay leaves
Salt and pepper to taste

Cook onion and garlic in butter and oil until clear. Add meat and brown. Stir in sliced mushrooms. Combine tomatoes, tomato paste, and all seasonings; add to meat mixture. Simmer, uncovered, until thick, at least 3 hours. When cool, put in refrigerator. Before reheating to serve, or freezing, skim off fat. Serve over very thin spaghetti. Serves 10–12.

Cook and Deal (Florida)

Picadillo II

2 medium onions, finely
  chopped
1 large green bell pepper, finely
  chopped
Olive oil
6 small tomatoes, chopped
  (or 2 small cans)
1 pound ground beef
1 pound ground pork
2 teaspoons salt

1 teaspoon garlic powder
Pepper to taste
1 tablespoon brown sugar
¼ cup vinegar
¼ cup stuffed green olives,
  chopped
½ cup raisins
1 tablespoon capers
½ cup red wine, or ½ cup
  tomato juice or bouillon

Sauté onions and green pepper in olive oil. Add chopped tomatoes, salt, garlic, pepper, and meat, stirring constantly to break into small bits. Add remaining ingredients slowly until meat is tender, about 1 hour. Serve over rice, mashed potatoes, or split, buttered, and toasted hamburger buns. Serves 10.

The Gasparilla Cookbook (Florida)

Classic Slow-Cooked Ribs

Delicious prepared with either beef or pork ribs!

1 cup vinegar
½ cup ketchup
2 tablespoons sugar
2 tablespoons Worcestershire
1 clove garlic, minced
1 teaspoon dry mustard

1 teaspoon paprika
½ teaspoon salt
⅛ teaspoon pepper
2 pounds boneless pork or beef
   ribs
1 tablespoon vegetable oil

Combine first 9 ingredients in slow cooker. Cut ribs into serving-size pieces, if needed. Brown ribs in vegetable oil in a skillet. Transfer to slow cooker. Cover and cook on LOW 4–6 hours or until tender. Serves 4.

Dining Under the Carolina Moon (South Carolina)

Citrus Spareribs

4–5 pounds spareribs, cut in
   serving pieces
1 (6-ounce) can frozen orange
   concentrate, thawed,
   undiluted
¾ cup ketchup

2 tablespoons molasses
1 teaspoon Worcestershire sauce
½ teaspoon Tabasco sauce
2 teaspoons salt
4 teaspoons grated onion

Place spareribs in large pot. Cover with water and bring to a boil. Reduce heat and simmer, covered, for 30 minutes. Drain and refrigerate until ready to grill.

Mix orange concentrate with remaining ingredients. Place spare-ribs on grill set about 8 inches from heat. Cook 15 minutes. Turn and brush with orange sauce. Cook 15–30 minutes longer, turning and brushing frequently with sauce. Serves 4–6.

Citrus Lovers Cook Book (Florida)

Oven-Cooked Spareribs

3 pounds lean pork spareribs
1 cup ketchup
1 tablespoon dry mustard
4 tablespoons brown sugar
1 teaspoon nutmeg
1 teaspoon allspice

½ teaspoon cinnamon
1 teaspoon salt
1 teaspoon white pepper
1 small onion, chopped, browned
   in 1 tablespoon margarine

Trim and cut spareribs into serving pieces. Wash; pat dry. Lightly salt and pepper. Put into covered roasting pan. Cook 1 hour at 300°. Drain, and add sauce made from remaining ingredients. Coat each piece; turn over after ½ hour and coat other side. Cook another ½ hour. Total cooking time is 2 hours. Serves 4.

The Sandlapper Cookbook (South Carolina)

Cumberland Island, Georgia's largest and southernmost barrier island, is largely unspoiled. On this National Seashore, the animals rule and people are only visitors. Wild horses run free through the marshes and wind-swept dunes, while the inland forests shelter deer, alligator, armadillo, and mink. There is no bridge to the island; the most convenient access is by ferry from the town of St. Marys. Once privately owned, large areas were deeded to the National Parks Foundation by members or heirs of the Carnegie family in 1971. The ruins of the once magnificent Carnegie Estate "Dungeness" still stand on the south end of the island.

Southern Pork Barbecue

**1 (5- to 6-pound) pork roast,
shoulder or Boston butt**

Season pork with Barbecue Dry Rub, if desired. Light fire in smoker. When coals are ashen, add hickory or oak chips that have been soaked in water for an hour and then drained. Add wood chips onto the mound of coals every hour for first 4 hours of grilling. Add more charcoal as needed. Keep temperature at 325°–350°. Place pork, fat side up, on grill over a drip pan, away from fire, or place pork on a rack in an aluminum pan on grill. Lower cover on grill to seal in smoke flavor. Barbecue until nicely browned and cooked through, 4–6 hours, or longer, until internal temperature reaches 195° and meat is tender. You can shorten the cooking time by wrapping roast in foil the last few hours.

Move cooked pork to a clean cutting board and cover meat with foil until cool enough to handle. Pull pork into pieces; discard skin, fat, and bones. With fingers or fork, pull into shreds about 2 inches long and ¼-inch wide (or you can also finely chop pork with a cleaver). Put pulled pork into a metal or foil pan and stir in some of the Vinegar Barbecue Sauce, enough to keep meat moist and flavorful. Cover with foil, and place on grill to keep warm until time to serve. Serve with additional Vinegar Barbecue Sauce.

BARBECUE DRY RUB:

2 tablespoons salt
2 tablespoons sugar
2 tablespoons ground cumin
2 tablespoons ground black
  pepper

2 tablespoons chili powder
4 tablespoons paprika
1 tablespoon garlic powder
1 teaspoon cayenne pepper
½ teaspoon dry mustard

Combine and rub on the pork roast before placing on the grill.

VINEGAR BARBECUE SAUCE:

1 cup vinegar
½ cup water
¼ cup ketchup
1 onion, sliced thin
1 large garlic clove, minced

½ teaspoon crushed red
  pepper
2 tablespoons brown sugar
½ teaspoon pepper
½ teaspoon salt

Bring all ingredients to a boil over high heat. Reduce heat to low, and simmer 10 minutes or until reduced to 1 cup. Serve over barbecue pork.

Our Best Home Cooking (Georgia)

Glorified Boston Butt

1 (3½- to 4-pound) Boston
  butt roast
2 tablespoons vegetable oil
1 (10¾-ounce) can cream of
  mushroom soup
½ cup water
1 cup chopped onions
1 teaspoon salt

¼ teaspoon pepper
⅛ teaspoon red pepper
1 bay leaf
1 tablespoon paprika
1½ pounds potatoes, peeled,
  quartered
4 medium carrots, peeled, sliced
1 tablespoon Worcestershire

Brown roast in hot oil in large Dutch oven. Pour off fat. Combine soup and next 7 ingredients. Pour over roast. Cover and simmer 1½ hours, stirring occasionally.

Add potatoes, carrots, and Worcestershire. Cover and simmer 30 minutes or until vegetables are done. Remove bay leaf. Remove pot roast and vegetables to a serving platter, reserving drippings. Cook pan drippings over medium heat until slightly reduced. Serve gravy over rice.

Bountiful Blessings from the Bauknight Table
(South Carolina)

Fruited Pork

8 small pork tenderloins
1 tablespoon oil
1 small onion, thinly sliced
Salt, pepper, thyme, paprika
½ cup apple juice

7–8 dried apricots
7–8 dried pitted prunes
⅓ cup sweet cream or
  non-dairy creamer

On medium to high heat, brown tenderloins in oil. Add onion; sprinkle with seasonings, being especially generous with paprika and continue to cook until browned on both sides, about 8–10 minutes in all. Lower heat, add apple juice and dried fruits. Cover and simmer 7–8 minutes or until meat is well done. Add cream, stir well, and cook a minute or two longer.

Galley Gourmet III (Florida)

Citrus Pork Chops

6 pork chops (½–¾ inch
  thick)
2 tablespoons shortening
1 teaspoon salt
⅛ teaspoon pepper
½ cup orange juice
1 teaspoon lemon juice

2 tablespoons honey
¼ teaspoon cinnamon
¼ teaspoon ginger
1 teaspoon sugar
2 oranges, sectioned
Flour for thickening

Brown chops in shortening. Pour off drippings. Season chops with salt and pepper. Combine juices, honey, spices, and sugar. Pour over chops. Cover tightly, and cook slowly 45 minutes, or till done. Add orange sections and cook just until heated through. Remove chops. Thicken pan liquid with flour for gravy, and spoon over hot chops.

Citrus Lovers Cook Book (Florida)

Pork Chop Casserole

6 pork chops
½ cup flour
Salt and pepper to taste
4 sweet potatoes, peeled, sliced,
  divided

½ cup brown sugar
1½ cups sliced apples, divided
Sugar
½ cup apple juice

Coat chops with flour, salt, and pepper. Brown in heavy skillet. Arrange in greased 2-quart casserole. Arrange ½ of sweet potato slices over top. Sprinkle with brown sugar. Top with ½ the sliced apples. Sprinkle with sugar. Top with remaining potatoes and apples, and pour juice over all. Cover. Bake at 350° for 1½ hours. Remove cover for last 15 minutes.

Cooking with 257 (Florida)

While searching for the legendary Fountain of Youth, Hernando de Soto discovered the historic Espiritu Santo Springs or "Springs of the Holy Spirit" in 1539 in Safety Harbor, Florida. The springs are still thought to have curative powers. Safety Harbor was first homesteaded by Count Odet Philippe, a Frenchman who is credited with introducing the grapefruit to Florida in 1823.

"Pickin' Pork"

Fresh pork ham, whole or
   shoulder or butt ham (must
   be a fresh ham, not smoked
   or cured)

Vinegar
Seasoned pepper

Trim ham, leaving small amount of fat for flavor during cooking. All skin and brine should be removed. Rub fresh ham with a liberal amount of vinegar. Cover ham completely with seasoned pepper; pressing pepper into sides so most of it adheres. Wrap ham in heavy-duty foil tightly. Place in roasting pan and bake at 200° overnight—at least 10 hours. When unwrapped, the pork should fall apart, or shred when pulled with a fork. Place on a large wooden platter on a buffet table and your guests will "pick" at it forever. Serve with your favorite barbecue sauce. Also great for sandwiches.

Seasons in the Sun (Florida)

Quick Draw's
Ham and Sweet Potatoes

6 medium sweet potatoes
½ teaspoon salt
3 tablespoons butter or
  margarine
⅛ teaspoon pepper
⅛ teaspoon nutmeg
Milk
2 cups diced, cooked ham

1 (8-ounce) can pineapple
  chunks, drained, reserve juice
½ cup green pepper strips
2 tablespoons brown sugar
1 tablespoon cornstarch
2 tablespoons vinegar

Cook and mash sweet potatoes; add salt, butter, pepper, nutmeg, and enough milk to whip potatoes. Pan-fry ham in butter until golden brown. Add pineapple and green peppers. Cook 3 minutes. Combine sugar and cornstarch; blend in reserved pineapple juice and vinegar. Cook, stirring constantly, until clear and thickened. Pour mixture in shallow casserole dish. Drop spoonfuls of whipped sweet potatoes on top. Bake at 400° for 20 minutes, or until thoroughly heated. Serves 4–5.

Wanted: Quick Draw's Favorite Recipes (Georgia)

Country Ham and Red-Eye Gravy

1 thick slice cured country
  ham

1 cup boiling black coffee or
  water

Take a slice of uncooked country ham about ½–¾ inch thick, with most of the fat left on around the edges. Fry ham slice in a black iron skillet over medium to medium-high heat in its own fat until nicely browned on both sides. When browned, transfer ham to a warm platter. Add boiling black coffee or water to the skillet, scraping bottom to dissolve particles that cling to the bottom. Drizzle several spoonfuls of gravy over ham, and serve remaining red-eye gravy with thick creamy grits.

South Carolina Ladies & Gents Love to Cook! (South Carolina)

Atlanta Baked Ham

1 (7-pound) half or whole
  ham

2 tablespoons prepared
  mustard

⅓ cup firmly packed brown
  sugar

2 tablespoons peanut butter

1 teaspoon horseradish

18–20 whole cloves

½ cup Coca-Cola

Preheat oven to 325°. Bake ham 25 minutes per pound for half ham, or slightly less for a whole ham. Combine mustard, brown sugar, peanut butter, and horseradish, mixing well. Set aside. When about 45 minutes baking time remains, remove ham from oven. Trim off rind and fat; pour excess fat from pan. Stud top of ham with cloves, and spread with mustard sauce. Pour Coca-Cola in pan and return to oven, basting ham several times with pan juices. Easy, can prepare ahead, can freeze. Serves 8–10.

Atlanta Cooknotes (Georgia)

Festive Baked Ham

1 cup apple cider
½ cup water
1 (5-pound) uncooked ham half
12 whole cloves
1 cup firmly-packed brown
  sugar

1 (21-ounce) can cherry pie
  filling
½ cup raisins
½ cup orange juice

Combine apple cider and water in a saucepan; bring to a boil. Set aside. Remove skin from ham. Place ham, fat side up, on a cutting board; score fat in a diamond design, and stud with cloves. Place ham in a shallow baking pan, fat side up; coating top with brown sugar.

Insert meat thermometer, making sure it does not touch fat or bone. Bake, uncovered, at 325° for about 2 hours (22–25 minutes per pound) or until meat thermometer registers 160°, basting every 30 minutes with cider mixture.

Combine remaining ingredients in a saucepan; bring to a boil. Serve sauce with sliced ham. Serves 10.

Sawgrass and Pines (Florida)

Veal Parmigiana

1 pound veal cutlets
1 egg, slightly beaten
½ cup fine dry bread crumbs
2 tablespoons oil
1 (10¾-ounce) can tomato
  soup
¼ cup water
¼ cup minced onion

1 clove garlic, crushed
⅛ teaspoon thyme
8 mushrooms, sliced
4 ounces mozzarella cheese,
  grated
2 tablespoons freshly grated
  Parmesan cheese

Dip veal in egg, then in bread crumbs, and fry in oil until brown on each side. Place veal in a 7½x12-inch shallow baking dish. Blend soup, water, onion, garlic, and thyme. Pour over meat. Top with mushroom slices, mozzarella cheese, and sprinkle with Parmesan cheese. Bake in 350° oven about 30 minutes, or until hot and bubbling. Serves 4.

A Taste of South Carolina (South Carolina)

Lamb Shanks in Red Wine

3 slices bacon
4 lamb shanks
Flour
Salt and pepper to taste
1 (14½-ounce) can tomatoes
1 cup chopped celery
½ cup chopped parsley

2 medium-size onions, chopped
1 clove garlic, chopped
1 teaspoon Worcestershire
1 tablespoon grated horseradish
1 cup dry red wine (Burgundy preferred)
½ pound fresh mushrooms

Render 3 slices of bacon, diced, and remove bacon. Coat lamb shanks thickly with seasoned flour. Brown slowly in bacon fat, turning until nicely browned. Use a deep iron kettle (Dutch oven). When shanks are browned, add tomatoes, bacon bits, celery, parsley, onions, garlic, Worcestershire, horseradish, and wine. Cover and simmer 2 hours. Add mushrooms, separating stems from tops and, if large, halve or quarter. Cook ½–¾ hour longer. If gravy has not thickened, just before serving, add flour paste (flour and small amount of water). Yields 4 servings.

Quail Country (Georgia)

Darlington Raceway near Darlington, South Carolina, is known as the track "too tough to tame." The track opened in 1950, and is still remembered as the original superspeedway, and one of the pillars of the NASCAR establishment. It was the first superspeedway built with NASCAR racing in mind and is of a unique, somewhat egg-shaped design, an oval with the ends of very different configurations. This condition supposedly arose from the proximity of one end of the track to a minnow pond the owner refused to relocate. The design of the track makes it very challenging for the crews to set up their cars' handling in a way that will be effective at both ends.

Venison Steaks with Shrimp and Asparagus Sauce

1 pound asparagus
1 envelope béarnaise sauce
  mix
1 tablespoon butter
2 tablespoons olive oil

Several green onions, sliced
1 pound venison loin steaks
¼ cup all-purpose flour
½ pound shrimp, cooked,
  peeled, chopped

Steam asparagus until tender-crisp, then drop into ice water to stop cooking. Prepare béarnaise sauce according to package directions.

Melt butter with olive oil in a nonstick skillet, and sauté green onions until tender. Drain and add to béarnaise.

Flatten steaks with a meat mallet until very thin. Coat with flour, and brown quickly in drippings in skillet. Add shrimp and asparagus to béarnaise and heat gently. Serve steaks topped with shrimp and asparagus sauce. Makes 2–4 servings.

Wild Fare & Wise Words (South Carolina)

Pat's Meat Rub

Nice to give away small bottles to your friends.

¼ cup garlic salt
¼ cup salt
¼ cup celery salt
¼ cup onion salt
1 cup sugar

3 tablespoons black pepper
½ teaspoon cayenne pepper
½ cup paprika
2 tablespoons chili powder
1 teaspoon MSG (optional)

Mix ingredients well. Store in sealed container in dark cabinet. Rub generously on all types of meat. Especially good on Boston butt. Yields 3 cups.

A Carolina Country Collection II (South Carolina)

Pat's Barbecue Sauce

1 cup sugar
1 teaspoon cornstarch
½ teaspoon oregano
½ teaspoon thyme
2 teaspoons salt
¼ teaspoon cayenne pepper
1 teaspoon black pepper
¾ cup distilled vinegar
1½ cups molasses
1¼ cups ketchup
2 cups prepared yellow mustard
¼ cup canola oil

Mix all dry ingredients in medium saucepan; add vinegar slowly to make a paste. Mix remaining ingredients together; add to vinegar paste. Bring to a boil, stirring constantly. Reduce heat and simmer 10 minutes. Cool and store in refrigerator.

A Carolina Country Collection II (South Carolina)

Lat's Gourmet Sauce for Beef

The crowning glory!

3 tablespoons butter, melted
3 tablespoons flour
2 teaspoons prepared mustard
   or ½ teaspoon dry mustard
2 teaspoons Worcestershire
1¼ cups beef broth
1 cup Burgundy
4 scallions, thinly sliced
1 (3-ounce) can mushrooms,
   drained, sliced
Arrowroot (cornstarch)

Over low heat, blend butter with flour. Stir in mustard and Worcestershire. Add beef broth, a small amount at a time, blending well after each addition. Stir in Burgundy. Cook, stirring constantly until thickened. Add scallions and mushrooms. If more thickening is desired, add small amount of arrowroot. If too thick, add small amount of Burgundy. Serve over beef tenderloin slices. Yields 2 cups.

Fare by the Sea (Florida)

POULTRY

PHOTO © GEORGIA DEPARTMENT OF ECONOMIC DEVELOPMENT.

Located just south of Atlanta, Georgia, off I-75, Indian Springs is one of the oldest state parks in the nation. It became an official "State Forest Park" in 1927. Indian Springs was first visited by Creek Indians who believed the natural spring water had healing qualities.

Company Chicken 'n Beef

1 (6-ounce) jar chipped beef
1 whole fryer, cut up, or 4
  chicken breast halves
  (boneless breasts good for
  company)

Bacon slices
1 (10¾-ounce) cream of
  mushroom soup
1 (8-ounce) carton sour cream

Put chipped beef in bottom of lightly greased casserole dish. Place chicken pieces in next. Lay bacon slices on top of chicken. Bake uncovered 30 minutes at 350°. Mix soup and sour cream together and pour over top. Bake 25–30 minutes more. (May want to cover loosely at this time.) The gravy is very good over rice.

Feeding the Faithful (South Carolina)

Roast Chicken Dinner

1 (2½- to 3-pound) fryer
  chicken
½ teaspoon black pepper
1–2 medium onions, wedged

6–8 medium carrots, left whole
6 medium potatoes, quartered
  or halved
1 teaspoon salt

Heat oven to 375°. Spray a 9x13-inch baking dish with vegetable spray. Split chicken in half, lengthwise. Arrange in baking dish, skin side up (for less fat, remove skin). Sprinkle chicken with pepper. Arrange vegetables around chicken. Season with salt. Roast, covered, 1¼–1½ hours. Makes 6 servings.

The Bishop Family Heirloom Cookbook (South Carolina)

Each year thousands of purple martins return to Bomb Island on Lake Murray, South Carolina, to roost for the summer. As you near the island, hundreds of thousands of birds blacken the sky, then swoop down in a funnel formation, just missing the top of your boat. As they near the island, they charge back up into the air, circle, and swoop again, as if there to entertain—they are actually stopping at the island to gather, eat, and gain strength for the long journey back to their winter habitat in Brazil. The phenomenon has gained national attention since the island was designated as a bird sanctuary.

Chicken with Drop Dumplin's

1 (3- to 4-pound) chicken,
  cut up
2 stalks celery, diced
2 tablespoons chicken bouillon
  granules
1 bay leaf
8 cups water
2 cups all-purpose flour
4 teaspoons baking powder
1 teaspoon salt

¾ cup milk
½ cup chopped green onion
  tops
Pinch of cayenne pepper
½ cup chopped fresh parsley
¼ teaspoon freshly grated
  nutmeg
1 (10¾-ounce) can cream of
  chicken soup
Salt and pepper to taste

Place the chicken pieces, celery, bouillon, and bay leaf in a stockpot. Add the water and bring to a boil over medium-high heat. Reduce the heat and cook for 45–60 minutes, or until the chicken is tender. Remove the chicken and let it cool slightly. Pick the meat off of the bones, discarding the bones and skin; set aside.

Sift the flour, baking powder, and salt into a large bowl. Add the milk and mix well. Add the onions and cayenne; mix. Drop batter by tablespoons into the boiling broth until all the batter is used up. Gently shake the pot. (Never stir dumplings with a spoon, as this will tear them.) Add parsley and nutmeg; shake pot again. Cover, reduce the heat, and simmer gently for about 15 minutes without lifting the lid. While the dumplings are cooking, heat soup with 1 can water in a small saucepan. When the dumplings are done, carefully pour the soup into the dumpling pot. Shake the pot gently. Return the chicken to the pot and again shake the pot, this time in a rotating motion. Season to taste with salt and pepper. Serves 6–8.

The Lady & Sons, Too! (Georgia)

Chicken Key West

1 stick butter or margarine
1 broiler-fryer chicken, cut in
  parts, skinned
1 teaspoon salt
1 teaspoon freshly-ground
  pepper
¼ teaspoon paprika
1 large onion, thinly sliced
3–4 cloves garlic, crushed
¼ cup Key lime juice

Melt butter over medium heat in large frying pan with cover. Add chicken and cook until light brown on all sides. Sprinkle with salt, pepper, and paprika. Add onion and garlic. Cook, stirring occasionally, 5 minutes. Pour lime juice over chicken. Cover and simmer 25 minutes or until fork can be inserted with ease. Remove cover and cook a few minutes until chicken is a golden color.

Margaritaville Cookbook (Florida)

Barbecued Chicken

½ stick margarine or butter
2½ cups water
½ cup vinegar
2 teaspoons dry mustard
2 teaspoons sugar
½ teaspoon onion salt
½ teaspoon garlic salt
2½ teaspoons chopped onion
1 teaspoon Tabasco
2 teaspoons black pepper
1 tablespoon salt
1 tablespoon Worcestershire
1 tablespoon chili powder
2 chickens, quartered

Melt margarine in frying pan; add all ingredients except chicken and simmer ½ hour. Lay chicken pieces in roaster pan and butter well. Broil a minute or 2 on both sides. Then pour in part of sauce, basting well, later adding more sauce. Bake slowly, basting often in medium oven of 325° at least 2–3 hours until meat begins to pull away from bone.

Southern Cooking (South Carolina)

Chicken Asparagus with Tarragon

Tarragon and balsamic vinegar add a special touch.

2 large whole chicken breasts, deboned, skinned, split in half lengthwise
1½ teaspoons salt, divided
¾ teaspoon black pepper, divided
¼ cup all-purpose flour
2 tablespoons olive oil
2 tablespoons butter
1 cup chopped onion
2 cloves garlic, pressed
1 pound asparagus, trimmed, cut diagonally

½ pound mushrooms, sliced
2 cups chopped fresh tomatoes
½ cup chicken broth
2 tablespoons chopped fresh tarragon, or 1½ teaspoons dried tarragon
1 tablespoon balsamic vinegar
1 teaspoon sugar
1 cup freshly grated Parmesan cheese, divided
1 pound fettuccine or linguine, cooked

Flatten chicken by pounding lightly between 2 pieces of wax paper. Sprinkle with ½ teaspoon salt and ¼ teaspoon pepper. Coat lightly in flour; set aside.

Heat olive oil and butter in large skillet over medium heat. Sauté onion and garlic until onion is golden. Add chicken; cook on both sides until golden. Remove chicken; set aside. Add asparagus to drippings. Sauté 3 minutes. Add mushrooms, and sauté 2 more minutes. Add tomatoes, chicken broth, tarragon, vinegar, sugar, remaining 1 teaspoon salt and remaining ½ teaspoon pepper. Cook and stir about 8 minutes over low heat. Stir ¾ cup Parmesan cheese into asparagus mixture. Cook and stir until thickened. Add cooked chicken. Heat through. Toss cooked fettuccine or linguine lightly with remaining ¼ cup Parmesan cheese. Arrange chicken over pasta, and pour sauce over fettuccine or linguine. Makes 4 servings.

The Best of Sophie Kay Cookbook (Florida)

Spinach-Stuffed Chicken in Apricot Sauce

1 (10-ounce) package frozen, chopped spinach, thawed
½ cup 1% fat cottage cheese
⅓ cup bread crumbs
1 tablespoon minced shallot
1 egg white
⅛ teaspoon garlic powder
⅛ teaspoon nutmeg
Salt to taste

6 (4-ounce) boneless, skinless chicken breast halves
1 tablespoon vegetable oil
1 cup apricot nectar
3 tablespoons Dijon mustard
1 tablespoon tarragon vinegar
2 teaspoons brown sugar
6 (2-ounce) unpeeled fresh apricots, cut into wedges

Press spinach between paper towels to remove excess moisture. Combine with cottage cheese, bread crumbs, shallot, egg white, garlic powder, nutmeg, and salt in a bowl and mix well. Rinse chicken and pat dry. Spoon spinach mixture onto chicken and roll to enclose filling; secure with wooden picks. Chill in refrigerator for 1 hour.

Brown chicken rolls in heated oil in a large skillet for 7 minutes on each side. Remove chicken to a warm platter. Add apricot nectar, mustard, vinegar, and brown sugar and mix well. Bring to a boil and reduce heat. Simmer for 7 minutes. Add apricots. Simmer until sauce thickens to desired consistency. Serve over chicken. Serves 6.

Tropical Settings (Florida)

People pay a lot for famous signatures. Among the famous men who signed the Declaration of Independence are Thomas Jefferson, John Hancock, and Ben Franklin, but it is Georgia's own Button Gwinnett who nets the highest price for a signature, mostly because only eight are known to exist. A representative of Georgia in the Continental Congress at the time, Gwinnett later became the second governor of Georgia. Signers Monument in Augusta, Georgia, memorializes Gwinnett and the other two Georgians who signed the Declaration of Independence—George Walton and Lyman Hall.

Florida Orange Chicken

1½ cups uncooked
  long-grain rice
4 boneless, skinless chicken
  breasts
½ cup sliced fresh
  mushrooms

2 cups orange juice
1 cup fat-free chicken broth
½ teaspoon salt and pepper
2 oranges, sectioned, membrane
  removed

Spread rice in greased, shallow 3-quart baking dish. Top with chicken and mushrooms. Pour orange juice and broth over all. Sprinkle with salt and pepper. Cover with foil and bake at 350° for 50 minutes or until rice is tender. Makes 4 servings.

Country Club Cooks (Florida)

Simply Delicious
Southern Fried Chicken

The southern specialty! Mrs. Smith, wife of a past chairman of the National Broiler Council Board, has perfected this recipe after many years of close association with poultry and the poultry industry.

Salt
6 chicken breast halves, or
  3½ pounds assorted chicken
  pieces, or 1 pound chicken
  livers, halved

1 cup buttermilk
2 cups self-rising flour
1 teaspoon lemon-pepper
  seasoning
Oil for frying

Lightly salt chicken to taste. Place buttermilk in shallow dish, and place flour on wax paper. Dip each piece of chicken into buttermilk, sprinkle with lemon-pepper, and roll in flour, coating well; shake off excess flour. Heat 2-inch depth of oil in large skillet to 350°. Place chicken, a few pieces at a time, in oil. (Take care to add extra chicken pieces slowly enough that oil temperature does not drop below 325°.) Cook until chicken is crisp and richly browned, turning once. Drain well on absorbent toweling. To keep hot, hold in warm oven. Serves 6.

Perennials (Georgia)

Chicken Savannah!

1 egg
1½ cups bread crumbs
½ teaspoon garlic powder
¼ teaspoon pepper
6 chicken breasts, boneless
  and skinless
¼ cup margarine
1 (14-ounce) can artichoke
  hearts, drained, cut into
  quarters
12 small new red potatoes

1 (6-ounce) jar mushrooms,
  drained
1 (10¾-ounce) can cream of
  mushroom soup
2 cups sour cream
½ cup dry white wine
2 tablespoons tarragon
¼ cup grated Parmesan
  cheese
Paprika to taste

Beat egg in a shallow dish. Combine bread crumbs, garlic powder, and pepper in a shallow dish and mix well. Dip chicken in beaten egg. Dredge in bread crumb mixture. Brown chicken on both sides in margarine in a skillet. Remove chicken and place in a 9x13-inch baking dish.

Arrange artichokes, potatoes, and mushrooms around chicken. Add soup, sour cream, wine, and tarragon to pan drippings and mix well. Pour over chicken and vegetables. Sprinkle with Parmesan and paprika. Bake, covered, at 350° for 45 minutes. Yields 6 servings.

From Black Tie to Blackeyed Peas (Georgia)

Cashew Chicken with Snow Peas

⅓ cup sherry
3 tablespoons water
1 tablespoon cornstarch
1 tablespoon brown sugar
1 tablespoon soy sauce
2 teaspoons minced fresh
  ginger root

4 split chicken breasts
½ pound fresh mushrooms
6 green onions
¼ pound fresh snow peas
2 tablespoons peanut oil
¾ cup cashew nuts

In a medium-size bowl, combine sherry, water, cornstarch, brown sugar, soy sauce, and ginger root, mixing well. Bone, skin, and dice chicken. Place chicken in bowl and marinate in the mixture for at least 1 hour. Wipe mushrooms with a damp cloth, trim stems and cut mushrooms into thin slices. Slice green onions into 1-inch pieces. Trim snow peas and remove strings. Set aside.

Heat oil in a large skillet or wok. Drain chicken, reserving marinade. Cook chicken in oil over medium-high heat 5 minutes, or until done. Add mushrooms and cook until tender, 3–4 minutes. Add reserved marinade, green onions, and snow peas. Cook until sauce is thickened. Sprinkle with cashews. Makes 4 servings.

The Sandlappers' Salvation Cookbook (South Carolina)

Chicken Hmmmmmm

Simple, but elegant served alone or on a slice of ham.

4 half-breasts of chicken,
  boned
4 teaspoons parsley flakes
Garlic salt to taste

¼ cup butter or margarine,
  melted
1 cup herb stuffing mix

Sprinkle breasts with parsley and garlic salt. Roll up and secure with a toothpick. Roll in butter, then dressing mix. Place in a heavily greased baking dish. Sprinkle remaining crumbs over chicken and moisten lightly with water. Bake at 325° for 30–40 minutes.

Tea-Time at the Masters® (Georgia)

Plantation Chicken and Shrimp

¼ cup plus 3 tablespoons
  butter, divided
½ cup sliced green onions
2 teaspoons dried tarragon
  leaves, divided
2 red bell peppers, diced into
  bite-size pieces
½ pound mushrooms,
  thickly sliced

¾ cup dry white wine, divided
4 chicken breasts, cubed
1 pound medium shrimp,
  peeled, deveined
2 tablespoons flour
2 cups half-and-half, scalded
Salt and white pepper to taste
Paprika for garnish

Melt ¼ cup butter in saucepan; add onions and 1 teaspoon tarragon. Sauté about 5 minutes, until onions are wilted. Add bell peppers, mushrooms, and ½ cup wine, and sauté until vegetables are crisp-tender. Remove vegetables from pan; leave liquids in pan. Add chicken, and sauté until opaque. Add chicken to vegetables; leave most of liquid in pan. Now add shrimp and remaining tarragon. Sauté about 2 minutes, until shrimp just turn pink. Add shrimp and liquid to vegetables-chicken mixture.

In another saucepan, melt remaining 3 tablespoons butter; stir in flour, and sauté about 2 minutes, stirring frequently. Add scalded half-and-half; whisk over low heat until smooth and thick. Add rest of wine and liquid from vegetables. Heat well, and adjust seasonings. Add chicken, shrimp, and vegetables. Simmer 20–30 minutes; do not allow to boil. Serve over biscuits, rice, or puff pastry shells. Garnish with paprika. Makes 5–6 servings.

Culinary Memories of Merridun, Volume 1 (South Carolina)

Michael's Marvelous Chicken

Time well spent!

1 (8-ounce) carton sweet
  unsalted whipped butter
4 large scallions, chopped
  fine, divided
6 mushrooms, chopped fine
½ pound white crabmeat
¼ pound shrimp
½ teaspoon ground basil
  leaves

¼ teaspoon garlic
¼ teaspoon poultry seasoning
½ lemon
Salt to taste
6–8 boned chicken breasts,
  pounded thin
½ cup white wine
Paprika and soft butter
4 mushrooms, sliced

Preheat oven to 350°. Mix butter, 3 chopped scallions, chopped mushrooms, crabmeat, and shrimp. Add spices, lemon juice, and salt to taste. Place 2 tablespoons of mixture on each breast and fold corners to cover. Turn over and place in casserole. Pour white wine over, then dab each with butter and sprinkle with paprika. Bake 15 minutes, covered. Uncover and bake additional 10 minutes.

Pour liquid from casserole into small sauté pan and bring to a boil. Add 1 chopped scallion and sliced mushrooms and bring to a boil again. Lower heat to simmer and reduce liquid to half.

Deglaze the sauce—stir in 1 tablespoon butter at a time (3 tablespoons total) with a whisk. Allow sauce to cool. Sauce can be spooned over each chicken breast. Serve with curried rice. Serves 6–8.

Charleston Receipts Repeats (South Carolina)

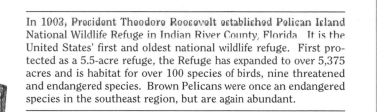

In 1903, President Theodore Roosevelt established Pelican Island National Wildlife Refuge in Indian River County, Florida. It is the United States' first and oldest national wildlife refuge. First protected as a 5.5-acre refuge, the Refuge has expanded to over 5,375 acres and is habitat for over 100 species of birds, nine threatened and endangered species. Brown Pelicans were once an endangered species in the southeast region, but are again abundant.

Sweet and Sour Chicken

1 (8-ounce) bottle Thousand
  Island dressing
1 package dry onion soup mix

1 (12-ounce) jar apricot or
  peach preserves
1 chicken, cut up

Mix dressing, onion soup mix, and preserves together and pour over chicken, which has been placed in a large baking pan or dish. Bake at 350° for 1½ hours. Do not cover.

Note: This is delicious served over yellow rice.

Through Our Kitchen Windows (Florida)

Savory Chicken Squares

3 ounces cream cheese,
  softened
2 tablespoons margarine,
  softened
2 cups diced, cooked chicken
  or turkey
¼ teaspoon salt
⅛ teaspoon pepper
2 tablespoons milk

1 tablespoon chopped onion
1 tablespoon chopped pimento
1 (8-ounce) can crescent rolls
Melted butter
Italian bread crumbs
1 (10¾-ounce) can cream of
  chicken soup
Half-and-half

Blend cream cheese and margarine. Mix next 6 ingredients together. Separate crescent rolls. Form into rectangular shape by sealing the 2 rolls together. Roll dough a little to make thinner. Spoon ½ cup of the chicken mixture in the center of the dough. Bring the 4 corners together and pinch together to seal. Brush top with melted butter and sprinkle with Italian bread crumbs. Bake on greased baking sheet for 20–25 minutes at 350°.

Serve with cream sauce made with cream of chicken soup diluted with half-and-half. Use only enough half-and-half to make a cream sauce.

Olivia's Favorite Menus and Recipes (South Carolina)

Hot Chicken Sandwich

1¾ cups diced cooked
  chicken
½ cup sliced pitted ripe olives
½ cup mayonnaise
4 slices bread

Butter
3 hard-cooked eggs, sliced
1 (10¾-ounce) can cream of
  chicken or celery soup
1 cup sour cream

Combine chicken, olives, and mayonnaise. Trim crusts from bread; butter both sides. Place 2 slices bread in glass baking dish; spread with chicken mixture. Add egg slices. Top with remaining bread. Blend soup and sour cream. Pour over sandwiches. Bake at 350° for 25 minutes or until top is lightly browned. Serves 2.

Perennials (Georgia)

Ham and Chicken Casserole

½ pound spaghetti
2–3 cups diced chicken
1 cup diced ham
½ cup chopped pimento
½ cup chopped green bell
  pepper
2 (10¾-ounce) cans cream of
  chicken soup

1 cup chicken broth
¼ teaspoon celery salt
¼ teaspoon pepper
1 large onion, grated
2 cups grated Cheddar cheese,
  divided

Break spaghetti into 1-inch pieces and cook according to package directions until just tender. Mix all ingredients together, except 1 cup cheese, and pour into a lightly greased 3-quart casserole. Add remaining cheese to top of casserole. Bake at 350° for 1 hour. Serves 15.

A Taste of South Carolina (South Carolina)

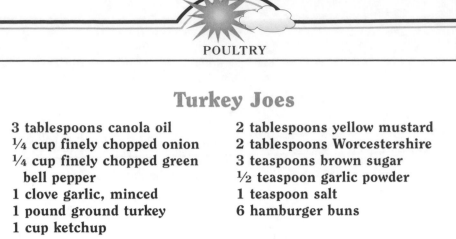

Turkey Joes

3 tablespoons canola oil
¼ cup finely chopped onion
¼ cup finely chopped green
  bell pepper
1 clove garlic, minced
1 pound ground turkey
1 cup ketchup

2 tablespoons yellow mustard
2 tablespoons Worcestershire
3 teaspoons brown sugar
½ teaspoon garlic powder
1 teaspoon salt
6 hamburger buns

In a medium skillet, heat oil over medium-high heat. Add onion and bell pepper; sauté until onions are slightly translucent. Add garlic and stir. Add ground turkey, stirring to crumble. Continue to sauté until turkey is browned. Add remaining ingredients; mix well. Reduce heat, cover, and simmer for 30 minutes, stirring occasionally. Serve on hamburger buns.

Collard Greens and Sushi (Georgia)

Turkey à la King

3 tablespoons butter
2 tablespoons chopped green
  bell pepper
2 tablespoons chopped
  pimento
3 tablespoons flour
1 (10¾-ounce) can cream
  of mushroom soup

¼ teaspoon salt
1 tablespoon sweet relish
2 cups diced, cooked turkey
2 egg yolks
Patty shells or toast

Melt butter in saucepan, and add green pepper and pimento. Cook slowly until slightly brown. Add flour and blend well. Add mushroom soup and salt, and stir until thick. Add relish and turkey, and heat thoroughly. Add well-beaten egg yolks, and continue cooking only 2 or 3 minutes more. Serve in baked patty shells or on toast. Yields 4 servings.

Boarding House Reach (Georgia)

Good-Bye Turkey Casserole

7½ tablespoons sifted
 all-purpose flour
⅜ teaspoon onion salt
1½ teaspoons salt, divided
⅜ cup butter, melted (6
 tablespoons)
3¾ cups light cream or
 half-and-half
¼ cup sherry
2½ cups cubed, cooked turkey
 or chicken

2¼ cups instant rice
2¼ cups turkey or chicken
 broth
¾ cup shredded American
 cheese, divided
1½ (15-ounce) cans asparagus
 spears
3 tablespoons toasted slivered
 almonds

Stir flour, onion salt, and half the salt into butter. Stir in half-and-half. Cook over hot water, stirring occasionally, until thickened. Let cool, add the sherry, and set aside. Add turkey or chicken and rice, and put into a 2-quart shallow baking dish. Combine turkey or chicken broth with remaining salt and pour over rice mixture. Sprinkle half of the cheese over rice mixture. Place asparagus on top and pour reserved sauce over this. Sprinkle with remaining cheese and top with almonds. Bake at 375° until bubbly, approximately 20 minutes. Serves 8–10.

A Pinch of Sunshine (Florida)

WWW.WIKIPEDIA.COM

Erskine Caldwell was born December 17, 1903, near Moreland, Georgia. As one of the first authors to be published in mass-market paperback editions, he is a key figure in the history of American publishing. By the late 1940s, Caldwell had sold more books than any writer in the nation's history. He is the author of 25 novels, 150 short stories, and 12 nonfiction books. The stage adaptation of Caldwell's *Tobacco Road* (which opened on Broadway on December 4, 1933) made American theatre history when it ran for 3,182 consecutive performances over a period of seven-and-a-half years. Three of Caldwell's books have been made into movies: *Tobacco Road* (1941), *God's Little Acre* (1958), and *Claudelle Inglish* (1961). The house in which he was born has been moved to Moreland's town square where it serves as a museum. Caldwell died in 1987.

Black Walnut-Crusted Turkey

1 pound wild turkey breast
   cutlets
½ cup oil and vinegar salad
   dressing
⅓ cup finely chopped black
   walnuts

½ cup fresh bread crumbs
1 tablespoon finely chopped
   fresh chives
1 tablespoon margarine
2 tablespoons olive oil

Pound cutlets with a meat mallet to a uniform thickness. Combine with salad dressing in a plastic zip-top bag. Refrigerate 6–8 hours. Process walnuts and bread crumbs in a food processor until finely chopped. Add chives, and pulse to blend.

Heat margarine and olive oil in a large skillet over medium-high heat. Drain cutlets, and coat with walnut mixture, pressing mixture into cutlets so it will adhere. Place turkey in skillet, and lower heat to medium. Cook until golden brown outside and no longer pink inside, 4–6 minutes per side. Serve immediately. Makes 4 servings.

Wild Fare & Wise Words (South Carolina)

Watson Mill Bridge State Park is a 1,018-acre Georgia state park located near Comer and Carlton on the South Fork of the Broad River. The park is named for the Watson Mill Bridge, the longest original-site covered bridge in Georgia, which spans 229 feet across the South Fork River. The bridge, built in 1885, is supported by a town lattice truss system held firmly together with wooden pins. Georgia once had over 200 covered bridges, but only 20 remain.

Turkey Dressing

2 cups diced celery
¾ cup minced onion
½ cup butter
4 cups dry bread crumbs
4 cups cornbread, crumbled
Salt and pepper to taste

1 tablespoon poultry seasoning
(optional)
3 cups turkey broth (cook turkey
giblets in saucepan and use
broth for dressing)
2 eggs, beaten

Cook celery and onion 5 minutes in butter. Add to bread crumbs; add seasonings. Mix remaining ingredients, except eggs, thoroughly; then add eggs. Stir lightly. If dressing seems dry, add enough water to moisten well. Stuff turkey and bake remainder in baking dish, uncovered, for 45 minutes to a hour at 400°. Serve this in spoonfuls around turkey. Serves 12.

Nell Graydon's Cook Book (South Carolina)

Stuffed Carolina Quail

1 cup spinach, wilted in butter
4 ounces smoked Gouda
cheese
6 shallots, roasted in oven

4 semi-boneless quail
2 tablespoons extra virgin olive
oil
½ cup seasoned flour

Combine first 3 ingredients. Divide mixture into 4 portions, and stuff into body cavity of quail. Brush each bird liberally with extra virgin olive oil, then lightly dredge in flour. In a hot pan, sear quail on both sides to achieve a golden crust. Transfer to a 425° oven and roast 8–10 minutes, or until firm to touch. Yields 2 servings.

Recipe from Poogan's Porch, Charleston
Lowcountry Delights II (South Carolina)

Mary Ann's Cornish Game Hens

4 Cornish game hens
1 (14-ounce) can Le Sueur
  peas, drained
4 medium potatoes, sliced

4 large carrots, sliced
3–4 medium onions, sliced
1 (10-ounce) bottle soy sauce
1 (10-ounce) bottle A-1 sauce

Place hens in the middle of a large piece of 18-inch aluminum foil. Fill the cavities of the hens with peas. Make a packet of the aluminum foil by tightly closing the two sides. Place pieces of potatoes, carrots, and onions around the edges of the hens. Pour ¼ bottle soy sauce over each hen, coating the entire top. Next pour ¼ bottle A-1 sauce over each hen, coating the top of each. (You may use a little more of the sauce if you desire. I usually do because it makes the most unbelievably good gravy-type sauce, but thinner.) Put 1 tablespoon water in each foil packet, salt and pepper to taste; tightly seal top of foil so that no steam or juice can escape. Bake at 350° for 1½ hours. Just before serving, fold back foil just enough to brown tops of hens. Serve on a plate in the foil packet with foil folded down so that the sauce cannot run out. Serve with salad and French bread for a complete meal.

Seasoned with Sunshine (Florida)

SEAFOOD

PHOTO © ANDY NEWMAN / FLORIDA KEYS TDC.

Known as the "Sportfishing Capital of the World," Islamorada in the Florida Keys offers some of the most competitive and diverse fishing in the world.

Shrimp Delight

1½ pounds medium raw
  shrimp
4 tablespoons butter
1 teaspoon Worcestershire
1 clove garlic, minced
2 tablespoons chopped chives

2 tablespoons parsley flakes
¼ teaspoon salt
⅛ teaspoon freshly ground
  black pepper
¼ cup grated Parmesan cheese
¼ cup dry bread crumbs

Shell and devein shrimp. Pat dry with paper towels. Melt butter in a medium skillet. Add shrimp, Worcestershire sauce, garlic, chives, parsley flakes, salt, and pepper. Sauté for about 5 minutes, stirring constantly, until shrimp just turn pink.

With a slotted spoon, transfer shrimp to a casserole dish. Sprinkle with cheese and bread crumbs. Pour butter in which shrimp were cooked over all. Bake in a preheated 400° oven for 8–10 minutes, until golden brown. Serve with drawn butter, garnished with a sprig of parsley and a lemon wedge. Serves 4.

Cookin' in the Keys (Florida)

Memree's Soppin' Shrimp

Memree makes a special trip to the Florida panhandle around Memorial Day and gets the fresh shrimp for this memorable meal.

3 pounds raw shrimp, in shells
1 stick butter
⅔ cup lemon juice
1 teaspoon grated lemon rind

1½ cups Italian dressing
2½ teaspoons black pepper,
  more to taste

Wash shrimp and remove heads, but leave in shells. Drain. In a medium saucepan, melt butter and add lemon juice, lemon rind, Italian dressing, and black pepper; bring to a boil. Add shrimp and simmer about 6 minutes or just until tender.

Serve with crusty French bread. Ladle shrimp into individual bowls with plenty of sauce for soppin' the bread in. You peel your own shrimp, which guarantees the pleasure of slow eating. Serves 4.

Cross Creek Kitchens (Florida)

Shrimp in Tomato and Feta Cheese Sauce à la Grecque

This recipe originated in the Tarpon Springs area, where a small but colorful Greek community carries on the sponge-fishing industry started in the early years of this century. Flavorful Greek ingredients are combined with tomatoes, shrimp, and feta cheese to make a dish that is good for serving a crowd because it is easily multiplied. Chunks of fish can be substituted for the shrimp or mixed with the shrimp for variety.

½ cup olive oil
2 cloves garlic, crushed
1 large onion, sliced thin
⅔ cup dry white wine
4 large tomatoes, peeled and
  chopped
1 teaspoon chopped fresh
  oregano, or ½ teaspoon
  dried

¼ cup chopped Italian
  (flat-leaf) parsley
1 teaspoon salt
½ teaspoon ground pepper
2 pounds shrimp, shelled,
  deveined, and halved
  lengthwise
½ pound feta cheese
Sprigs of parsley

In a shallow oven-proof casserole, heat oil and sauté garlic and onion until transparent. Add wine, tomatoes, herbs, and seasonings; simmer about 30 minutes or until mixture has thickened. Add shrimp and stir to coat thoroughly.

Crumble feta cheese over top of casserole. Preheat oven to 450° and bake for about 15 minutes or until shrimp is cooked and cheese has melted. Garnish with parsley sprigs and serve over rice or with crusty bread. Serves 6.

Gulf Coast Cooking (Florida)

Daufuskie Island Shrimp Creole

4 green onions, or 1 Vidalia
  onion, chopped
½ cup chopped celery
¾ cup chopped green bell
  pepper
1 garlic clove, minced
2 tablespoons butter or
  margarine
1 (16-ounce) can whole
  tomatoes, or 4 fresh
  tomatoes, chopped
1 (16-ounce) can tomato
  sauce

1 teaspoon salt
2 teaspoons dried parsley
¼ teaspoon cayenne
2 teaspoons Worcestershire
2 teaspoons soy sauce
1 teaspoon hot sauce
1 tablespoon lemon juice
2 teaspoons curry powder
  (optional)
3 bay leaves (optional)
1 cup golden raisins (optional)
1 pound shrimp, peeled

Sauté onions, celery, pepper, and garlic in butter in large saucepan until onions are transparent. Add tomatoes, tomato sauce, salt, parsley, cayenne, Worcestershire, soy sauce, hot sauce, lemon juice, curry powder, bay leaves, and raisins; mix well. Bring to a simmer; simmer for 30 minutes. Add shrimp; cook over medium-low heat until shrimp turn pink. Remove the bay leaves. Serve over rice. Yields 4–6 servings.

From Black Tie to Blackeyed Peas (Georgia)

Atlanta was briefly named Marthasville from 1843–1844, after the daughter of Georgia's governor at that time. However, the business community was concerned that such a name wouldn't attract commerce, and so a new name, "Atlanta," was chosen in 1845 as being much more marketable. I'd say that was a good decision! Internationally known as a top business city and transportation hub, Atlanta has the nation's third largest concentration of Fortune 500 companies (only New York City and Houston have more), and more than 75% of the Fortune 1000 companies have a presence in the Atlanta Metro. Additionally, the region accounts for two-thirds of Georgia's economy and 72% of its job and population growth. Hartsfield-Jackson Atlanta International Airport is the busiest airport in the world.

Coconut Fried Shrimp
with Mango Sauce

MANGO SAUCE:

2 cups cider vinegar
1 cup firmly packed light
  brown sugar
2 mangoes, peeled, seeded,
  and chopped
4 shallots, thinly sliced
4 cloves garlic, thinly sliced
½ ounce fresh gingerroot

1 ounce tamarind paste
2 inches sliced lemon peel
2 inches sliced orange peel
1 teaspoon cayenne pepper
⅓ teaspoon cinnamon
⅓ teaspoon ground cardamom
1 tablespoon kosher salt
8 bananas, peeled

In heavy, stainless steel saucepan (not aluminum), place vinegar and sugar; bring to a boil. Reduce heat and simmer until thick syrup forms and thickens (238° on candy thermometer). Add all other ingredients except bananas; simmer 45 minutes, stirring frequently. Remove from heat and chill.

In blender or food processor, purée mango mixture and bananas until smooth and well blended. Store, covered, in a glass container in refrigerator until needed. Serve cold with hot, freshly cooked coconut shrimp. Dip and enjoy.

2 pounds raw shrimp
1 cup all-purpose flour
½ teaspoon sugar
½ teaspoon salt

1 egg, slightly beaten
2 tablespoons vegetable oil
⅔ cup grated coconut

Thaw shrimp, if they are frozen; shell and devein, leaving tails intact. Blot shrimp dry with paper towels. In large bowl, combine flour, sugar, salt, egg, and oil. Dip shrimp into batter, then into coconut. Fry in deep fat fryer at 375° until golden brown. Serve with Mango Sauce. Serves 4–6.

Florida Seafood Cookery (Florida)

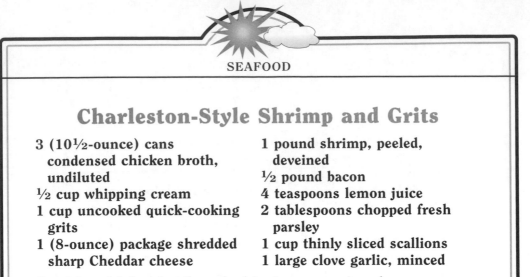

Charleston-Style Shrimp and Grits

3 (10½-ounce) cans
   condensed chicken broth,
   undiluted
½ cup whipping cream
1 cup uncooked quick-cooking
   grits
1 (8-ounce) package shredded
   sharp Cheddar cheese

1 pound shrimp, peeled,
   deveined
½ pound bacon
4 teaspoons lemon juice
2 tablespoons chopped fresh
   parsley
1 cup thinly sliced scallions
1 large clove garlic, minced

Combine chicken broth and whipping cream in a large saucepan; bring to a boil. Stir in grits, and return to a boil. Cover, reduce heat, and simmer 5–7 minutes; stir in cheese. Remove from heat and prepare shrimp.

Rinse shrimp and pat dry. Fry bacon in large skillet until browned; drain well, and chop. Add shrimp to bacon drippings in skillet, and cook just until pink. Add lemon juice, chopped bacon, parsley, scallions, and garlic. Sauté 3 minutes. Spoon shrimp mixture over cheese grits, and serve immediately.

Note: If you do not have quick grits, use 2⅓ cups instant grits. Otherwise, you can use 1 cup regular grits, then cover and cook 18 minutes, or until grits are thickened.

A Collection from Summerville Kitchens (South Carolina)

JOHN HELD, JR.

The Charleston is a dance named for the city of Charleston. Its rhythm was popularized in the United States by a 1923 tune called *Charleston* by composer/pianist James P. Johnson. It debuted in the Broadway show *Runnin' Wild* and became the definitive dance number of the Roaring 20s. The Charleston dance that consequently developed is most frequently associated with flappers and speakeasies where young women would dance alone or together as a way of mocking the citizens who supported the Prohibition Amendment; the dance was considered quite immoral and provocative at the time. Many variations of the dance have developed over the years.

Grits a Ya Ya
(Shrimp and Grits)

CHEESE GRITS:

2 cups chicken stock
1 quart heavy cream
8 ounces grits

½ stick butter
½ pound smoked Gouda
  cheese, diced

Bring stock and cream to boil. Add grits and cook on high heat for 5 minutes, stirring rapidly. Add butter and cook on low heat for 10 minutes. Add smoked Gouda cheese. Stir to incorporate to smooth consistency.

SAUCE:

8 strips bacon
1 tablespoon minced garlic
1 tablespoon minced shallots
3 tablespoons butter
White wine
1 pound peeled and deveined
  jumbo shrimp

1 portabello mushroom cap,
  sliced
¼ cup diced scallions
2 cups chopped fresh spinach
2 cups heavy cream
Salt, pepper, and hot sauce to
  taste

Heat a large saucepan over medium heat. Add bacon and cook for about 3 minutes, then add garlic and shallots. Sauté, then add butter and a splash of white wine. When butter is half melted, add shrimp. When the down sides of shrimp become white, flip them and add mushroom slices, scallions, and spinach. Sauté for 2 minutes. Remove shrimp. Pour in heavy cream and let simmer while stirring. When reduced by ⅓, add salt, pepper, and hot sauce to taste. Return shrimp to sauce and combine. Spoon sauce and shrimp onto heaping mounds of Cheese Grits.

Recipes and Remembrances (Florida)

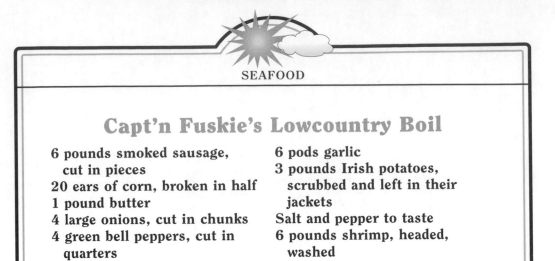

Capt'n Fuskie's Lowcountry Boil

6 pounds smoked sausage,
   cut in pieces
20 ears of corn, broken in half
1 pound butter
4 large onions, cut in chunks
4 green bell peppers, cut in
   quarters

6 pods garlic
3 pounds Irish potatoes,
   scrubbed and left in their
   jackets
Salt and pepper to taste
6 pounds shrimp, headed,
   washed

In huge pot, cook sausage in water about 20 minutes. Add remaining ingredients except headed shrimp. Cook until potatoes are almost done. Add shrimp and cook until just tender. Drain off water.

   Cover table(s) with newspaper. Take pot of "boil" and throw it out on the table(s) as though you were throwing out a bucket of water. Let everyone help himself, using paper plates. Have plenty of iced tea on hand and if you like, some slices of Vienna or French bread smeared with garlic butter. Plenty of paper towels will be needed as this "boil" is "drippin'-lickin'-good!"

Stirrin' the Pots on Daufuskie (South Carolina)

Chow Shia

The Chinese word "chow" means "stir." "Shia" means "shrimp." Assemble all ingredients before you start. This cooks very quickly.

1½ pounds raw shrimp (or frozen raw) peeled, deveined
2 tablespoons cornstarch, divided
½ teaspoon Ac'cent
1½ tablespoons vegetable oil (to coat pan)
2 tablespoons water
2 tablespoons soy sauce
Salt to taste (about ½ teaspoon)
½ package frozen green peas
1 (4-ounce) can mushrooms bits and juice
2 teaspoons sherry

Coat raw shrimp with 1 tablespoon cornstarch; add Ac'cent. Warm frying pan with oil until hot. Add remaining 1 tablespoon cornstarch to 2 tablespoons water and set aside to dissolve. Put shrimp in hot pan and cook about 1 minute over high heat, stirring constantly. Add soy sauce (this gives color to shrimp). Add salt, then remove from heat and put in bowl. Set aside.

Add raw peas, mushrooms and juice to same skillet. Salt. Cook about 1 minute over high heat, stirring constantly. Remove from heat. Return shrimp to peas in skillet. Add sherry. Stir cornstarch-water mixture well and add to shrimp for thickening. Return to heal just for a minute to cook thickening. It is now ready to serve over rice or Chinese noodles

Cypress Gardens Cookbook (Florida)

The Gullah are African Americans who live in the Lowcountry region of South Carolina and Georgia. Most of the Gullahs' ancestors were brought to the South Carolina and Georgia Lowcountry through the ports of Charleston and Savannah during the slave trade. The Gullah are best known for preserving their African linguistic and cultural heritage. The Gullah language is an English-based Creole language containing many African loan words. Over the years, the Gullahs have attracted many historians, linguists, folklorists, and anthropologists interested in their rich cultural heritage.

Jekyll Stuffed Shrimp

CRABMEAT STUFFING:

2 tablespoons butter
2 tablespoons finely chopped
  green bell pepper
1 tablespoon minced onion
2 tablespoons flour
½ cup milk
½ cup soft bread crumbs

1 teaspoon Worcestershire
½ teaspoon seasoned salt
Dash of cayenne
1 (7½-ounce) can crabmeat
20 large raw shrimp (1½
  pounds)

In hot butter, sauté green pepper about 2 minutes. Remove from heat; stir in minced onion, flour, and gradually stir in milk. Cook, stirring constantly, until very thick and mixture begins to boil. Remove from heat. Add bread crumbs, Worcestershire, salt, cayenne, and crabmeat; mix well. Set aside.

Shell shrimp, leaving on tails. Split each shrimp lengthwise along back being careful not to cut completely through. Devein, wash, and drain dry. Put 2 shrimp together, sandwich-style, using about a tablespoon of crabmeat stuffing as filling. Fasten with toothpicks; be sure tails are sticking up. Fill all shrimp, place in shallow baking pan and refrigerate 1 hour.

BARBECUE SAUCE:

¼ cup salad oil
2 tablespoons vinegar
¼ cup light brown sugar
2 (8-ounce) cans tomato sauce
1 tablespoon Worcestershire

½ teaspoon salt
Dash of Tabasco
Dash of cayenne
4 cups hot cooked rice

Make Barbecue Sauce by combining all ingredients except rice. Bring to a boil, stirring. Reduce heat; simmer uncovered 5 minutes. Place shrimp in preheated 350° oven. Brush sauce lightly over shrimp. Cover pan lightly with foil; bake 20 minutes. Spread cooked rice on serving platter, and carefully arrange shrimp on rice (remove toothpicks). Reheat remaining sauce and pass separately. Serves 6–8.

Golden Isles Cuisine (Georgia)

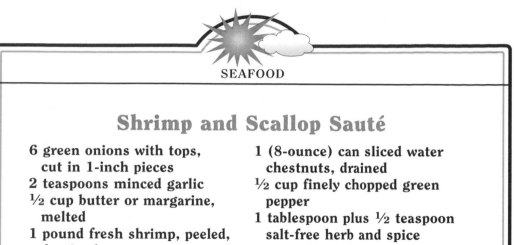

Shrimp and Scallop Sauté

6 green onions with tops,
  cut in 1-inch pieces
2 teaspoons minced garlic
½ cup butter or margarine,
  melted
1 pound fresh shrimp, peeled,
  deveined
¾ pound fresh scallops
½ pound lump crabmeat
½ pound fresh mushrooms,
  sliced

1 (8-ounce) can sliced water
  chestnuts, drained
½ cup finely chopped green
  pepper
1 tablespoon plus ½ teaspoon
  salt-free herb and spice
  seasoning
1 tablespoon Worcestershire
2 tablespoons chopped fresh
  parsley
Hot cooked rice (optional)

Sauté green onions and garlic in butter in a large, heavy skillet 1 minute. Add remaining ingredients except parsley and rice. Cook over medium heat 6–8 minutes, stirring occasionally. Stir in chopped parsley. Serve mixture over rice, if desired. Serves 6.

The Museum Cookbook (South Carolina)

Shrimp Étouffée

1 stick butter
½ cup chili sauce
¼ cup chopped onion
¼ cup chopped celery
⅛ teaspoon salt
⅛ teaspoon pepper

2 pounds medium shrimp,
  peeled, deveined
¼ cup white wine
¼ cup chopped fresh parsley
2 tablespoons minced shallots
1 cup freshly cooked rice

Melt butter in a large skillet over low heat. Add chili sauce, onion, celery, salt, and pepper; sauté until tender. Add shrimp and wine, sauté 3 minutes on each side. Add parsley and shallots, simmer 3 minutes. Serve hot over cooked rice. Serves 4.

Vincent Russo's Seafood Cookbook (Georgia)

Sweet and Sour Shrimp

These deep fried shrimp, when combined with green pepper, pineapple, and tomato, provide an eye as well as a taste pleaser. The sweet and sour sauce is especially good.

1½ pounds shrimp, cleaned, deveined
1 tablespoon soy sauce
½ teaspoon salt
½ cup cornstarch
Peanut oil

2 onions, cut in wedges
2 green bell pepper, cut in chunks
1½ cups Sweet and Sour Sauce
1 cup pineapple chunks
2 tomatoes, cut in wedges

Combine shrimp, soy sauce, and salt. Coat shrimp with cornstarch. Deep fry shrimp about 3 minutes. Drain on paper towels.

In wok or large fry pan, heat 1 tablespoon oil. Add onion and pepper; cook 1 minute. Add Sweet and Sour Sauce and pineapple. Add shrimp and tomato wedges. Cook until heated. Place on serving dish.

SWEET AND SOUR SAUCE:

½ cup sugar
1 tablespoon cornstarch
2 teaspoons salt
½ cup red wine vinegar

¼ cup orange juice
¼ cup pineapple juice
3 ounces tomato paste

Blend sugar, cornstarch, and salt. Stir in vinegar, fruit juices, and tomato paste. Cook, stirring constantly until thickened.

Gourmet Cooking (Florida)

Almost twice the size of Delaware, the Florida Everglades encompass some 4,000 square miles. Everglades National Park is the only subtropical preserve in North America. Unlike most other U.S. national parks, the Everglades was created to protect a fragile ecosystem instead of safeguarding a geographic feature. A swamp such as the Fakahatchee Strand in the Everglades functions in three major ways. First, its vegetation serves as a filter to clean the water as it makes its slow journey southward. Secondly, it is a major habitat for wildlife and plant life. Finally, it actually prevents flooding by slowing down the flow of water after heavy rains.

Seafood Crêpes Mornay

8 ounces small shrimp, peeled and deveined
1 tablespoon butter
1 tablespoon olive oil
Salt and pepper to taste
Herbes de Provence to taste
8 ounces lump crabmeat, shells and cartilage removed
¼ cup Madeira
5 tablespoons butter
5 tablespoons flour
1 cup whipping cream

1 cup half-and-half
⅓ cup shredded Gruyère cheese
¼ cup dry white wine
½ teaspoon Worcestershire
Nutmeg to taste
1 teaspoon tomato paste
12 crêpes
1 bunch fresh asparagus spears, blanched and drained
½ cup slivered almonds, toasted

Reserve a few shrimp for garnish. Heat butter and olive oil in a medium sauté pan over medium-high heat. Add remaining shrimp, salt, pepper, and herbes de Provence and mix well. Stir in crabmeat. Cook for 4 minutes or until the shrimp turn pink, stirring frequently. Stir in Madeira. Let stand until cool.

Heat 5 tablespoons butter in 2½-quart saucepan over medium heat. Whisk in flour until blended. Cook until a soft paste forms, whisking constantly. Add whipping cream and half-and-half gradually, whisking constantly until smooth. Cook until slightly thickened, stirring frequently. Stir in cheese. Add white wine and mix well. Cook until thickened, stirring frequently. Season with salt, pepper, Worcestershire sauce, and generously with nutmeg. Combine ⅓ cup of sauce with tomato paste in a bowl and mix well. Keep both sauces warm.

To serve, layer each crêpe with 2 asparagus spears, some shrimp mixture and some mornay sauce and roll to enclose filling. Arrange crêpes in baking dish and warm to serving temperature in a 350° oven. Remove to serving platter and drizzle with tomato paste sauce. Sprinkle with almonds and reserved shrimp. Serves 6.

Bay Fêtes (Florida)

Grilled Marinated Shrimp

Simple, divine and always a hit. For a different presentation that is also aromatic, thread the shrimp on the woody end of rosemary branches, leaving some of the leaves on the end.

½ cup vegetable or canola oil
¼ cup soy sauce
¼ cup lemon juice
2 tablespoons chopped fresh
  gingerroot

2 garlic cloves, minced
2 pounds fresh jumbo shrimp,
  peeled, deveined

Combine oil, soy sauce, lemon juice, gingerroot, and garlic in a bowl and mix well. Add shrimp to the mixture, tossing to mix well. Chill, covered, for 2–3 hours. Thread shrimp onto skewers. Grill over hot coals for 3–4 minutes on each side or until shrimp turn pink. If using wooden skewers, soak in water for 15 minutes before threading. Yields 8–10 servings.

The Life of the Party (Florida)

Shrimp and Crabmeat au Gratin

1 stick butter, divided
3 heaping tablespoons flour
2 tablespoons sugar
1 teaspoon salt
½ teaspoon pepper
1 tablespoon paprika
2 cups milk

Sherry to taste
½ pound crabmeat
½ pound shrimp, cooked
1 cup grated sharp Cheddar
  cheese
Slivered almonds

Melt ⅔ stick butter in a saucepan and gradually add flour, milk, sherry, sugar, salt, and pepper. Allow to come to a boil and keep warm. Grease a casserole dish with remaining ⅓ cup butter. Place half the shrimp and crab in casserole and half the cheese followed by a layer of sauce. Repeat layers and sprinkle top with paprika and almonds. Bake at 325° for approximately 45 minutes.

Bay Leaves (Florida)

SEAFOOD

Savannah Crab Cakes

1 pound crabmeat, picked free
  of shell
½ cup crushed Ritz Crackers
3 green onions with tops,
  finely chopped
½ cup finely chopped bell
  pepper
1 teaspoon salt
Dash of cayenne pepper

¼ cup mayonnaise
1 egg
1 teaspoon Worcestershire
1 teaspoon dry mustard
Juice of ½ lemon
¼ teaspoon garlic powder
Flour for dusting
½ cup peanut oil

Mix all ingredients together except flour and peanut oil. Shape into
patties and dust with flour. Pan fry in hot peanut oil over medium
heat until browned, 4–5 minutes. Flip and pan fry other side until
golden brown. Serves 4–6.

TARTAR SAUCE:

½ cup chopped green onion
½ cup chopped dill pickle

1 cup mayonnaise
½ teaspoon House Seasoning

In a bowl, combine chopped onion, pickle, mayonnaise, and House
Seasoning; mix well. Serve alongside crab cakes with lemon
wedges.

Variation: Substitute ⅓ cup capers for ½ cup pickles; add a dash of
cayenne pepper.

HOUSE SEASONING:

1 cup salt
¼ cup pepper

1 cup garlic powder

Mix well. Store in shaker near stove for convenience.

The Lady & Sons Savannah Country Cookbook (Georgia)

McClellanville Crab Cakes

1 pound lump crabmeat,
  picked clean of shell
½ cup mayonnaise
2 green onions, chopped fine
2 dashes Tabasco
1 dash Worcestershire

½ cup coarse bread crumbs,
  plus more for coating
½ ounce fresh lemon juice
½ teaspoon ground thyme
2 eggs
¼ cup half-and-half

Combine all ingredients, except eggs and half-and-half. Form into desired cake size, about 4 ounces each. Make egg wash by combining eggs with half-and-half. Dip crab cakes into egg mixture, then roll into more bread crumbs. Sauté cakes in butter or olive oil until golden brown. Serve with Roasted Red Pepper Cream Sauce.

ROASTED RED PEPPER CREAM SAUCE:

1 stick butter
½ cup flour
2 cups milk
2 cups fish stock
¼ cup sherry
2 red bell peppers, seeded,
  peeled, roasted, puréed

¼ teaspoon cayenne pepper
Salt and white pepper to taste
1 teaspoon paprika
¼ cup bacon grease

In a saucepan, melt butter over low heat. Add flour, and whisk until a roux is formed. Add next 3 ingredients, and bring to a boil. Reduce heat, to a simmer. Add peppers and remaining ingredients. Simmer 10 minutes; strain through a strainer. Add more milk, if too thick. Yields 6 servings.

Recipe from 82 Queen, Charleston
Lowcountry Delights III (South Carolina)

Lucille's Crab Savannah

2 tablespoons butter
2 tablespoons flour
1 cup chicken stock
Salt to taste
White pepper to taste
Dash of dry mustard
Dash of dry white wine

1 (10-ounce) can white
  asparagus
1 pound fresh lump crabmeat
½ cup grated mozzarella
  cheese
4–6 egg whites, beaten
2–3 tablespoons mayonnaise

Make a sauce by melting butter in small saucepan and stirring in flour. Mix well and gradually add chicken stock. Cook until thick, stirring constantly. Season to taste with salt and pepper. Stir in mustard and wine.

Preheat oven to 350°. Cover bottom of a 1½-quart baking dish with half the sauce. Top with a layer of asparagus. Pick over crabmeat to remove any shell; place crabmeat over asparagus. Sprinkle with grated cheese and top with rest of sauce. Bake at 350° for 20 minutes.

While casserole is baking, prepare a meringue by beating egg whites until stiff, gradually adding mayonnaise. Take casserole from oven and spread meringue evenly over top. Place back in hot oven and bake another 5 minutes, or until meringue is lightly browned. Serves 4.

Recipes from the Olde Pink House (Georgia)

Deviled Crab

½ stick margarine
½ small onion, chopped
1 stem celery, chopped
3 eggs, beaten
12 Ritz Crackers, crumbled
  slightly
1 heaping tablespoon
  mayonnaise
1 teaspoon prepared mustard

1 tablespoon Worcestershire
1 dash Tabasco
½ teaspoon salt
Black pepper
¼ cup milk
1 pound claw crabmeat
Additional cracker crumbs for
  topping
Paprika for garnish

Melt margarine in heavy saucepan. Sauté onion, celery, and pepper until tender, but not browned. Beat eggs; add other ingredients, and toss together lightly until well mixed. Turn into a 1-quart casserole dish, sprinkle with additional cracker crumbs, and paprika. Bake at 325° about 25–30 minutes or until firm. Serves 6.

Strictly for Boys (South Carolina)

Imperial Crab Casserole

1 pound backfin crabmeat
1 tablespoon chopped pimento
1 tablespoon chopped green
  pepper
6 saltine crackers, crushed

2 tablespoons mayonnaise
1 tablespoon prepared mustard
1 egg, beaten
Old Bay Seasoning

Grease 9x13-inch casserole. Mix together all ingredients, except Old Bay Seasoning. Pile ingredients loosely in casserole. Sprinkle seasoning on top.

TOPPING:
2 egg yolks
2 cups mayonnaise

Paprika

Beat egg yolks with mayonnaise. Spread mixture over crabmeat mixture. Sprinkle paprika on top. Bake at 425° for 20–25 minutes.

Sing for Your Supper (Florida)

Catch of the Day Casserole

1 (6-ounce) box quick wild
  rice mix
⅔ cup sliced fresh mushrooms
¼ cup chopped onion
2 tablespoons olive oil, divided
1 pound crabmeat

Flour
1 pound bay scallops
½ cup milk
½ (10¾-ounce) can cream
  of mushroom soup
2 tablespoons cooking sherry

Cook rice as directed on package, omitting butter; set aside. In large skillet, sauté mushrooms and onion in 1 tablespoon oil for 5 minutes. Add crab and cook 2 more minutes. Remove vegetables and crab from skillet. Add remaining oil to skillet and sauté lightly floured scallops for 2 minutes. Blend together milk, soup, and sherry. Add to scallops along with vegetables and crab mixture. Cook 1 more minute; remove from heat. Combine seafood mixture together with rice, and spoon into a greased 2-quart baking dish. Bake at 350° for 30 minutes. Serves 8.

Traditions (Georgia)

The Edgefield area of South Carolina is endowed with rich clay resources, including large amounts of kaolin, sands, feldspars, and pine trees, all necessary for making pottery. In the early 19th century, a new tradition of alkaline-glazed stoneware was developed using local materials to produce inexpensive containers for local use. By 1850, at the height of Edgefield stoneware production, five large-scale factories existed in the area. Now, the mere mention of Edgefield is synonymous with pottery. The Old Edgefield Pottery Museum offers visitors a look at original Edgefield pottery, as well as a look at the history of local pottery.

Coquilles Saint-Jacques

1½ pounds scallops, cut in
  chunks
1 tablespoon chopped shallots
¼ teaspoon salt
Dash of white pepper
½ cup dry vermouth or
  sauterne

1 cup heavy cream
1 tablespoon flour
4 tablespoons butter, softened
Freshly grated Parmesan
  cheese
Fresh parsley, chopped
  (optional)

In 2-quart saucepan, bring scallops, shallots, salt, pepper, and vermouth to a boil. Cover; simmer 2 minutes. Remove scallops with slotted spoon. Reduce remaining liquid to half by cooking about 10 minutes. Add cream. Boil rapidly till syrupy. Lower heat. Combine flour and butter, then stir into liquid, cooking till thickened.

Remove saucepan from heat. Return scallops to cream sauce, stirring to coat evenly. Divide equally among shell ramekins (ideal molds for homemade pastry shells), purchased pastry shells, or shallow casserole. Top with Parmesan and parsley. Heat at 450° for 5 minutes or until golden and bubbly. Serves 4– 8.

Variation: This recipe is exceptional with chunks of fish, crab, or shrimp. May be frozen for later use.

Catch-of-the Day (South Carolina)

GEORGIA DEPARTMENT OF ECONOMIC DEVELOPMENT

The Soque River in northeast Georgia is ranked as one of the top trout fishing streams in the eastern United States. It's the only river in Georgia that begins and ends in its home county.

Florida Lime Seviche

Use any variety of white meat fish, cleaned and cut into bite-size pieces. The less adventurous eaters reject the thought of eating "raw" fish, but in reality seviche is not raw at all but is rather "cooked" by the lime acid.

Diced raw fish	**1 teaspoon salt**
2 cups lime juice	**1 teaspoon sugar**
⅓j cup finely chopped onion	**¼ teaspoon oregano**
3 cloves garlic, finely chopped	**Freshly ground black pepper**
2 hot peppers, finely chopped	**¼ cup olive oil**
1 teaspoon chili powder	

Combine all ingredients and mix well. Add fish pieces, cover tightly and allow to marinate in refrigerator overnight.

Note: You can serve seviche as an appetizer or as an accompaniment to end-of-the-day cocktails. It's great for lunch or at pool side. In place of fish, you may substitute scallops.

Maurice's Tropical Fruit Cook Book (Florida)

Georgia Mountain Trout in Wine

6 pieces trout	**2 medium onions, thinly sliced**
Salt and pepper to taste	**½ cup chopped parsley**
Juice of 2 fresh lemons	**½ cup dry white wine**
3 large tomatoes, peeled and sliced	**¼ cup chicken bouillon**

Oil shallow baking dish; place trout in dish; season with salt, pepper, and lemon juice (sprinkle outside and rub inside cavity). Cover trout with sliced tomatoes, then cover tomatoes with sliced onions. Sprinkle with chopped parsley. Pour wine and chicken bouillon over all. Bake uncovered 30 minutes at 400°. Garnish with lemon slices and parsley. Serve with brown rice. Serves 6.

Flavors of the Gardens (Georgia)

Marinated Grouper with Fruit Salsa

½ cup lime juice
¼ cup tequila
2 tablespoons chopped cilantro

1 medium shallot, chopped
1 garlic clove, chopped
4 grouper fillets

Combine lime juice, tequila, cilantro, shallot, and garlic in a small bowl, and mix well. Let stand at room temperature to enhance flavors. Brush lime mixture over grouper fillets 15–20 minutes before grilling. Place grouper fillets on a grill over hot coals. Grill until grouper flakes easily. Place on individual serving plates. Spoon Fruit Salsa over top. Yields 4 servings.

FRUIT SALSA:

½ fresh pineapple, finely chopped
½ cup finely chopped strawberries
¼ cup finely chopped kiwi fruit
1 medium shallot or green onion, chopped

Cilantro to taste
Juice of 1 lime or lemon
Salt to taste
2 tablespoons chopped jalapeño pepper

Combine pineapple, strawberries, kiwi fruit, shallot, cilantro, lime juice, salt, and jalapeño pepper in a bowl, and mix well.

Note: You may substitute seasonal fruits for pineapple, strawberries, and kiwi fruit.

Tapestry (South Carolina)

Grilled Marinated Grouper

⅓ cup lemon juice
1 teaspoon lemon rind
2 teaspoons prepared
  horseradish
½ garlic clove
½ teaspoon oregano
½ teaspoon basil

½ teaspoon salt
¼ teaspoon pepper
⅓ cup olive oil
8 (4-ounce) grouper fillets or
  other white fish
Vegetable cooking spray

In electric blender or food processor, combine lemon juice, lemon rind, horseradish, garlic, oregano, basil, salt and pepper. Turn blender or processor on low, and gradually add olive oil in a slow, steady stream. Set aside.

Arrange fish in a 9x13x2-inch baking dish. Pour marinade over fish, turning to coat both sides. Cover and refrigerate 8 hours or overnight.

Arrange fish in a fish grill basket coated with cooking spray. Grill, covered, over medium hot coals 7–8 minutes on each side, or until fish flakes easily when tested with a fork, basting frequently with marinade. Yields 8 servings.

Cookin' on Island Time (Florida)

In the 1960s, Aiken, South Carolina, was hailed as the "Polo Center of the South." Today, polo is still played at Whitney Field, the site of the longest consecutive period of play on one field in the United States.

Pecan-Crusted Grouper

½ cup pecan pieces
½ cup bread crumbs
1 (1-pound) grouper fillet, cut
   diagonally into 4 (4-ounce)
   pieces
Salt and pepper to taste
¼–⅓ cup flour

2 eggs, beaten
¾ cup butter or margarine,
   divided
Juice of 1 lemon
1 bunch Italian parsley,
   chopped

Process pecans and bread crumbs in a food processor just until a coarse mixture forms. Season fillet pieces with salt and pepper. Dredge in flour; dip in egg. Coat with pecan mixture. Melt ¼ cup butter in a nonstick oven-proof skillet over medium-high heat. Sauté fish on one side until brown; turn fish. Place skillet in oven; bake at 400° for 10 minutes or until fillet pieces flake easily. Remove fish to a warm platter; wipe skillet. Add remaining butter to skillet. Cook over high heat until butter is foamy and dark brown, stirring constantly. Add lemon juice and parsley, stirring until combined. Pour over grouper. Serve immediately. Serves 4.

True Grits (Georgia)

Broiled Flounder

This cook and her husband created this dish together, from several recipes. The "puffy sauce" is also good on broiled chicken, she has found.

2–2½ pounds flounder
Salt and pepper to taste
2 tablespoons pickle relish
2 tablespoons chopped parsley
1 tablespoon lemon juice
¼ teaspoon salt

Dash of cayenne pepper
½ cup shredded Cheddar
   cheese (optional)
2 egg whites
Grated Parmesan cheese

Sprinkle flounder with salt and pepper. Place in shallow buttered pan and broil 6–10 minutes or until nearly cooked through. Stir together all other ingredients except egg whites which have been beaten until stiff but not dry. Then fold in egg whites and spread sauce over fish. Sprinkle with Parmesan cheese and broil 3–5 minutes longer or until sauce is puffed and lightly browned.

Good Cookin' (Georgia)

Flounder with Crabmeat

1 (1½- to 2-pound) flounder
Salt and pepper to taste
1 stick butter, melted
Juice of 1 lemon
2 teaspoons dill weed

Have flounder prepared and cut for stuffing. Season fish with salt and pepper. Mix butter, lemon, and dill weed and baste generously over fish while cooking.

STUFFING:

2 tablespoons chopped bell
  pepper
½ stick butter
1 cup crabmeat
1½ teaspoons Worcestershire
½ teaspoon seasoning salt
¼ teaspoon black pepper
1 teaspoon lemon juice
1 tablespoon chopped parsley
Dash of Tabasco
1 cup bread crumbs mixed with
  ½ stick melted butter

Sauté bell pepper in butter and add to crabmeat with remaining ingredients except bread crumbs. Stuff flounder and cover top of crabmeat where exposed with buttered bread crumbs. Bake at 350° for 5 minutes (baste with lemon, dill sauce). Then turn on broiler for approximately 4–6 minutes to brown.

"Don't Forget the Parsley . . . ." (South Carolina)

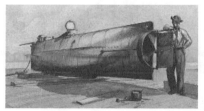

The first submarine ever used in warfare was the *H. L. Hunley,* which was used by the Confederates on the night of February 17, 1864, in Charleston Harbor, South Carolina. On that night, the *Hunley* became the first submarine ever to sink an enemy ship, but she suddenly disappeared, not to be found for more than one hundred years. She was finally discovered buried under twenty-five feet of sediment on May 3, 1995. The South Carolina Hunley Commission and a private, nonprofit group called the Friends of the Hunley are still solving the mystery of why she disappeared. Like a puzzle that reveals new information one piece at a time, they are engaged in the single most important underwater archaeological expedition of the century. For more information, visit www.hunley.org.

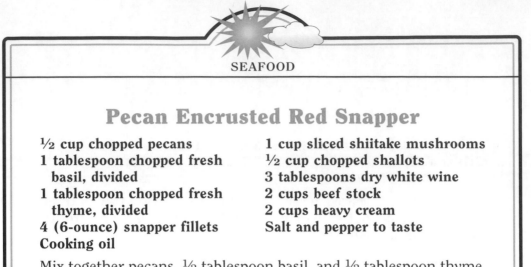

Pecan Encrusted Red Snapper

½ cup chopped pecans
1 tablespoon chopped fresh
  basil, divided
1 tablespoon chopped fresh
  thyme, divided
4 (6-ounce) snapper fillets
Cooking oil

1 cup sliced shiitake mushrooms
½ cup chopped shallots
3 tablespoons dry white wine
2 cups beef stock
2 cups heavy cream
Salt and pepper to taste

Mix together pecans, ½ tablespoon basil, and ½ tablespoon thyme. Rub mixture into flesh side of fillets. Heat small amount of oil in sauté pan over medium heat. With pecan side down (skin side up), brown fillets quickly in hot oil, no more than 10–20 seconds. Remove fillets from pan and transfer to a baking dish with pecan side up; reserve oil. Bake fillets 5–10 minutes in 350° oven.

Cook mushrooms and shallots with remaining basil and thyme over medium heat in same sauté pan about 5 minutes. Deglaze pan with white wine; add beef stock and reduce to half. Stir in remaining ingredients. Spread sauce, vertically, over half of snapper, leaving pecan crust on other half of fish exposed. Allow sauce to flow over onto serving plate—just a little bit above and below the fish. Yields 4 servings.

Recipe from Carriage House Restaurant, Pawleys Island
Lowcountry Delights III (South Carolina)

Potato Crusted Snapper

½ cup low-fat buttermilk
¼ teaspoon salt
¼ teaspoon black pepper
2 garlic cloves, minced
¾ cup instant potato flakes
   (not granules)

4 (6-ounce) red snapper or mahi
   mahi fillets
1 tablespoon butter or
   margarine
4 lemon wedges

Combine first 4 ingredients in a shallow dish. Place potato flakes in another shallow dish. Dip fillets in buttermilk mixture, then dredge in potato flakes. Melt butter in a large nonstick skillet on medium-high heat. Add fish; cook 3 minutes on each side or until golden and fish flakes easily when tested with a fork. Serve with lemon wedges.

Good Cooking (Florida)

Snapper with Sour Cream Stuffing

SOUR CREAM STUFFING:
¾ cup chopped celery
½ cup chopped onion
¼ cup margarine, melted
   (or oil)
4 cups dry bread cubes

½ cup sour cream
¼ cup lemon, peeled, diced
2 tablespoons lemon rind
1 teaspoon paprika
1 teaspoon salt

Sauté celery and onion in margarine. Combine all ingredients and mix thoroughly.

3–4 pounds fresh snapper,
   cut into fillets
1½ teaspoons salt

2 tablespoons margarine, melted
   (or oil)

Cut a pocket in each fillet in order to stuff. Sprinkle fish inside and out with salt. Stuff fish loosely with Sour Cream Stuffing. Close opening with skewers or wooden picks. Place fish on a greased baking pan. Brush with margarine. Bake at 350° for 40–60 minutes, or until fish flakes easily. Baste while cooking. Serves 6.

Sugar Beach (Florida)

Roasted Spice Glazed Salmon

¼ cup pineapple juice
2 tablespoons fresh lemon juice
4 (8-ounce) salmon fillets
2 tablespoons brown sugar
4 teaspoons chili powder

¾ teaspoon ground cumin
½ teaspoon salt
¼ teaspoon ground cinnamon
2 tablespoons grated lemon rind
  (optional)

Combine pineapple juice, lemon juice, and salmon fillets in a zip-lock plastic bag; seal and marinate in refrigerator 1 hour, turning occasionally. Remove fish from bag and discard marinade.

Preheat oven to 400°. Combine remaining ingredients in a bowl. Rub over fish. Place in a 7x11-inch baking dish coated with cooking spray. Bake 12–14 minutes. Serves 4.

INN the Kitchen at Abingdon Manor (South Carolina)

Pan-Seared Tilapia
with Chile-Lime Butter

CHILE-LIME BUTTER:
½ stick unsalted butter,
  softened
1 tablespoon finely chopped
  shallots
2 teaspoons fresh lime juice

1 teaspoon finely grated fresh
  lime zest
1 teaspoon minced serrano
  chile, including seeds
½ teaspoon salt

Stir together butter, shallots, lime juice, lime zest, chile, and salt in a bowl; set aside.

6 (6-ounce) pieces skinless
  tilapia fillets

½ teaspoon salt
2 tablespoons vegetable oil

Pat fish dry, and sprinkle with salt. Heat oil in 12-inch skillet until just smoking, then sauté 3 fillets, turning just once until golden and cooked through, 4–5 minutes. Repeat with remaining fillets. Top each fillet with a dollop of Chile-Lime Butter.

Savor Summerville (South Carolina)

Pompano Baked in Sour Cream Sauce

This recipe is of Russian origin. Pompano, red snapper and yellowtail are often caught in Florida waters and are perfect for this dish.

SOUR CREAM SAUCE:

½ stick butter

2 tablespoons flour

1 cup meat or vegetable stock,
  warmed

1 cup sour cream

Salt to taste

In a medium saucepan, melt butter, then add flour and blend until smooth. Gradually add warmed stock, stirring to blend, then add sour cream and blend thoroughly. Add salt as desired and simmer gently for 5–10 minutes.

2 pounds pompano fillets,
  boned and skinned

2 tablespoons flour

½ stick butter, divided

2 hard-boiled eggs, peeled
  and sliced

1 cup sliced mushrooms

1½ pounds potatoes, peeled
  and sliced

Salt and pepper to taste

Sour Cream Sauce

½ cup grated Cheddar cheese

Preheat oven to 350°. Cut fish fillets into 4 portions and roll in flour. In a large skillet, melt ¼ stick butter and sauté fillets for 3–4 minutes on both sides. Place fillets in a buttered baking dish and layer egg slices on top. In same large skillet, saute mushrooms for 4–5 minutes. Spoon mushrooms on top of eggs.

In same skillet, melt remaining butter; add potatoes and cook until tender. Arrange potatoes around fish, eggs, and mushrooms. Sprinkle with salt and pepper. Pour Sour Cream Sauce over casserole, then sprinkle top with Cheddar cheese. Bake for 20–25 minutes.

Florida Cook Book (Florida)

Mahi Mahi with Spicy Mango Cilantro Sauce

½ cup chopped, dried mango
2 fresh serrano chiles, seeded
  and chopped
5 cloves garlic, chopped
½ white onion, chopped
¾ cup dry white wine
¼ cup orange juice
1 cup chopped fresh cilantro

8 (¾-inch-thick) mahi mahi
  fillets
Salt and pepper to taste
1 tablespoon olive oil
½ cup skim milk
2 tablespoons chopped
  macadamia nuts

Combine mango, chiles, garlic, onion, wine, and orange juice in a medium saucepan. Bring to a boil over medium heat. Cook 5 minutes. Reduce heat, and simmer until ingredients are tender and liquid is reduced by about half. Add cilantro. Purée mixture in a blender. Set aside.

Season fillets with salt and pepper. In a large skillet, heat oil. Add fillets, and cook 2 minutes on each side or until lightly browned. Turn off heat and cover. Add milk to sauce and purée again. Reduce sauce. Place fillets on a serving platter. Pour sauce over top, and sprinkle with nuts. Yields 8 servings.

Treasures of the Tropics (Florida)

PHOTO COURTESY OF JULES UNDERSEA LODGE.

A diver greets a guest staying at the Jules' Undersea Lodge in Key Largo, Florida. The lodge is the first and only underwater hotel. Accommodating up to six people, the cottage-sized building has two bedrooms, a living room, showers, and a kitchen. The lodge actually began its existence as a research laboratory.

Grilled Tuna with Tomato Basil Vinaigrette

6 (8-ounce) tuna steaks
¼ cup virgin olive oil
¼ cup dry white wine

1 tablespoon minced garlic
Salt and freshly ground pepper
   to taste

Arrange steaks in a single layer in a nonreactive dish. Whisk olive oil, white wine, garlic, salt and pepper in a bowl. Pour over steaks, turning to coat. Marinate, covered, at room temperature for 1 hour or up to 6 hours in refrigerator. Drain, reserving marinade. Bring reserved marinade to a boil in a saucepan. Boil for 2 minutes.

Grill steaks over hot coals for 5–7 minutes or until steaks flake easily, basting occasionally with cooked, reserved marinade. Drizzle with Tomato Basil Vinaigrette. Serves 6.

TOMATO BASIL VINAIGRETTE:

½ cup virgin or light olive oil
4 medium tomatoes, peeled,
   seeded, chopped
¼ cup finely chopped red
   onion
¼ cup drained finely chopped
   sun-dried tomatoes

¼ cup minced fresh basil
¼ cup drained small capers
1 teaspoon minced garlic
½ teaspoon salt
½ teaspoon freshly ground
   pepper

Combine olive oil, tomatoes, onion, basil, sun-dried tomatoes, capers, garlic, salt and pepper in a bowl, and mix gently.

Note: The vinaigrette may be prepared a day in advance and stored, covered, in the refrigerator, adding the basil and salt just before serving.

Made in the Shade (Florida)

Seafood Medley

A Sarasota favorite.

¾ cup all-purpose flour
¾ cup butter, melted
3 cups half-and-half
1½ teaspoons salt
½ teaspoon red pepper
2 cups grated sharp Cheddar
  cheese
3 teaspoons onion juice
½ cup sherry
⅔ cup water or milk
1 pound crabmeat

1 pound shrimp, cooked, peeled,
  deveined
1 pound scallops, steamed 2–3
  minutes
2 (8-ounce) cans water
  chestnuts, drained
2 (14-ounce) cans artichoke
  hearts, halved
1 cup slivered almonds
Parmesan cheese, grated

Preheat oven to 325°. In saucepan, add flour to butter. Stir over low heat 3 minutes. Add half-and-half, salt, and red pepper. Stir constantly; continue cooking until thickened. Add Cheddar cheese; stir until cheese melts. Add onion juice, sherry, and water or milk. Mix well. Line 2 (6x12-inch) buttered baking dishes with crabmeat, shrimp, scallops, water chestnuts, and artichoke hearts. Add cream sauce. Sprinkle with almonds and Parmesan cheese. Bake 30 minutes. Serves 16–18.

Fare by the Sea (Florida)

Lobster Tails Grilled in Foil

6 spiny lobster tails, fresh or
  frozen
¼ cup butter or margarine,
  melted
2 tablespoons lemon or lime
  juice

½ teaspoon salt
Pepper, freshly ground
Melted butter for dipping

Thaw lobster tails in refrigerator (if frozen). Start fire in grill 30 minutes before cooking time. If lobster is fresh, remove swim-merettes and sharp edges. Cut 6 (12-inch) squares of heavy-duty aluminum foil. Place each lobster tail on half of each square of foil. Combine ¼ cup butter, lemon or lime juice, salt and pepper. Baste lobster meat with sauce. Fold other half of foil over lobster tail; seal edges by making double folds in foil.

  Place packages of lobster tails on barbecue grill, shell-side-down, 5 inches above hot coals. Cook 20 minutes. Remove lobster tails from foil. On well-greased grill, place lobster tails, meaty-side-down, for 2–3 minutes, or until nicely browned. Serve at once with melted butter. Serves 6.

Note: This is equally good with 2 or 3 pounds fresh shrimp substituted for the lobster. For easy removal, place shelled shrimp on skewers before wrapping in foil and browning over the coals. You may also eliminate lemon butter, and instead combine white wine, soy sauce, and ground ginger with the black pepper for the marinade, for oriental-style shrimp.

Florida Seafood Cookery (Florida)

 More than 80 million visitors have explored the mysteries of the sea at SeaWorld Adventure Park in Orlando, Florida, with up-close animal encounters with killer whales, dolphins, sea lions, stingrays and more. Since opening in 1973, SeaWorld Orlando has made many contributions to Florida wildlife conservation. Scientists, trainers and 24-hour on-call animal rescue teams actively participate in research and wildlife preservation. Recently, teams have helped saved beached whales, dolphins, seals, and helped raise the awareness of endangered manatees.

Lobster Thermidor

3 lobsters
2 cups heavy cream
¾ cup butter
3 tablespoons flour
1½ teaspoons salt
Freshly ground pepper
½ cup milk
¼ cup prepared mustard
½ cup grated Parmesan cheese

Boil lobsters and remove from shells; cut into bite-size pieces. Heat cream to a simmer, stirring occasionally; do not boil. Melt 4 tablespoons butter. Stir in flour, salt, pepper, and milk, stirring constantly until thick. Mix in warmed cream. Combine lobster and sauce and pour into a baking dish that has been rubbed well with mustard. Sprinkle with Parmesan cheese, dot with butter and bake in 400° oven, uncovered, for 10 minutes. A very rich dish.

Note: Mixture may be placed in cleaned lobster shells or served over pastry shells or rice. Chicken may be substituted for variation.

Florida Flavors (Florida)

Oyster Club Sandwich

½ tablespoon flour
½ cup milk
1 egg
¼ pint oysters
2 tablespoons butter
¼ cup rolled cracker crumbs
6 slices buttered toast
Lettuce
1 tomato, sliced
Mayonnaise
4 slices crisp bacon
Salt and pepper to taste

Blend flour in milk smooth and add a well beaten egg. Drain and dry oysters. Dip into batter and roll in cracker crumbs, then simmer in butter until golden brown. Make a two-layer sandwich, the first layer consisting of lettuce, tomato, mayonnaise, and bacon; the second layer of oysters, salt and pepper.

Ode to the Oysters (Florida)

Dolphin Street Broiled Oysters

This deserves to be served with a glass of chilled dry Chablis.

½ cup chopped green onions
1 cup chopped celery
¼ cup chopped parsley
1 cup butter
1 quart oysters, diced
¼ teaspoon salt

¼ teaspoon black pepper
½ teaspoon dry mustard
3 eggs, beaten
1 cup dry bread crumbs
4 teaspoons dry Chablis

Sauté onions, celery, and parsley in butter until brown. Then add diced oysters, salt, pepper, dry mustard, and eggs. Cook over a low heat about 15 minutes. Stir in bread crumbs and dry Chablis, then remove from heat. Place mixture in shells or ramekins and stick under the broiler for 2 minutes. Makes 10 servings.

Ode to the Oysters (Florida)

Scalloped Oysters

½ cup stale bread crumbs
1 cup cracker crumbs
½ cup butter, melted
1 pint oysters

Salt and pepper
4 tablespoons oyster liquor
4 tablespoons milk or cream

Mix bread and cracker crumbs; stir in butter. Put a thin layer of this mixture in bottom of shallow, buttered baking dish; cover with oysters and sprinkle with salt and pepper. Add half each, oyster liquor and milk or cream. Repeat and cover top with remaining crumbs. Bake 30 minutes at 450°. Use only 2 layers of oysters. You may sprinkle each layer with mace or nutmeg.

Recipes from Pawleys Island (South Carolina)

Oysters Rockefeller Casserole

6 tablespoons butter, divided
2 (10-ounce) packages frozen
  chopped spinach, thawed,
  drained
1 tablespoon lemon juice
1 tablespoon Worcestershire
Black pepper to taste
Hot pepper sauce to taste
½ medium onion, grated
1 cup saltine or butter cracker
  crumbs

2 cloves garlic, minced
6 crackers
3 quarts oysters, drained
¼ cup grated Parmesan cheese
1 (12-ounce) package grated
  Cheddar cheese
1 (12-ounce) package grated
  mozzarella cheese

Preheat oven to 350°. Heat 2 tablespoons butter over medium heat. Add spinach, and stir until excess butter evaporates. Mix in lemon juice, Worcestershire, black pepper, and pepper sauce.

In a mixing bowl, combine remaining 4 tablespoons butter with onion, cracker crumbs, and garlic. Mix in spinach mixture. Crumble 6 crackers over bottom of a greased shallow baking dish. Layer spinach mixture, oysters, and cheeses, ending with layers of cheeses. Bake 45 minutes. Serve immediately. Makes 8–12 servings.

Faithfully Charleston (South Carolina)

CAKES

PHOTO © CHARLESTON CVB.

Morris Island lighthouse stands all alone about 300 yards offshore from the island of Folly Beach, South Carolina. Since 1938, over 1600 feet of land surrounding the tower has been lost. The changing tidal currents caused severe erosion on Morris Island, and the lighthouse is now completely surrounded by water.

Florida Key Lime Pudding Cake

¾ cup sugar	¼ teaspoon grated Key lime peel
¼ cup all-purpose flour	¼ cup Key lime juice
Dash salt	3 egg yolks
3 tablespoons butter or	1½ cups milk
margarine, melted	3 egg whites

In medium bowl, combine sugar, flour, and salt. Add melted butter, lime peel, and lime juice. Stir until blended. Set aside. Separate eggs into 2 bowls, being careful not to get any yolk in the whites. Beat egg yolks, then add the milk, stirring with a wooden or plastic spoon; stir into lime mixture.

In glass or china bowl (not plastic), beat egg whites until stiff. Fold gently into lime mixture. Pour batter into greased 8x8x2-inch baking pan. Pour hot water into a large, shallow baking pan to 1-inch depth. Set pan of pudding batter into the hot water. Bake in 350° oven 40 minutes or until lightly browned. Serve warm or chilled, topping with whipped cream or softened vanilla ice cream. Serves 6.

Florida Seafood Cookery (Florida)

Lemonade Cake

CAKE:

1 (3-ounce) package lemon	¾ cup cooking oil
gelatin	1 (18¼-ounce) package yellow
¾ cup boiling water	cake mix
4 eggs	

Dissolve lemon gelatin in boiling water. Let cool. In a large mixing bowl, beat eggs thoroughly. Add cooking oil. Alternately add cake mix and dissolved lemon gelatin mixture. Pour into a greased tube pan. Bake in a 350° oven for 1 hour.

GLAZE:

1 (6-ounce) can lemonade	½ cup sugar
concentrate	

Dissolve sugar in heated lemon concentrate. Remove cake from oven, and leave in tube pan; drizzle with Glaze. Leave in pan 1 hour before removing.

Under the Canopy (Florida)

Tearoom Lemon Cake

Easy, beautiful, and delicious!

1 (18¼-ounce) package yellow
   cake mix
½ cup butter, softened
6 eggs
½ cup heavy cream
½ cup water

1 tablespoon lemon zest
1 teaspoon vanilla
¾ cup raspberry preserves
1½ cups sliced almonds,
   toasted

Preheat oven to 350°. Grease 2 (9-inch) springform pans with 2¾-inch sides. Combine cake mix, butter, eggs, cream, water, lemon zest, and vanilla. Beat about 2 minutes, or until smooth. Divide batter between prepared pans. Bake 25–30 minutes or until a toothpick inserted in the center comes out clean. Cool thoroughly on racks. After cooling, cut around side of pans to loosen; release sides, and remove cakes. Cut each cake in half horizontally, resulting in 4 layers.

   Place one layer, cut side up, on a cake plate. Spread with ¼ cup preserves, then ¾ cup Lemon Frosting. Repeat layers twice. Top with final cake layer, cut side down. Frost sides and top with remaining Lemon Frosting. Press almonds into sides of cake, and chill at least 2 hours or until frosting sets.

LEMON FROSTING:

3 (8-ounce) packages cream
   cheese, softened
1 (11¾-ounce) jar lemon curd

1 cup powdered sugar
3 tablespoons fresh lemon juice
1 tablespoon lemon zest

Cream together all ingredients until smooth.

Faithfully Charleston (South Carolina)

"The Tree that Owns Itself," is located at the corner of Dearing and Finley Streets in Athens, Georgia. Legend holds that Colonel William H. Jackson, a professor at the University of Georgia, owned the land on which the large white oak stood, and enjoyed its shade and "magnificent proportions" so much that he willed the tree eight feet of land on all sides around its base. The original tree fell in 1942; a new tree was grown from one of its acorns and planted in the same location. The current tree is sometimes referred to as the "Son of the Tree that Owns Itself."

Sunshine Island

⅓ cup butter, softened
⅓ cup Crisco
1½ cups sugar
3 eggs
2¼ cups sifted all-purpose
   flour
2½ teaspoons baking powder

1 teaspoon salt
½ cup milk
½ cup orange juice
1 cup coconut flakes
1½ teaspoons grated orange
   rind

Cream together butter, Crisco, and sugar until fluffy. Beat in thoroughly the eggs. Sift together flour, baking powder, and salt; stir in, alternating with milk and orange juice. Add coconut and rind. Bake in 2 (9-inch) greased and floured pans for 25–30 minutes at 350°. Put cooled layers together with Clear Orange Filling. Frost top and sides with Orange Mountain Icing. Decorate with fresh orange sections (membranes removed) nestled in coconut.

CLEAR ORANGE FILLING:

1 cup sugar
4 tablespoons cornstarch
½ teaspoon salt
2 tablespoons butter

1 cup orange juice
2 tablespoons grated orange
   rind
1½ tablespoons lemon juice

Mix together in saucepan and bring to rolling boil and boil 1 minute, stirring constantly. Cool.

ORANGE MOUNTAIN ICING:

2 egg whites
1 cup sugar
⅛ teaspoon cream of tartar

¼ cup orange juice
Dash of salt
2 tablespoons light corn syrup

Combine all ingredients in top of double boiler. Place over boiling water stirring occasionally for about 2 minutes. Then with mixer on HIGH speed, beat until mixture holds its shape.

The Gasparilla Cookbook (Florida)

Blueberry Cake

Serve this beautiful dessert with the whipped cream as suggested here, or omit the whipped cream for a delicious breakfast or brunch treat.

½ cup butter or margarine, softened	3½ cups fresh blueberries
1 cup sugar, divided	16 ounces sour cream
1 egg	2 egg yolks
1½ cups flour	1½ cups whipping cream
1½ teaspoons baking powder	¾ cup sifted confectioners' sugar
2 teaspoons vanilla extract, divided	Blueberries for garnish

Cream butter in a mixer bowl until light. Add ½ cup sugar gradually, beating at MEDIUM speed until fluffy. Beat in egg. Combine flour and baking powder. Add to creamed mixture, and mix just until moistened. Stir in 1 teaspoon vanilla. Spoon into a greased, 9-inch springform pan. Sprinkle with blueberries.

Combine sour cream, egg yolks, remaining ½ cup sugar, and remaining 1 teaspoon vanilla in a bowl, and mix well. Spoon over batter in pan. Bake at 350° for 1 hour or until edges are light brown. Cool in pan on wire rack. Chill, covered, in refrigerator. Place on a serving plate and remove side of pan.

Beat whipping cream in a mixer bowl until soft peaks begin to form. Add confectioners' sugar gradually, beating constantly. Spoon half the whipped cream over cake. Pipe remaining whipped cream around edge. Garnish with additional blueberries. Serves 8.

Tropical Settings (Florida)

Peach-Glazed Almond Cake

2¾ cups all-purpose flour,
  divided
¾ cup plus 2 tablespoons
  sugar, divided
¾ teaspoon salt, divided
½ cup butter
1 tablespoon water
3 eggs, separated
¾ cup peach preserves,
  divided

⅛ teaspoon cream of tartar
½ cup finely chopped
  unblanched almonds
½ cup milk
⅓ cup vegetable oil
1½ teaspoons baking powder
1¼ teaspoons almond extract
1 (28-ounce) can cling peach
  slices, drained

Preheat oven to 350°. In large bowl, mix 1½ cups flour, 2 table-spoons sugar, and ¼ teaspoon salt. With pastry blender or 2 knives used scissor-fashion, cut butter into flour mixture until mixture resembles coarse crumbs. Stir in water and 1 egg yolk. With hands, work dough until smooth. Press dough evenly and firmly on bottom and sides of a 9-inch round cake pan. Brush dough with ¼ cup peach preserves.

In small bowl with mixer at HIGH speed, beat 3 egg whites and cream of tartar until stiff peaks form; set aside. In large bowl with mixer at LOW speed, beat almonds, milk, oil, baking powder, almond extract, and remaining ½ teaspoon salt, 2 egg yolks, 1¼ cups flour, and ¾ cup sugar until smooth; fold in beaten egg whites. Pour into dough-lined cake pan, spreading batter evenly. Bake 45 minutes, or until cake springs back when touched with finger. Cool cake 20 minutes on wire rack, or until side of cake shrinks from pan. Remove cake from pan and cool completely on rack. Place cake onto platter. Brush top of cake with ¼ cup peach preserves. Arrange peach slices on top of cake; brush with remaining ¼ cup peach preserves. Serves 10.

Peachtree Bouquet (Georgia)

Miss Lucy's Coconut Cake

1 cup butter, softened
2 cups sugar
4 eggs
3 cups all-purpose flour
3 teaspoons baking powder
  (scant)

½ teaspoon salt
½ cup buttermilk
½ cup water
1 teaspoon vanilla

Cream butter and sugar. Add eggs, one at a time, beating well after each addition. Sift together dry ingredients and add alternately with buttermilk and water, which have been mixed. Add vanilla and blend thoroughly. Turn into 3 greased, paper-lined cake pans. Bake in a 375° oven for about 20 minutes. Remove from oven; let stand in pans a few minutes, then turn out on rack to cool slightly before putting together with Filling.

FILLING FOR COCONUT CAKE:

Large fresh coconut, grated
  (reserve milk from coconut)
2 cups sugar
2 tablespoons cornstarch

1 cup coconut milk (supplement
  with sweet milk, if necessary,
  to make 1 cup)

Reserve ¾-cup grated coconut, then mix remaining coconut with other ingredients. Place over medium heat and cook, stirring until thickened. Cool slightly. Spread between layers, sprinkling a bit of grated coconut on top of Filling on each layer. Spread over top and sides of cake. Sprinkle reserved grated coconut on top of cake.

Seasoned with Light (South Carolina)

Apricot Rum Cake

4 eggs
¾ cup vegetable oil
¾ cup apricot nectar (canned)
1 (18¼-ounce) box yellow
  cake mix

5 ounces margarine
¾ cup sugar
½ cup rum
Confectioners' sugar

In a large bowl, beat eggs lightly and combine with oil, apricot nectar, and cake mix. Beat at MEDIUM speed 4 or 5 minutes until smooth. Pour into large greased and floured Bundt or deep cake pan. Bake at 350° for 50 minutes.

Melt margarine and sugar in pan over low heat and stir in rum. As soon as cake is done, place pan on cooling rack and pour rum mixture over cake, allowing it to soak in well. Cool 1 hour before removing from pan. Sift confectioners' sugar over top. Yields 12–16 servings.

Friendly Feasts Act II (Florida)

Southern Gingerbread
with Caramel Sauce

½ cup sugar
½ cup butter and lard,
  softened, mixed
1 egg
1 cup dark syrup
1 teaspoon cinnamon

½ teaspoon salt
1 teaspoon ginger
½ teaspoon cloves
2½ cups all-purpose flour
1½ teaspoons baking soda
1 cup hot water

Cream sugar into butter mixture. Add egg and syrup. Sift dry ingredients; add to creamed mixture alternately with water. Pour into greased 9-inch square pan. Bake at 350° for 25–30 minutes. Test for doneness with toothpick.

CARAMEL SAUCE:
3 tablespoons butter, softened
3 tablespoons flour

1½ cups sugar
2 cups water

Cream butter and flour. Caramelize sugar by melting over low heat, stirring until browned. Add water slowly. Cook until bubbly. Add to butter and flour. Pour over gingerbread to serve.

Betty Talmadge's Lovejoy Plantation Cookbook (Georgia)

Lady Baltimore Cake

CAKE:

1 cup butter, softened
1½ cups sugar
6 eggs
1¼ cups self-rising flour, sifted
1¼ cups plain flour, sifted

1 cup milk
1 cup seedless raisins
½ teaspoon ground cinnamon
½ teaspoon ground cloves
½ teaspoon ground allspice
Chopped pecans

Cream butter and sugar, and add eggs one at a time, beating well after each addition. Alternately add sifted flour and milk. Pour enough batter into 3 layer cake pans to make 3 plain layers, and save enough batter to make 2 spice layers. To remaining batter, add raisins, cinnamon, cloves, and allspice. Divide spice mixture into 2 layers. This cake makes a total of 5 layers—3 plain and 2 spice. Bake at 400° about 20 minutes; allow to cool.

Frost cake with Caramel Icing, starting with a plain layer first, then a spice layer, a plain layer, a spice layer, and a plain layer on top. Sprinkle chopped pecans on Caramel Icing between each layer and on top of cake.

CARAMEL ICING:

1 cup butter
1 (1-pound) box brown sugar
½ cup evaporated milk

1 teaspoon vanilla
1 (1-pound) box confectioners' sugar

Melt butter in saucepan and add brown sugar. Stir until thoroughly melted. Add milk, and boil 2 minutes, stirring constantly. Remove from heat and allow to cool. Add vanilla and confectioners' sugar until it reaches spreading consistency.

South Carolina Ladies & Gents Love to Cook!

WWW.WIKIPEDIA.COM

Owen Wister (1860–1938), a popular novelist, picked Charleston, South Carolina, as the setting of his novel, *Lady Baltimore*, published in 1906. He modeled the central character, Lady Baltimore, after one of the city's former belles, Alicia Rhett Mayberry. In the novel, Lady Baltimore created a cake also called "Lady Baltimore." Wister's description of the cake sent readers of his novel scrambling to find the recipe. The cake has become a southern specialty with many recipe variations.

Italian Cream Cake

1 teaspoon baking soda	5 eggs
1 cup buttermilk	1 teaspoon vanilla
½ cup butter, softened	1 (3-ounce) can coconut
2 cups sugar	1 teaspoon baking powder
½ cup shortening	2 cups all-purpose flour

Preheat oven to 350°. Grease 3 (9-inch) round cake pans. Dissolve baking soda in buttermilk. Cream butter, sugar, and shortening together until light and fluffy. Mix in eggs, buttermilk, vanilla, coconut, baking powder, and flour. Stir until just combined. Pour batter into prepared pans. Bake at 350° for 30 minutes. Let cakes cool before frosting and assembling.

FROSTING:

1 (8-ounce) package cream cheese, softened	4 cups confectioners' sugar
	Cream
½ cup butter, softened	Chopped nuts
1 teaspoon vanilla	Flaked coconut

Cream together the cream cheese, butter, vanilla, and confectioners' sugar until light and fluffy. Mix in a small amount of cream to attain the desired consistency. Stir in chopped nuts and flaked coconut to taste. Spread between layers and on top and side of cooled cake.

A Taste of Heaven (Florida)

Carrot Cake

Pineapple and coconut make this an outstanding cake.

2 cups sifted all-purpose flour
2 teaspoons baking powder
1½ teaspoons baking soda
1 teaspoon salt
2½ teaspoons cinnamon
2 cups sugar
4 eggs
1½ cups oil
2 cups finely grated carrots
⅓ cup chopped pecans
1 (8-ounce) can crushed
  pineapple, drained
1 (3½-ounce) can flaked
  coconut

Sift together first 5 . Add sugar, eggs, and oil; mix well. Stir in carrots, pecans, pineapple, and coconut; blend thoroughly. Pour into 3 greased and floured 9-inch cake pans. Bake at 350° for 35–40 minutes. Cool briefly in pans, then turn onto racks. Cool completely. Combine frosting ingredients. If frosting is too thick, add small amount of milk. Spread frosting between layers and on top of cake. Serves 10.

CREAM CHEESE FROSTING:

1 stick butter or margarine,
  softened
1 (8-ounce) package cream
  cheese, softened
1¼ teaspoons vanilla
1 (1-pound) box confectioners'
  sugar

Combine all ingredients well.

Sunny Side Up (Florida)

WWW.DISCOVERSOUTH-CAROLINA.COM

Huntington Beach is the best preserved beach on the Grand Strand in South Carolina. It is also the site of Atalaya Castle, the winter home of philanthropist Archer Huntington and his wife, sculptress Anna Hyatt Huntington. In 1930, the couple purchased three plantations, including an extensive beach-front area where they built their castle, now a National Historic Landmark. Atalaya stands as a monument to the creativity and generosity of Archer and Anna Hyatt Huntington.

Butter Pecan Cake

1⅓ cups chopped pecans
1¼ cups butter, divided
3 cups sifted all-purpose flour
2 teaspoons baking powder
½ teaspoon salt

2 cups sugar
4 unbeaten eggs
1 cup milk
2 tablespoons vanilla

Toast pecans in ¼ cup butter in a 350° oven 20–25 minutes. Stir frequently. Sift flour with baking powder and salt. Cream 1 cup butter; gradually add sugar, creaming well. Blend in eggs; beat well after each. Add dry ingredients alternately with milk, beginning and ending with dry ingredients. Blend well after each addition. Stir in vanilla and pecans. Turn into 3 (8- or 9-inch) round layer cake pans, greased and floured on bottoms. Bake at 350° for 25–30 minutes. Cool 15 minutes. Remove from pans. Wait until completely cooled before frosting between layers and on top.

BUTTER PECAN FROSTING:

¼ cup butter, softened
1 pound confectioners' sugar, sifted
1 teaspoon vanilla

4–6 tablespoons evaporated milk
⅔ cup pecans

Cream butter. Add sifted confectioners' sugar, vanilla, and evaporated milk or heavy cream until of spreading consistency. Stir in pecans.

The Sandlappers' Salvation Cookbook (South Carolina)

Cola Cake

2 cups sugar
2 cups all-purpose flour
1½ cups small marshmallows
½ cup butter or margarine
½ cup vegetable oil
3 tablespoons cocoa

1 cup Coca-Cola
½ cup buttermilk
1 teaspoon baking soda
2 eggs
1 teaspoon vanilla extract

Preheat oven to 350°. In a bowl, sift sugar and flour. Add marshmallows. In saucepan, mix butter, oil, cocoa, and Coca-Cola. Bring to a boil and pour over dry ingredients; blend well. Add buttermilk, baking soda, eggs, and vanilla; mix well. Pour into a well-greased 9x13-inch pan; bake 45 minutes. Remove from oven and frost immediately.

FROSTING:

½ cup butter
3 tablespoons cocoa
6 tablespoons Coca-Cola
1 (16-ounce) box confectioners' sugar

1 teaspoon vanilla extract
1 cup chopped pecans

Combine butter, cocoa, and Coca-Cola in a saucepan. Bring to a boil and pour over confectioners' sugar, blending well. Add vanilla and pecans. Spread over hot cake. When cool, cut into squares and serve. Serves 12.

Atlanta Cooknotes (Georgia)

GEORGIA DEPT. OF ECONOMIC DEVELOPMENT

Coca-Cola was invented in May 1886 by John S. Pemberton, a druggist and chemist in Atlanta. It was intended to stop headaches and calm nervousness, but others insist he was attempting to create a pain reliever for himself and other wounded Confederate veterans. The name was suggested by Dr. Pemberton's bookkeeper, Frank Robinson. Frank penned the name in the flowing script that is still famous today. Discover the history of Coca-Cola and see the world's largest collection of Coke memorabilia at the World of Coca-Cola in Atlanta. First served at a small soda fountain in Jacob's Pharmacy in Atlanta by Willis Venable, it is now served over a billion times a day and enjoyed in over 200 countries across the globe.

Chocolate Cake

There is no other!

1 cup butter, softened
2 cups sugar
4 eggs
2 cups all-purpose flour, sifted
¼ teaspoon salt
1½ teaspoons baking soda

⅔ cup buttermilk
1 teaspoon vanilla extract
3 (1-ounce) squares
  unsweetened chocolate, melted
  in ⅔ cup boiling water

Preheat oven to 325°. Cream butter and sugar with electric beater until light and fluffy. Add eggs, one at a time, and beat well after each addition. Sift flour with salt. Mix baking soda with buttermilk and add alternately with flour to creamed mixture, starting and ending with flour. Add vanilla and melted chocolate with water; stir until smooth. Grease a 9x13-inch pan. Pour batter into pan and bake with Chocolate Frosting. Makes about 20 (2-inch) squares. The cake freezes well.

CHOCOLATE FROSTING:

½ cup margarine
1½ cups sugar
⅓ cup milk
¾ cup semisweet chocolate
  pieces

1 cup chopped pecans or
  walnuts (optional)

In a heavy saucepan cook margarine, sugar, and milk to a full rolling boil. Boil 2 minutes. Remove from heat; add chocolate pieces and nuts. Blend quickly. Beat until a spreading consistency. (It won't take more than a minute or two.) Spread at once over chocolate cake.

Cook and Deal (Florida)

Sunken Treasure Cake

1 (18¼-ounce) package
  Pillsbury Plus German
  chocolate cake mix
1 cup water

⅓ cup oil
3 eggs
1 bag Heath bars, crushed

Preheat oven to 350°. Grease a 9x13-inch pan. In large bowl, combine all cake ingredients, except candy bars, at LOW speed until moistened; beat 2 minutes at highest speed. Pour into prepared pan. Sprinkle batter with crushed Heath bars. Bake at 350° for 30–40 minutes. Cool completely.

GLAZE:

1 cup powdered sugar
5 teaspoons water

1 teaspoon vanilla

In small bowl, blend Glaze ingredients. Drizzle over cooled cake.

Seasoned with Light (South Carolina)

Fourteen-Layer Chocolate Cake

This recipe is one of this cook's mother's, and it's especially good, she says.

½ cup margarine, softened
½ cup vegetable oil
2 cups sugar
6 eggs

1 cup milk
3 cups self-rising flour, sifted
2 teaspoons vanilla

Cream margarine, oil, and sugar well. Add eggs, one at a time. Alternate, adding milk and flour, beating at LOW speed. Add vanilla last. Put 3 tablespoons batter on iron griddle at a time. Cook only a few minutes (until bubbles appear on top). Do not turn or flip. (Take up on wax paper until ready to stack.)

FILLING:

2 cups sugar
1½ sticks margarine
1½ cups evaporated milk

6 heaping tablespoons cocoa
  with enough water to make
  paste

Cook in saucepan until it begins to thicken. Spread over each cake layer—do not frost sides.

Good Cookin' (Georgia)

Chocolate Roll

6 eggs, separated
1 cup sugar
½ cup all-purpose flour

½ cup cocoa
1 teaspoon baking powder
2 cups whipping cream

Beat egg yolks and sugar until thick and lemon colored. Add flour, cocoa, and baking powder. When blended, fold in beaten egg whites. Put mixture in a 12½ x 17½ x 1½-inch greased pan lined with greased wax paper. Bake at 400° for 12–15 minutes. Turn out onto towel or smooth surface. Remove wax paper and roll tightly. When cold, unroll and spread with whipped cream. Roll up and spread top with Icing.

ICING:

2½ squares bitter chocolate
½ stick butter
2 cups powdered sugar

¼ teaspoon salt
1 teaspoon vanilla
2 tablespoons evaporated milk

Melt chocolate and butter. Add powdered sugar, salt, and vanilla. Put in electric mixer and add canned milk for proper consistency to spread.

"Don't Forget the Parsley . . . ." (South Carolina)

Candy Bar Pound Cake

A great favorite!

1 cup butter, softened
2 cups sugar
4 eggs
2½ cups cake flour
¼ teaspoon baking soda

1 cup buttermilk
8 Hershey's bars
2 teaspoons vanilla
1 cup chopped pecans

Cream butter until light and fluffy, gradually adding sugar. Add eggs, one at a time, beating well after each addition. Add sifted dry ingredients alternately with buttermilk. Add melted Hershey's bars, vanilla, and pecans (rolled in flour until lightly coated).

Grease and flour tube pan or Bundt pan and bake at 325° for 1½ hours or until done.

Country Cakes (Georgia)

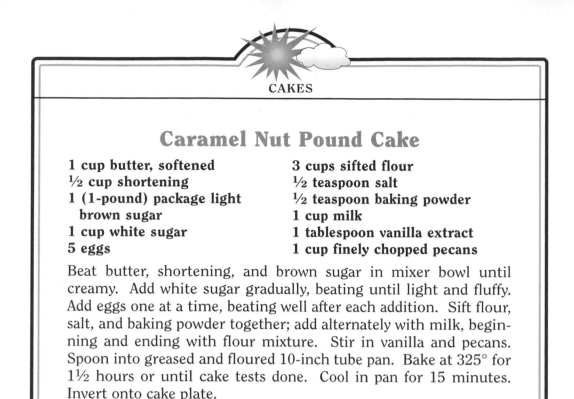

Caramel Nut Pound Cake

1 cup butter, softened
½ cup shortening
1 (1-pound) package light
  brown sugar
1 cup white sugar
5 eggs

3 cups sifted flour
½ teaspoon salt
½ teaspoon baking powder
1 cup milk
1 tablespoon vanilla extract
1 cup finely chopped pecans

Beat butter, shortening, and brown sugar in mixer bowl until creamy. Add white sugar gradually, beating until light and fluffy. Add eggs one at a time, beating well after each addition. Sift flour, salt, and baking powder together; add alternately with milk, beginning and ending with flour mixture. Stir in vanilla and pecans. Spoon into greased and floured 10-inch tube pan. Bake at 325° for 1½ hours or until cake tests done. Cool in pan for 15 minutes. Invert onto cake plate.

ICING:

½ cup butter or margarine
1 cup packed light brown sugar

¼ cup milk
1¾–2 cups confectioners' sugar

Heat butter in saucepan until melted. Stir in brown sugar. Boil over low heat for 2 minutes, stirring constantly. Add milk; mix well. Bring to a boil, stirring constantly. Remove from heat. Let stand until cool. Add confectioners' sugar gradually, beating until of spreading consistency. Spread over top and side of cake. Makes 18 servings.

Home Sweet Habitat (Georgia)

Florida is the number one destination state for overseas visitors. New York is second and California, third.

Mama's Crunch Pound Cake

Cake has a crunchy top.

1 cup shortening	1½ teaspoons lemon flavoring
2 cups sugar	⅔ teaspoon vanilla
6 eggs	¾ teaspoon salt
2 cups all-purpose flour	2 tablespoons sour cream

Cream shortening and sugar at MEDIUM speed. Add eggs, one at a time, beating well. Add flour in 3 parts; mix well. Add flavorings, salt, and sour cream. Pour into a greased and floured Bundt or tube pan. Place into a cold oven. Set oven temperature to 300° and bake for 1 hour. Test for doneness with a toothpick.

Thoroughbred Fare (South Carolina)

Mocha Cheesecake

CRUST:

1½ cups graham cracker crumbs	6 tablespoons butter, melted
	¼ cup sugar

Place crumbs in mixing bowl; add butter and sugar; blend well. Press into bottom and up sides of a well-greased 9-inch springform pan. Place in freezer until ready to fill.

1 (6-ounce) package semisweet chocolate chips	2 large eggs
	1 cup heavy cream
3 (8-ounce) packages cream cheese, softened	⅓ cup double-strength coffee
	1 teaspoon vanilla
½ cup sugar	

Preheat oven to 350°. Melt chocolate in double boiler. Beat together cream cheese and sugar until light. Add eggs one at a time, beating thoroughly after each. Beat in cream. Pour melted chocolate slowly into cheese mixture, and add coffee and vanilla. Mix to blend ingredients thoroughly. Pour mixture into prepared Crust; bake 45 minutes, or until edges of cake are puffed slightly. Cool to room temperature in oven with door cracked open. Chill.

The McClellanville Coast Cookbook (South Carolina)

Black Forest Cheesecake

CRUST:

1½ cups chocolate cookie crumbs

¼ cup butter, melted

Combine crumbs and butter; blend well. Press into bottom and 1 inch up sides of a 9-inch springform pan.

FILLING:

3 (8-ounce) packages cream cheese, softened

1½ cups sugar

4 eggs

⅓ cup cherry-flavored liqueur

Beat cream cheese with mixer until fluffy; add sugar gradually, blending well. Add eggs, one at a time, mixing well. Add liqueur, continuing to beat until mixed. Spread into prepared Crust, and bake at 350° for 55–60 minutes or until set. Cool completely.

TOPPING:

4 (1-ounce) squares semisweet chocolate

½ cup sour cream

12 maraschino cherries with stems

In the top of a double boiler, melt chocolate; allow to cool, then stir in sour cream. Spoon over top of cheesecake, and chill thoroughly before serving. Slice and garnish each slice with a cherry.

Christmas Memories (Florida)

Fort Sumter is a coastal fortification located in Charleston Harbor, South Carolina. Construction began in 1827, and the structure was still unfinished in 1860, when the American Civil War began. The fort is best known as the site upon which the shots initiating the American Civil War were fired, April 12–13, 1861. When the Civil War ended, Fort Sumter was in ruins. The U.S. Army worked to restore it as a useful military installation.

Irish Cream Cheesecake

CRUMB CRUST:

½ pound cookies (vanilla wafers, coconut cookies, ginger snaps, or any other cookies of choice)

¼ pound butter (1 stick)

Crush cookies to crumbs with a rolling pin, food processor, or blender. Melt butter; add crumbs and mix well. Press mixture onto base and sides of an 8-inch springform cake pan. Chill while preparing the Filling.

FILLING:

½ pound cottage cheese
½ pound cream cheese, softened
2 tablespoons cold water
1 teaspoon plain gelatin
Juice and rind of 2 lemons
6 tablespoons Irish cream liqueur

1 cup heavy whipping cream
2 egg whites
½ cup castor sugar* (or regular sugar)
2 ounces melted chocolate

Push cottage cheese through sieve, then combine in mixing bowl with cream cheese. Beat together well. Put cold water into a cup and sprinkle gelatin on top. Leave about 5 minutes to soak, then put the cup over or in a small amount of hot water until gelatin has dissolved completely. Blend into creamed mixture with lemon juice and rind. Continue beating until mixture is very smooth. Beat in liqueur. Whip cream until thick, and fold into creamed mixture. Whisk egg whites until stiff, then gradually whisk in sugar. Fold them carefully into cake batter. Pour into prepared Crumb Crust. Refrigerate 6 hours or overnight.

Just before serving, drizzle melted chocolate over surface of cheesecake. Serves 8.

Note: *Castor sugar is very fine sugar often used in baking. If not available, place sugar in a blender or food processor and work for about a minute or two. You may also use regular sugar, if preferred.

Let's Talk Food from A to Z (Florida)

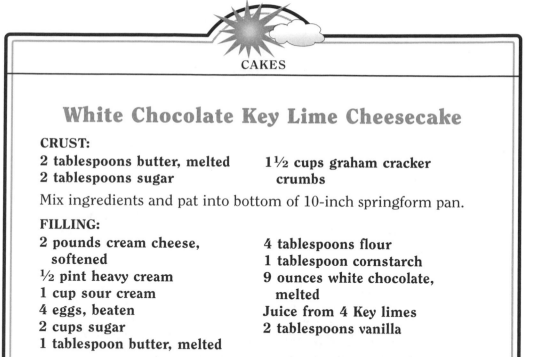

White Chocolate Key Lime Cheesecake

CRUST:

2 tablespoons butter, melted

2 tablespoons sugar

1½ cups graham cracker crumbs

Mix ingredients and pat into bottom of 10-inch springform pan.

FILLING:

2 pounds cream cheese, softened

½ pint heavy cream

1 cup sour cream

4 eggs, beaten

2 cups sugar

1 tablespoon butter, melted

4 tablespoons flour

1 tablespoon cornstarch

9 ounces white chocolate, melted

Juice from 4 Key limes

2 tablespoons vanilla

Beat cream cheese until smooth and add remaining ingredients. Pour into crumb-lined springform pan. Bake at 350° for 1 hour; turn oven off and leave for ½ hour. Chill for 12 hours.

Roberts Ranch Museum Cookbook (Florida)

Toffee Cheesecake Temptations

Creamy and rich bite-size cheesecakes. Ideal to serve on a buffet.

⅔ cup butter or margarine,
   softened
¾ cup packed brown sugar
2 cups flour
½ cup chopped pecans
16 ounces cream cheese,
   softened

¾ cup sugar
2 large eggs
1 tablespoon lemon juice
2 teaspoons vanilla extract
1 (7-ounce) Heath Bar, crushed

Beat butter at MEDIUM speed in mixing bowl until light. Add brown sugar gradually, beating until fluffy. Add flour and mix well. Stir in pecans. Set aside 1 cup mixture. Press remaining mixture over bottom of a greased 9x13-inch baking pan. Bake at 350° for 14–15 minutes or until light brown.

Beat cream cheese at MEDIUM speed in mixing bowl until smooth. Add sugar gradually, beating until light and fluffy. Beat in eggs one at a time. Stir in lemon juice and vanilla. Pour over hot crust. Sprinkle reserved crumb mixture evenly over batter. Bake at 350° for 25 minutes or until nearly set; cheesecake will firm when chilled. Sprinkle candy over hot cheesecake. Cool on a wire rack. Chill, covered, for 8 hours. Cut into bars to serve. Makes 3 dozen.

Savor the Moment (Florida)

COOKIES and CANDIES

PHOTO © GEORGIA DEPARTMENT OF ECONOMIC DEVELOPMENT.

The walls are covered with murals at the Road to Tara Museum in Jonesboro, Georgia—the setting for Margaret Mitchell's acclaimed novel and film, Gone with the Wind. *The museum contains original props, costume reproductions, and other memorabilia associated with the movie.*

Wongalara Lemon Fingers

This is a perfect choice for a hot day, as it requires no baking whatsoever. Serve these lemon fingers with a cool glass of lemonade!

8 ounces vanilla wafer cookies
2⅔ cups flaked coconut
⅔ cup butter, melted
½ cup plus 2 tablespoons
  sweetened condensed milk

Juice of 1 lemon
1½ cups confectioners' sugar

Crush vanilla wafers with a rolling pin in a sealable plastic bag. Remove to a bowl. Add coconut and melted butter and stir to mix. Add sweetened condensed milk and mix thoroughly. Press into bottom of a 9x9-inch baking pan. Combine lemon juice and confectioners' sugar in a bowl; mix until smooth. Pour over crumb mixture. Chill for one hour. Cut into squares. Yields 2–3 dozen bars.

An American Celebration (Florida)

Crunchy Key Lime Cookies

Mouth-watering cookies with a tropical flair, made with the juice and rind of the Key lime—a small yellow lime native to Florida.

½ cup (1 stick) butter or
  margarine, softened
1½ cups confectioners' sugar
1 egg
1 tablespoon Key lime juice

2 teaspoons grated Key lime zest
1 cup flour
1 teaspoon baking powder
¼ teaspoon salt
2 cups cornflakes, crushed

Cream butter and confectioners' sugar in a mixing bowl until light and fluffy. Stir in egg, Key lime juice, and zest (mixture may appear curdled). Add flour, baking powder, and salt, and mix well.

Drop dough by teaspoonfuls into cornflakes, and turn to coat. Place on ungreased cookie sheets. Bake at 350° for 16 minutes. Remove to a wire rack to cool. Makes 2 dozen.

Savor the Moment (Florida)

Florida Sunshine Cookies

2 cups all-purpose flour
2 cups sugar
4 teaspoons baking powder
1 teaspoon salt
1 teaspoon nutmeg

1 cup corn oil
2 large eggs
2 tablespoons orange juice
4 teaspoons grated orange rind
3 cups uncooked rolled oats

Sift flour, sugar, baking powder, salt, and nutmeg together into a large bowl. Add eggs, corn oil, orange juice, and orange rind; mix well. Add rolled oats and again mix well. Drop by level table-spoonfuls on greased baking sheet about 2 inches apart. Bake at 375° for 12–15 minutes. Remove from pans as soon as done and allow to cool thoroughly before storing.

Gator Country Cooks (Florida)

World's Best Cookies

2 sticks margarine, softened
1 cup light brown sugar
1 cup white sugar
1 egg
1 cup salad oil
1 cup regular oats
1 cup Rice Krispies

½ cup flaked coconut
3½ cups plain flour
1 teaspoon salt
1 teaspoon baking soda
2 teaspoons vanilla
½ cup chopped pecans

Cream margarine and sugars. Add egg; mix well. Add oil; contin-ue beating. Add oats, Rice Krispies, and coconut; mix well. Add flour, salt, baking soda, and vanilla. Stir in pecans. Form mixture into small balls. Place on ungreased cookie sheet. Flatten with fork dipped in water. Bake at 325° for 10–12 minutes.

Grandma Mamie Jones' Family Favorites (Georgia)

Lace Cookies

1 cup sifted all-purpose flour
1 cup chopped flaked coconut
  (or nuts)
½ cup light corn syrup
½ cup firmly packed brown
  sugar
½ cup margarine
1 teaspoon vanilla

Mix flour and coconut. Combine syrup, sugar, and margarine in heavy saucepan. Bring to a boil over medium heat, stirring constantly. Remove from heat; gradually blend in flour mixture, then vanilla. Drop onto foil-covered cookie sheets by scant teaspoonfuls, 3 inches apart. Bake at 350° for 8–10 minutes. Cool on wire racks until foil peels off easily. Place cookies on absorbent paper.

The Prima Diner (Florida)

Tea Time Tassies

CRUST:

1 (3-ounce) package cream
  cheese, softened
½ cup margarine, softened
1 cup all-purpose flour, sifted

Blend cream cheese and margarine; stir in flour. Chill about 1 hour; shape into 24 (1-inch) balls. Place in ungreased muffin pan. Press dough into bottom and sides, forming a pastry cup.

FILLING:

1 egg
¾–1 cup brown sugar
1 tablespoon margarine,
  softened
1 teaspoon vanilla extract
Dash of salt
⅔–¾ cup chopped pecans

Beat egg with sugar, margarine, vanilla, and salt until smooth. Combine egg mixture and nuts. Pour into Crust. Bake at 325° for 20–25 minutes. Cool in pan. Yields 24.

Feeding the Faithful (South Carolina)

Coconut Macaroons

3 egg whites
1 cup sugar
3 cups shredded coconut

2 tablespoons cornstarch
1 tablespoon vanilla

Beat egg whites until stiff, but not dry. Gradually beat sugar into egg whites. Fold in shredded coconut mixed with cornstarch. Cook in double boiler over hot water, stirring often, for 15 minutes. Add vanilla to mixture. Drop by teaspoonfuls onto greased cookie sheet, 1 inch apart. Bake at 300° for 20–25 minutes or until delicately browned. Yields 2½ dozen.

Historic Spanish Point: Cooking Then and Now (Florida)

Butterscotch Drops

1 (12-ounce) package
butterscotch chips
2 tablespoons peanut butter
½–1 cup slivered almonds,
toasted

2 cups cornflakes
½ teaspoon vanilla
Dash of salt

Melt butterscotch in top of a double boiler. Add peanut butter, and stir well. Add almonds, cornflakes, vanilla, and salt. Drop by teaspoonful onto greased cookie sheet. Chill until firm. Yields 4–6 dozen. Make be frozen for 2 weeks.

Stir Crazy! (South Carolina)

Eli Whitney invented the cotton gin near Savannah, Georgia, in 1793. After the invention of the cotton gin, the yield of raw cotton doubled each decade after 1800. By mid-century, America was growing three-quarters of the world's supply of cotton. Today, cotton is still a vital part of the agricultural economy. The South Carolina Cotton Trail meanders through a ninety-mile area in the state's northeast quadrant, tracing the crop's influence on the state.

Cherry Wink Cookies

2¼ cups all-purpose flour
1 teaspoon baking powder
½ teaspoon baking soda
½ teaspoon salt
¾ cup shortening
1 cup sugar
2 eggs
2 tablespoons milk
1 teaspoon vanilla
⅓ cup chopped maraschino
  cherries, drained
1 cup chopped pecans
1 cup chopped dates
2½ cups crushed cornflakes
⅓ cup maraschino cherries,
  halved

Sift dry ingredients together; set aside. Cream shortening and sugar, and blend in eggs. Add milk and vanilla. Mix in chopped cherries. Blend in dry ingredients; mix well.

Shape dough into balls using a level tablespoon for each. Roll each ball of dough in crushed cornflakes. Place on greased baking sheet; top each cookie ½ cherry. Bake 10–12 minutes at 350°.

Cherries Galore (Georgia)

Very Thin Benne Cookies

¾ cup melted butter (1½
  sticks)
1½ cups dark brown sugar
1 egg
¾ cup all-purpose flour
¼ teaspoon baking powder
¼ teaspoon salt
1 cup benne (sesame) seeds
1 teaspoon vanilla

Cream butter and sugar. Add egg slightly beaten; add flour with baking powder, salt, and benne seeds. Add vanilla. Drop with a coffee spoon in pan lined with aluminum foil. Bake in 300° oven till brown. Let cool before removing from pan.

Charleston Receipts (South Carolina)

Benne cakes are a food from West Africa introduced to South Carolina by slaves. "Benne" means sesame seeds, and are eaten for good luck.

Too-Good-To-Be-True Cookies

Every ingredient you love in a cookie all stirred into one.

2 sticks butter, softened
¾ cup light brown sugar,
  packed
¾ cup granulated sugar
1 teaspoon vanilla extract
1 egg
1½ cups rolled oats

1½ cups self-rising flour
1 cup dried cranberries,
  chopped
1 (8-ounce) package toffee bits
1 cup semisweet chocolate
  chips

Preheat oven to 350°. Beat butter, brown sugar, and granulated sugar until light and fluffy. Add vanilla and egg; stir to mix well. Stir in oats, flour, cranberries, toffee bits, and chocolate chips. Drop by teaspoonfuls onto greased baking sheet. Bake for 10 minutes. Remove to wire rack and let cool before removing from baking sheet. Makes 3 dozen cookies.

Par 3: Tea-Time at the Masters® (Georgia)

Butter Pecan Turtle Cookies

CRUST:

2 cups flour
1 cup packed brown sugar

½ cup sweet butter, softened
1 cup pecan halves

Preheat oven to 350°. Combine flour, brown sugar, and butter, and mix at MEDIUM speed for 2–3 minutes. Pat into 9x13-inch ungreased pan. Sprinkle pecans over Crust.

CARAMEL LAYER:

⅔ cup sweet butter (not
  margarine)

½ cup packed brown sugar
1 cup milk chocolate chips

Combine butter and brown sugar in saucepan. Cook over medium heat, stirring constantly until mixture boils. Boil 1½ minutes, stirring. Pour over Crust. Bake at 350° for 18–22 minutes. Remove from oven. Immediately sprinkle with chips. Swirl slightly. Do not spread. Cool, then cut into bars.

Tastes from Paradise: A Garden of Eating (Florida)

Savannah Cheesecake Cookies

These are a favorite among Savannahians.

CRUST:

1 cup all-purpose flour
½ cup packed light brown
  sugar

1 cup chopped pecans
½ cup (1 stick) butter, melted

Preheat oven to 350°. Combine flour, brown sugar, pecans, and butter in a bowl. Press dough into ungreased 9x13x2-inch pan. Bake for 12–15 minutes or until lightly browned.

FILLING:

2 (8-ounce) packages cream
  cheese, softened
1 cup granulated sugar
3 eggs

1 teaspoon pure vanilla or
  almond extract
Fresh berries and mint leaves
  for garnish

Beat cream cheese and granulated sugar together in a bowl until smooth, using a handheld electric mixer; add eggs and extract; beat well. Pour over Crust. Bake 20 minutes. Cool completely. Cut into squares before serving. Decorate tops with berries and mint leaves. Makes 24 squares.

The Lady & Sons Just Desserts (Georgia)

Pecan Crispies

½ cup shortening
½ cup butter, softened
1 cup sugar
1½ cups brown sugar
2 eggs, beaten

2½ cups all-purpose flour
¼ teaspoon salt
½ teaspoon baking soda
1 cup chopped nuts

Cream shortening, butter, and sugars; add eggs and beat well. Add sifted dry ingredients and nut meats. Drop from teaspoon about 2 inches apart onto greased baking sheet. Bake in moderate 350° oven for 12–15 minutes. Makes 5 dozen cookies.

The South Carolina Cook Book (South Carolina)

Crispy Pecan Sticks

½ cup butter, softened
¼ cup powdered sugar, plus
    extra for rolling
2 cups all-purpose flour
¼ teaspoon salt
1 cup coarsely chopped pecans
1 tablespoon vanilla extract
1 tablespoon ice water

Beat butter with mixer until creamy. Gradually add powdered sugar; beat well. Combine flour and salt; add to butter mixture, beating at LOW speed until blended. Stir in pecans, vanilla, and ice water. Shape dough into 3-inch sticks. Place sticks on lightly greased baking sheet. Bake 15–18 minutes at 350° or until browned. Roll in powdered sugar. Makes 3 dozen.

Georgia National Fair Blue Ribbon Cookbook (Georgia)

Sandies

1 cup margarine, softened
¼ cup powdered sugar
2 teaspoons vanilla extract
2 teaspoons water plus 2
    tablespoons water, divided
2 cups all-purpose flour
1 (6-ounce) package semisweet
    chocolate chips
1 cup chopped nuts

Cream margarine with sugar in medium bowl; blend in vanilla and 2 teaspoons water. Add flour and mix well; chill 1 hour. Shape dough into small fingers; place on cookie sheet. Bake at 325° for 20 minutes or until lightly browned. In top of double boiler melt together chocolate chips and 2 tablespoons water. Dip tips of cookies in chocolate and then in nuts. Makes 6 dozen.

Suncoast Seasons (Florida)

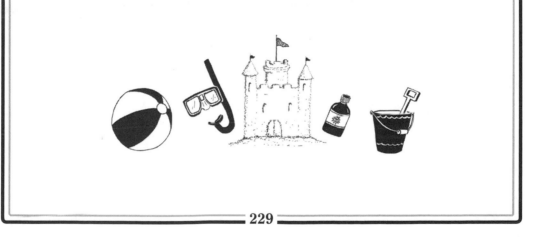

Kahlúa Nut Bars

½ cup (1 stick) butter,
  softened
2 eggs
2½ cups packed light brown
  sugar
¼ cup Kahlúa

1 teaspoon vanilla extract
1½ cups flour
2 tablespoons baking powder
1 teaspoon salt
1 cup chopped nuts
1 (4-ounce) can flaked coconut

Combine butter, eggs, and brown sugar in a bowl and mix well. Add Kahlúa, vanilla, flour, baking powder, and salt, and mix well. Stir in nuts and coconut. Spoon into a greased 9x13-inch baking pan. Bake at 350° for 25 minutes. Cool in the pan. Cut into squares. Yields 2 dozen.

Entirely Entertaining in the Bonnet House Style (Florida)

Chocolate Toffee Bars

1¾ cups crushed chocolate
  graham teddy bear cookies
½ cup butter or margarine,
  melted
1 (6-ounce) package milk
  chocolate chips
1 (6-ounce) package almond
  brickle chips

1 (6-ounce) package white
  chocolate chips
1 cup chopped walnuts
1 cup chopped pecans
1 (14-ounce) can sweetened
  condensed milk

Line a 9x13-inch pan with heavy-duty aluminum foil. Spread crushed cookies in pan, and pour melted butter over. Bake at 325° for 5 minutes. Remove from oven. Layer all chips and nuts over cookie layer, pressing into bottom layer. Pour sweetened condensed milk over all. Bake at 325° for 30 minutes. Cool completely. Cut into squares, removing foil.

Recipes for Lori's Lighthouse (Florida)

Chocolate Caramel Bars

1 package (50) Kraft caramels,
  unwrapped
⅔ cup evaporated milk, divided
1 (18¼-ounce) box German
  chocolate cake mix
¾ cup butter, melted
1 cup chopped nuts
1 cup chocolate chips

Melt caramels and ⅓ cup evaporated milk, stirring often. Mix German chocolate cake mix with remaining ⅓ cup evaporated milk, melted butter, and nuts. Put half of this mixture in bottom of lightly greased 9x13-inch pan. Bake at 350° for 6 minutes. Remove from oven. Sprinkle 1 cup chocolate chips over warm crust. Pour melted caramel mixture over chips. Spread remaining crust mixture over top. Bake at 350° for 15–20 minutes. Cut into bars.

Country Cupboard Cookbook (Georgia)

Toll House Marble Squares

½ cup butter or margarine,
  softened
¼ cup plus 2 tablespoons
  granulated sugar
¼ cup plus 2 tablespoons
  brown sugar, packed
½ teaspoon vanilla
1 egg
1 cup all-purpose flour
½ teaspoon baking soda
½ teaspoon salt
½ cup coarsely chopped
  walnuts (optional)
1 (6-ounce) package semisweet
  chocolate morsels

Heat oven to 375°. Grease 9x13-inch pan. Mix butter, sugars, and vanilla thoroughly. Beat in egg. Blend in flour, soda, and salt. Mix in walnuts. Spread in prepared pan. Sprinkle chocolate morsels over top of dough. Place in oven about 2 minutes. Remove from oven and run knife through dough to marbleize. Return to oven; bake 12–14 minutes. Cool. Cut into squares.

Windsor Academy Cookbook (Georgia)

An itinerant stonecutter traveling through the north Georgia hills in 1835 noticed an outcropping of particularly fine marble. The small quarry he founded near the present site of Jasper was the first exploitation of a vein estimated to be large enough to supply the world's building needs for 3,000 years. The town hosts the Georgia Marble Festival each year during the first full weekend of October.

Chocolate Mint Squares

CAKE LAYER:

½ cup butter, softened
1 cup sugar
2 eggs
½ cup all-purpose flour

2 (1-ounce) squares
   unsweetened chocolate, melted
½ cup chopped pecans

Cream butter and sugar until light and fluffy. Add eggs and beat thoroughly. Add flour and blend well. Add chocolate, blending thoroughly; stir in pecans. Pour into a greased 9x9-inch pan. Bake at 350° for 20 minutes. Cool in pan.

MINT FILLING:

1 tablespoon butter, softened   2 tablespoons crème de menthe
1 cup confectioners' sugar

Blend butter and sugar. Stir in crème de menthe until of spreading consistency. Spread filling over cake layer. Refrigerate.

CHOCOLATE GLAZE:

2 (1-ounce) squares semisweet   1 tablespoon butter
   chocolate

Melt chocolate and butter, stirring well. Spread Glaze over cold mint Filling. Chill. Cut into 1-inch squares. Store in refrigerator. Makes 4 dozen.

Heart of the Palms (Florida)

Snow Peak Lemon Squares

2½ cups graham cracker
  crumbs
1 stick butter or margarine,
  softened, divided
1¼ cups sugar, divided
1 (3-ounce) package lemon
  Jell-O
1 cup boiling water

1 (8-ounce) package cream
  cheese, softened
1 (12-ounce) can evaporated
  milk, chilled overnight
2 tablespoons lemon juice
½ pint whipping cream,
  whipped

Mix cracker crumbs, butter, and ½ cup sugar (reserve ¾ cup for topping) and press into a 9x13-inch dish. Dissolve Jell-O in boiling water and mix with cream cheese. Whip chilled evaporated milk, and add to remaining ¾ cup sugar and lemon juice. Fold into Jell-O mixture. Pour into crust and chill until set. Top with remaining crumbs and whipped cream. Garnish with a twist of lemon.

The Woman's Exchange Classic Recipes (Florida)

Gooies

Seven-layer cookies. Wonderful for waterfront outings where your appetite soars and your activities burn up the calories.

1 stick butter
Layer of graham crackers
  (total 16–18 crackers)
1 (6-ounce) package chocolate
  chips
1 cup pecans

1 (6-ounce) package
  butterscotch chips
1 (3½-ounce) can Angel Flake
  coconut
1 (14-ounce) can condensed
  milk

Preheat oven to 350°. Melt butter in 9x13-inch glass baking dish or pan. On top of melted butter place a layer of graham crackers, a layer of chocolate chips, a layer of butterscotch chips, layer of coconut, and a layer of chopped pecans. Dribble condensed milk on top and bake until a little brown around edge (about 30–40 minutes). Cut as soon as you remove from oven. Let stand at least 4 hours. Better to let stand overnight.

Sweet Surrender with Advice à la Carte (Florida)

Golden Eggnog Brownies

2¼ cups lightly packed vanilla
  wafer crumbs
1 teaspoon nutmeg
1 (14-ounce) can sweetened
  condensed milk
2 tablespoons golden rum

½ teaspoon rum extract
2 egg yolks, beaten
½ cup chopped golden raisins
½ cup finely diced walnuts
Extra nutmeg
Powdered sugar

Preheat oven to 350°. Butter 8-inch-square pan. In medium-size bowl, stir together vanilla wafer crumbs and 1 teaspoon nutmeg. Thoroughly blend in sweetened condensed milk. Stir in rum, rum extract, and beaten egg yolks. Mix well. Fold in raisins and walnuts. Spread batter evenly in pan. Sprinkle generously with extra nutmeg. Bake 20–25 minutes, or until toothpick comes out clean. Cool in pan. Lightly sift powdered sugar over top and cut into squares. Makes 16 brownies.

The Holiday Hostess (Georgia)

What is supposedly the world's largest peanut is in Turner County, Georgia. This 20-foot tall peanut monument symbolizes the importance of the peanut in Georgia history. Another peanut statue—12 feet tall—is located in Plains; this one honors the state's most famous peanut farmer, former U.S. president Jimmy Carter, and even boasts his grin.

Georgia Peanut Brittle

Use a candy thermometer and the brittle will be perfect!

3 cups sugar
1 cup white corn syrup
½ cup water
3 cups raw Georgia peanuts

3 tablespoons margarine
1 teaspoon salt
2 tablespoons baking soda

Grease 2 long pieces aluminum foil and have them ready (greased) on counter top. Combine sugar, syrup, and water in heavy 5- to 6-quart saucepan. On medium heat, stir until sugar melts, then add peanuts. Leave on medium to medium-high heat and stir occasionally. Cook until candy thermometer reaches 300—hard-crack stage. Syrup will be golden and peanuts will "pop" because they have roasted. Remove from heat and add margarine, salt, and soda, stirring well. Candy will "puff up." Pour candy on pieces of prepared, greased aluminum foil. Pour candy quickly and stretch, using a fork or hands, when cool enough. Cool and break into pieces. Yields 2½–3 pounds candy.

A Taste of Georgia (Georgia)

Microwave Peanut Brittle

1 cup sugar
1 cup dry raw peanuts
½ cup white corn syrup

1 teaspoon butter or margarine
1 teaspoon vanilla
1 teaspoon baking soda

Stir first 3 ingredients together in microwave-safe bowl, and microwave on HIGH 4 minutes. Stir, and cook on HIGH 4 more minutes. Add butter and vanilla. Stir, and cook 2 more minutes on HIGH. Remove from microwave and add baking soda. Stir quickly and pour onto greased or sprayed cookie sheet to cool.

The Best of Living in South Carolina (South Carolina)

Peanutty Balls

12 ounces crunchy peanut
  butter
1 cup margarine
2 cups graham cracker crumbs
1 pound powdered sugar

1 teaspoon vanilla
12 ounces chocolate chips
4 ounces paraffin
1 cup finely chopped nuts

Combine peanut butter, margarine, crackers crumbs, powdered sugar, and vanilla; mix until blended. Form into small balls and chill. Melt chocolate and paraffin in a double boiler. Using a pick, dip each ball into chocolate and sprinkle with nuts.

Holiday Favorites (Georgia)

Triple Chocolate Peanut Clusters

Simple, but elegant!

1 (12-ounce) package
  semisweet chocolate chips
1 (12-ounce) package milk
  chocolate chips

2 pounds white chocolate
1 (24-ounce) jar unsalted dry
  roasted peanuts

Melt all chocolate in an electric skillet on lowest setting, or in double boiler, stirring until melted. Cool for 5 minutes and stir in peanuts. Drop onto wax paper by tablespoons. Let cool completely. Wrap and keep in refrigerator until ready to serve. Makes 3 pounds.

Thymes Remembered (Florida)

©GATORADE

Gatorade was actually named for the University of Florida Gators (Gainesville) where the drink was first developed in order to help the football players combat dehydration.

Good Gracious, Charleston Toffee

40 saltine crackers
2 sticks butter (no substitute)
1 cup light brown sugar

1 (12-ounce) package milk
  chocolate chips
1 cup chopped pecans

Line jellyroll pan with aluminum foil, and spray with Pam. Lay saltines flat on foil. Melt butter and sugar together; heat until foamy. Pour mixture over crackers evenly. Put in oven and bake at 350° for 10 minutes. Remove from oven and sprinkle with chocolate chips. Let melt for 3 minutes, then spread with spoon to coat crackers. Sprinkle pecans over chocolate. Let cool; place in refrigerator until hard. Crack into pieces. Store in cool place.

Cooking with Faith (South Carolina)

Microwave Candy Bark

A great quick gift. Must do ahead.

¾ cup pecan chips or slivered
  almonds
1 cup sugar
½ teaspoon salt

1 stick unsalted butter
¼ cup water
1 (4-ounce) Hershey's chocolate
  bar

Butter cookie sheet and sprinkle nuts on sheet. Combine sugar, salt, butter, and water in medium size microwave bowl and cook in microwave for 8–8½ minutes on FULL POWER. Pour over nuts. In separate microwave bowl, cook chocolate bar for 2¼ minutes on level 6. Spread melted chocolate over nuts and caramelized sugar. Put in freezer for 20 minutes or refrigerate for 45–60 minutes. Break in pieces, bag, and refrigerate.

Culinary Arts & Crafts (Florida)

Key Lime Fudge

3 cups (18 ounces) white chocolate chips

1 (14-ounce) can sweetened condensed milk

2 tablespoons Key lime juice or lime juice

2 teaspoons finely grated lime zest

1 cup chopped macadamia nuts, toasted

Coarsely chopped macadamia nuts to taste

Line an 8x8-inch or 9x9-inch dish with foil, allowing a 4- to 5-inch overhang. Coat foil with butter. Combine white chocolate chips and condensed milk in heavy saucepan. Cook over low heat just until chocolate melts and mixture is smooth, stirring frequently. Remove from heat. Stir in lime juice and lime zest. Add 1 cup macadamia nuts and mix well. Spread chocolate mixture in prepared dish and sprinkle with coarsely chopped macadamia nuts. Chill, covered, for 2 hours or until firm. Lift fudge out of dish using edges of foil. Cut the fudge into squares and store in an airtight container at room temperature for 1 week or freeze for up to 2 months. Makes 64 squares.

Bay Fêtes (Florida)

PIES and OTHER DESSERTS

PHOTO © SOUTH CAROLINA DEPARTMENT OF PARKS, RECREATION, AND TOURISM, WWW.DISCOVERSOUTHCAROLINA.COM.

Built in 1981 in Gaffney, South Carolina, the Peachoid is a large water tower that resembles what else . . . a peach. The water tower, which holds one million gallons of water, is one of the most recognizable landmarks on the stretch of I-85 connecting Charlotte, North Carolina, and Atlanta, Georgia.

Margaritaville Key Lime Pie

This tropical dessert recipe comes from singer Jimmy Buffett's Margaritaville Café.

CRUST AND FILLING:

1 (9-inch) graham cracker pie
  crust
2 egg yolks
1 (14-ounce) can sweetened
  condensed milk

1 egg white
½ cup Key lime juice

Bake pie crust at 350° for 5 minutes. Beat egg yolks with an electric mixer 2 minutes. Blend yolks into milk. In separate bowl, beat egg white with electric mixer until fluffy. Gently fold white into mixture. Fold in lime juice. Pour filling into pie crust. Refrigerate 2–3 hours before adding Topping.

TOPPING:

5 egg whites
2 teaspoons cream of tartar

½ cup sugar

Whip egg whites and cream of tartar with electric mixer until foamy. Continue to whip while slowly adding sugar. Beat until peaks form. Score filling with a fork. Spread Topping over Filling. Bake at 425° for 5 minutes or until topping starts to brown. Yields 8 servings.

Calypso Café (Florida)

Key limes, abundant in the Florida Keys, are much smaller and rounder than regular limes, ranging in size from a ping-pong ball to a golf ball. The peel is thin, smooth and greenish-yellow when ripe. The flesh is yellow and quite juicy with a higher acidity than regular limes. The name comes from its association with the Florida Keys, where it is best known as the flavoring ingredient in Key lime pie.

No-Bake Key Lime Pie

1 (8-ounce) package cream
  cheese, softened
1 (14-ounce) can sweetened
  condensed milk
3 ounces Key lime juice
1 graham cracker pie shell,
  baked

Sliced strawberries, kiwi fruit,
  or other fresh fruit, or fruit
  pie filling
Whipped cream

Blend cream cheese and condensed milk (it will have some tiny lumps of cheese). Add one ounce of lime juice at a time, blend well each time. Pour into pie shell; chill.

At serving time, top with one or more of the fruit slices or pie filling. Then top with whipped cream.

The Cruising K.I.S.S. Cookbook II (Florida)

Margarita Pie

Tastes just like its namesake.

CRUST:

1½ cups crushed pretzel
  sticks

¼ cup sugar
¼ pound butter, melted

Combine crushed pretzels and sugar. Add melted butter. Press into 9-inch buttered pie plate and chill.

FILLING:

1 (14-ounce) can sweetened
  condensed milk
⅓ cup fresh lime juice
2 tablespoons tequila

2 tablespoons Triple Sec
1–2 drops green food coloring
1 cup heavy cream, whipped

Combine sweetened condensed milk, lime juice, tequila, and Triple Sec. Add food coloring, if desired. Fold whipped cream into mixture. Pour into chilled Crust and freeze for 3–4 hours or until firm. (Can be stored in freezer for several days.) Before serving, garnish each piece with thin slice of lime. Serves 8–10.

Sunny Side Up (Florida)

Cloister Lemon Meringue Pie

Recipe given to me by a long time baker for the Cloister Resort Hotel on St. Simons Island.

1½ cups sugar	1 teaspoon grated lemon peel
7 tablespoons cornstarch	2 tablespoons butter or
Dash of salt	margarine
1½ cups water	½ cup lemon juice
3 egg yolks, beaten	1 (9-inch) pie shell, baked

In a saucepan, combine sugar, cornstarch, and salt. Stir in water. Bring to boiling over medium heat and cook, stirring constantly until thick, about 5 minutes. Remove from heat, stir small amount of hot mixture into egg yolks, then return to remaining mixture in pan. Bring to a boil and cook 1 minute, stirring constantly. Remove from heat. Add lemon peel and butter. Slowly stir in lemon juice. Cool to lukewarm. Pour into cooled pie shell; top with Meringue.

MERINGUE:

3 egg whites	6 tablespoons sugar
1 teaspoon lemon juice	

Beat egg whites with lemon juice until soft peaks form. Gradually add sugar, beating until stiff. Spread Meringue over filling; seal to edges of pastry. Bake at 350° for 12–15 minutes or until Meringue is golden brown. Cool thoroughly before serving. Serves 6–8.

Southern Manna (Georgia)

The world's only double-barreled cannon was built in Athens, Georgia, and is displayed on the grounds of City Hall. The prototype was a spectacular failure in test firings, so it was never used in combat.

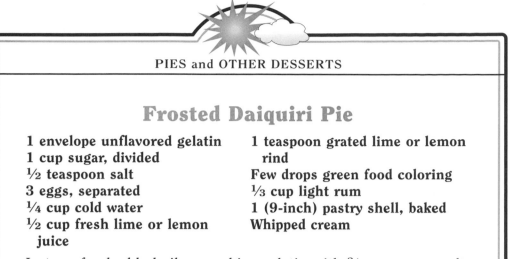

Frosted Daiquiri Pie

1 envelope unflavored gelatin
1 cup sugar, divided
½ teaspoon salt
3 eggs, separated
¼ cup cold water
½ cup fresh lime or lemon
  juice
1 teaspoon grated lime or lemon
  rind
Few drops green food coloring
⅓ cup light rum
1 (9-inch) pastry shell, baked
Whipped cream

In top of a double boiler, combine gelatin with ⅔ cup sugar, salt, egg yolks, water, and lime juice. With rotary beater beat until blended. Cook over boiling water, stirring until mixture coats a spoon. Remove from heat; add rind and food coloring to a pale green tint. Cool mixture; stir in rum. Refrigerate mixture until slightly thicker than unbeaten egg whites. In large bowl, beat egg whites until they form soft peaks; add remaining ⅓ cup sugar, 1 tablespoon at a time, beating until stiff. Fold in gelatin mixture. Turn mixture into baked pastry shell; refrigerate several hours. Top with whipped cream before serving.

Beyond the Bay (Florida)

Company's Coming Peach Pie

1 (8- or 9-inch) pie shell,
  unbaked
1 tablespoon butter, melted
2 teaspoons vanilla extract
1 (8-ounce) package cream
  cheese, softened
¼ cup sugar
¼ cup sour cream
½ cup apricot preserves,
  divided
1 (16-ounce) can sliced red
  freestone peaches, drained

Brush pie shell with butter. Bake according to package directions; let stand until cool. Process vanilla, cream cheese, sugar, sour cream, and ¼ cup preserves in blender or food processor until smooth. Pour into baked pie shell. Arrange peaches artfully in a spoke pattern over top. Drizzle remaining ¼ cup preserves (may have to heat slightly) over peaches. Chill in refrigerator. Serves 6.

Some Assembly Required (Georgia)

Strawberry Splendor Mile High Pie

The crust complements the delicious strawberry taste!

CRUST:

1 cup all-purpose flour	½ cup butter, melted
¼ cup firmly packed light brown sugar	½ cup finely chopped pecans

Preheat oven to 350°. In a large mixing bowl, combine all Crust ingredients until blended. Spread thinly onto an ungreased baking sheet. Bake 15 minutes, stirring occasionally. Cool slightly. Stir to crumble. Reserve ½ cup crumb mixture for garnish. Press remaining warm crumb mixture into a lightly buttered 9-inch glass pie plate. Cool.

FILLING:

1 (10-ounce) package frozen strawberries with syrup, thawed	2 egg whites
1 cup granulated sugar	1 (8-ounce) carton whipping cream, whipped
2 teaspoons freshly squeezed lemon juice	

Using an electric mixer, combine strawberries, sugar, lemon juice, and egg whites. Beat on HIGH speed 15 minutes until mixture is very stiff (beating is the secret!). Fold in whipped cream by hand. Turn Filling into prepared Crust. Sprinkle reserved crumb mixture over top. Freeze overnight before serving; serve frozen.

Bevelyn Blair's Everyday Pies (Georgia)

LIBRARY OF CONGRESS, NEW YORK WORLD-TELEGRAM & SUN COLLECTION

Civil rights activist Martin Luther King, Jr. was born in 1929 on Auburn Avenue in Atlanta, Georgia. The nine-room home that was owned by his grandfather, A. D. Williams, has been restored and is now one of the cornerstones of the Martin Luther King, Jr. National Historic Site. The Site, established on October 10, 1980, consists of several buildings surrounding his boyhood home, including Ebenezer Baptist Church, the church where King and his father Martin Luther King, Sr. pastored.

Florida Orange Pie

FILLING:

2 cups orange juice
1 cup sugar
2 tablespoons cornstarch
¼ cup water
1 tablespoon butter or
   margarine

½ teaspoon salt
3 egg yolks
3 tablespoons grated orange rind
1 cup orange sections
1 (9-inch) pie shell, baked

Combine orange juice and sugar, and boil until sugar dissolves. Mix cornstarch and water; add to orange juice mixture. Add butter and salt. Beat egg yolks and add a little of hot mixture and stir together, then combine and stir until thickened. Add grated orange rind and sections just before removing from heat. Pour into pie shell and let cool.

TOPPING:

3 egg whites
3 tablespoons ice water

Pinch of salt
6 tablespoons sugar

Beat egg whites until frothy; add ice water, then salt. Add sugar slowly while beating eggs until stiff, but not dry. Mound lightly on filled pie shell and spread to edge of crust. Bake at 300° for 15–20 minutes or until brown. Yields 8 servings.

Historic Spanish Point: Cooking Then and Now (Florida)

PHOTO © GEORGIA DEPARTMENT OF ECONOMIC DEVELOPMENT

Martin Luther King, Jr. National Historic Site

Grapefruit Grand Meringue Pie

A wonderful pie to make with a light and unusual flavor!

FILLING:

2 cups granulated sugar
6 tablespoons cornstarch
½ cup water
2 cups freshly squeezed
    grapefruit juice

3 eggs yolks, well beaten
1½ tablespoons butter
1 (9-inch) single plain pastry
    shell, baked and cooled

In a large saucepan, combine sugar, cornstarch, water, and juice; stir until blended and smooth. Cook over medium heat 5 minutes or until thickened, stirring constantly. Remove from heat. Quickly stir ⅓ cup hot mixture into beaten egg yolks; return to saucepan. Cook and stir for 2 minutes. Remove from heat. Add butter, stirring until melted. Spread evenly into shell; set aside to cool.

MERINGUE:

3 egg whites
⅛ teaspoon salt
¼ teaspoon cream of tartar

6 tablespoons granulated sugar
1 teaspoon grated grapefruit
    zest for garnish

Preheat oven to 375°. Using an electric mixer, beat egg whites until foamy. Gradually add salt, cream of tartar, and sugar, beating until stiff and shiny. Quickly spread over Filling to the edge. Sprinkle zest evenly over top. Bake 10 minutes or until light golden brown. Cool 3 hours on a wire rack before serving.

Bevelyn Blair's Everyday Pies (Georgia)

Sweetgrass basket making was brought from Africa to America by slaves, and has been a part of the South Carolina community of Mount Pleasant for more than 300 years. Sweetgrass basket weaving was an important tradition among African-Americans on Lowcountry plantations. Originally, these graceful products provided useful, practical objects for agricultural and household use on the plantations; today, they have evolved as treasured souvenirs by tourists.

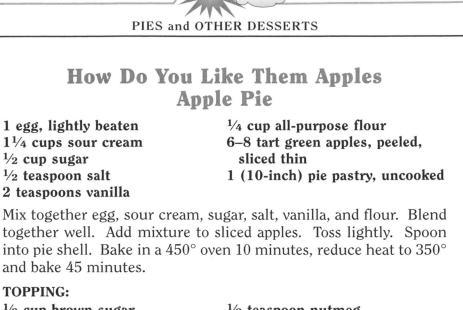

How Do You Like Them Apples Apple Pie

1 egg, lightly beaten
1¼ cups sour cream
½ cup sugar
½ teaspoon salt
2 teaspoons vanilla

¼ cup all-purpose flour
6–8 tart green apples, peeled,
  sliced thin
1 (10-inch) pie pastry, uncooked

Mix together egg, sour cream, sugar, salt, vanilla, and flour. Blend together well. Add mixture to sliced apples. Toss lightly. Spoon into pie shell. Bake in a 450° oven 10 minutes, reduce heat to 350° and bake 45 minutes.

TOPPING:

⅓ cup brown sugar
⅓ cup white sugar
⅛ teaspoon salt
1 teaspoon cinnamon

½ teaspoon nutmeg
½ cup all-purpose flour
1 cup chopped pecans
6 tablespoons butter, melted

Mix all Topping ingredients together. Spoon on top of hot pie, mix in lightly with apples, and bake an additional 10–15 minutes at 350° until golden. Serves 8.

Juicy Miss Lucy Cookbook (Florida)

Lost Creek Sawdust Pie

1½ cups flaked coconut
1½ cups graham cracker
  crumbs
1½ cups chopped pecans or
  walnuts

1½ cups sugar
1 cup egg whites (unbeaten)
1 unbaked pie shell

Combine coconut, graham cracker crumbs, nuts, and sugar. Mix with egg whites. Pour mixture into pie shell. Bake at 350° for 30–35 minutes. Serve warm with ice cream.

Let's ACT Up in the Kitchen (Florida)

Peanut Butter Pie

Peanut butter pie is fundamental to the serious dessert repertoire of the South, and that is especially true in the peanut-rich state of Georgia. This creamy peanut butter pie is on the dessert table every day at Blue Willow Inn. A guest once asked, "Who made the peanut butter pie? I want to marry her."

1 (8-ounce) package cream
 cheese, softened
1 cup confectioners' sugar
¾ cup crunchy peanut butter

2 (12-ounce) cartons whipped
 topping, divided
2 graham cracker pie crusts

In a large bowl, mix cream cheese, confectioners' sugar, and peanut butter together. Fold in 1 carton of whipped topping. Divide mixture between pie crusts and chill for several hours. Top each pie with half the remaining whipped topping. Makes 16 servings.

The Blue Willow Inn Bible of Southern Cooking (Georgia)

Chantilly Peanut Pie

1 quart vanilla ice cream,
 slightly softened
¾ cup creamy peanut butter
1 cup chopped unsalted
 peanuts, divided

1 tablespoon vanilla
1 (10-ounce) chocolate crumb
 crust
Whipped cream, sweetened
Hot fudge sauce

Combine ice cream, peanut butter, ½ cup peanuts, and vanilla in bowl. Mix well. Pour into prepared crust. Sprinkle with remaining nuts. Freeze. Remove from freezer about 10 minutes before serving. Garnish with whipped cream and serve hot fudge sauce drizzled over each slice.

Educated Taste (Georgia)

Every August, four and a half tons of peanuts are boiled in Pelion at the South Carolina Peanut Party, a weekend-long festival that celebrates the town's peanut heritage.

Kahlúa Pecan Pie

¼ cup butter, softened
¾ cup sugar
1 teaspoon vanilla
2 teaspoons flour
3 eggs

½ cup Kahlúa
½ cup corn syrup
¾ cup evaporated milk
1 cup chopped pecans
1 pie shell

Set oven at 400°. Mix butter, sugar, vanilla, and flour. Beat in eggs one at a time. Stir in Kahlúa, corn syrup, evaporated milk, and pecans; mix well. Pour into pie shell. Bake 10 minutes, then reduce heat to 325°. Continue cooking until firm, approximately 25 minutes. From the Player's Club.

Island Events Cookbook (South Carolina)

Ritz Pecan Pie

At Callaway Gardens there are so many good things served to eat . . . it's hard to decide what you like best . . . but one dessert you'll always enjoy is this delicious pie.

⅔ cup egg whites
1 cup sugar
½ teaspoon baking powder
¼ pound pecans, chopped

16 Ritz Crackers, crumbled
Whipped cream
Extra cracker crumbs and
   chopped pecans for garnish

Beat egg whites. Mix sugar and baking powder; add to egg whites. Beat until stiff peaks form. Fold in nuts and cracker crumbs. Bake in buttered pie pan 45 minutes at 300°. When cooled, top with whipped cream. Garnish with extra cracker crumbs and pecans.

Country Cookin' (Georgia)

Best Ever Sweet Potato Pie

1 cup whole milk, scalded
1 cup evaporated milk
1 cup cooked, mashed sweet
  potatoes
¾ cup white sugar
¾ cup brown sugar

3 tablespoons flour
½ teaspoon nutmeg
½ teaspoon cinnamon
½ teaspoon salt
3 eggs, separated
2 (9-inch) unbaked pie crusts

Scald whole milk. Mix together both milks, sweet potatoes, sugars, flour, spices, and salt. Add egg yolks. Whip egg whites until stiff and fold in last. Pour into pie crusts. Bake at 400° for 10 minutes, then 350° for 45 minutes. Makes 2 pies.

Variation: For crumb topping, mix 1 cup flour, 1 cup brown sugar, 1 cup oatmeal, and 1 stick softened butter. Add to top of pies before baking.

Montezuma Amish Mennonite Cookbook II (Georgia)

Candy Bar Pie

5 (2-ounce) Snicker candy
  bars
1 (9-inch) pie shell, baked
½ cup sugar
12 ounces cream cheese,
  softened
2 eggs

⅓ cup sour cream
⅓ cup peanut butter (crunchy
  or smooth)
⅔ cup semisweet chocolate
  chips
2 tablespoons whipping cream

Cut candy bars into ¼-inch pieces. Place candy bar pieces in baked pie shell; set aside. In a mixing bowl, beat sugar and cream cheese until smooth. Add eggs, sour cream, and peanut butter; beat on LOW speed just until combined. Pour mixture into pie shell; smooth over candy pieces. Bake at 350° for 35–40 minutes or until set. Cool on wire rack.

In small heavy saucepan, melt chocolate chips in whipping cream until smooth, spread over cooled pie filling and refrigerate overnight.

Jefferies Relay Team: Generating a Cure (South Carolina)

No Crust Coconut Pie

3 eggs
1½ cups sugar
2 tablespoons flour
1 (12-ounce) can evaporated
  milk

1 teaspoon vanilla
¾ stick butter or margarine,
  melted
1 (3½-ounce) can Angel Flake
  coconut

Beat eggs slightly. Add sugar and flour. Mix well and add milk, vanilla, margarine, and coconut. Pour into a well-greased and floured pan. Bake in a 375° oven for 30–35 minutes.

Cooking on the Go (South Carolina)

Buttermilk Custard Pie

¾ cup butter
½ cup sugar (about)
3 eggs, separated
3 tablespoons flour

Grated rind of 1 lemon
2 cups buttermilk
Pastry

Cream butter and sugar and add well-beaten egg yolks. Add flour, grated lemon rind, and then buttermilk. Fold in stiffly beaten egg whites and turn into 2 pie pans lined with pastry. The crust should be baked in a hot oven for 15 minutes before putting in the filling. Bake in a moderately hot (375°) oven for about 40 minutes. If the milk is very sour, add more sugar. We found that ⅔ cup sugar was needed when we tested this recipe.

Two Hundred Years of Charleston Cooking (South Carolina)

For decades, South Carolina's Grand Strand has been a Mecca for vacationers and retirees. Stretching for more than sixty miles along the Atlantic Coast, this string of beach resorts includes such ocean-side communities as Myrtle Beach, considered the Strand's hub.

Fried Pies

A southern specialty!

1 teaspoon salt	4 tablespoons sugar
1 teaspoon baking powder	½ cup milk
2 cups all-purpose flour, sifted	Dried fruit, cooked, sweetened
2 tablespoons solid shortening	Powdered sugar for sprinkling
1 egg yolk	

Sift salt and baking powder with sifted and measured flour. Blend in shortening. Combine egg yolk, sugar, and milk. Stir into flour mixture.

Roll out on a floured board to ¼-inch thickness. Cut into circles 4- to 5-inches in diameter. Spread a small amount of cooked and sweetened dried fruit on half of each round. Fold other half of crust over filling. Seal edges with a fork dipped in flour. Fry in deep fat at 360° until browned. Drain on absorbent paper and sprinkle with powdered sugar.

A Taste of Georgia (Georgia)

Peach Crisp

1 (21-ounce) can peach pie filling (or cherry)	1 stick margarine
1 (7½-ounce) box yellow cake mix (1 layer size)	½–1 cup chopped pecans

Preheat oven to 350°. Pour pie filling into 8x8-inch baking pan. Sprinkle dry cake mix over pie filling. Cut margarine into small slices and lay on top of cake mix. Sprinkle chopped nuts on top. Bake at 350° for 30–35 minutes.

Great with ice cream or Cool Whip served on top while warm.

Look Mom, I Can Cook (Georgia)

My Favorite Peach Cobbler

CRUST:

2 cups flour	**½ teaspoon salt**
1½ cups sugar	**1½ cups milk**
4 teaspoons baking powder	**1 teaspoon vanilla**

Combine flour, sugar, baking powder, and salt. Stir in milk and vanilla; set aside.

FILLING:

2 quarts peach slices, drained	**3 tablespoons cornstarch**
½ stick butter	**or clear gel**
2 teaspoons lemon juice	**¾ cup water**
½ cup sugar	

In saucepan, bring first 4 Filling ingredients to a boil. Mix together cornstarch and water to make a paste; gradually add to Filling mixture. Pour into 3-quart baking dish and put Crust mixture on top.

TOPPING:

1 stick butter	**1 teaspoon cinnamon**
¼ cup sugar	

Melt butter and pour over Crust. Mix together sugar and cinnamon; sprinkle over top. Bake at 350° for 40 minutes. Serve warm with milk. Serves 10.

Montezuma Amish Mennonite Cookbook I (Georgia)

Baseball legend Ty Cobb, nicknamed the "Georgia Peach," was born on December 18, 1886, in Narrows, Georgia. Cobb grew up in Royston. In 1936, he was the first player elected into the Baseball Hall of Fame. Cobb's lifetime batting average of .367 is the highest in baseball history. He won twelve batting titles.

Mango Cobbler

Anyone who has lived in the southern part of the United States knows fruit cobblers, the most popular ones being blackberry, dewberry, or peach. A warm cobbler served with cold heavy cream is summer's most delectable dessert. Along most of the Gulf Coast, mangoes are plentiful in the markets during the season, so for a change, try making the following cobbler from this delicious fruit.

6 cups sliced ripe mangoes
  (about 5, depending on size)
½ cup sugar
½ teaspoon cardamom seeds,
  crushed

2 tablespoons flour
4 tablespoons lime juice
Basic pastry dough

In a deep pie dish or other 2-quart baking dish, toss together mangoes, sugar, cardamom seeds, flour, and lime juice.

Roll out pastry dough to cover top of baking dish, crimping edges to seal. Cut slits for steam to escape. Preheat oven to 425° and bake for 45–50 minutes, or until crust is brown and crisp. If necessary, cover edges of crust with strips of foil to prevent burning. Serves 6–8.

Gulf Coast Cooking (Florida)

Peach Viennese Torte

A beautiful dessert!

¼ cup butter, softened
¼ cup confectioners' sugar
1 cup sifted flour
1 cup granulated sugar
2 tablespoons cornstarch

1 cup water
4 tablespoons cherry-flavored
  gelatin
8–10 large fresh peaches
1 cup whipping cream, whipped

Cream butter and gradually add confectioners' sugar. Add flour to mix, and form a soft dough. Pat on bottom and up sides of a 12-inch pizza pan. Bake at 325° for 20 minutes. Cool.

Combine sugar, cornstarch, and water. Cook over low heat, stirring constantly, until thick and clear. Stir in gelatin; allow to cool. While cooling, peel and slice peaches; arrange in a single layer over the baked shell. Spread the cooled gelatin glaze over the peaches; chill. When ready to serve, top with whipped cream.

Our Best Home Cooking (Georgia)

Callaway Shortbread
with Georgia Peaches Flambé

⅓ cup granulated sugar
2 cups all-purpose flour
2½ teaspoons baking
  powder
½ teaspoon salt
6 tablespoons butter

1¼ cups heavy cream
8 fresh peaches
1 cup honey
¼ cup Jack Daniels
  bourbon

In a bowl, combine sugar, flour, baking powder, and salt. Cut butter into small pieces and mix in with a fork. Make sure butter is incorporated, then add cream. Do not overwork the dough; the process should take less than 2 minutes. Let the dough rest for 10–15 minutes with a cloth on top to prevent drying. On floured surface, roll out dough to about ½-inch thickness and use a biscuit cutter to cut the dough. Bake on a greased cookie sheet at 350° for 10–15 minutes.

Peel and cut peaches into wedges. Pour honey in a pan and bring to a boil; add peaches. Stir for 3–4 minutes and flambé with Jack Daniels. To serve, place shortbread on a dish and scoop peaches on top. Serves 8.

Editor's Extra: Flambé is French for "flamed" or "flaming." It's the process of sprinkling certain foods with liquor, which, after warming, are ignited just before serving. (Be careful!)

Fine Dining Georgia Style (Georgia)

Colonized by James Edward Oglethorpe in 1733, Georgia was the last of the original thirteen English colonies. Named after King George II of England, Georgia became the fourth state to join the Union on January 2, 1788.

Another of the thirteen original colonies, South Carolina became the eighth state to ratify the Constitution in 1788, the first to secede from the Union in December 1860, and the site of the first shots fired in the Civil War, at Fort Sumter in Charleston Harbor on April 12, 1861.

Florida was not one of thirteen original colonies, but was admitted to the United States as a state on March 3, 1845, as the 27th state.

Peach Delight

This recipe takes a little extra time since every layer has to cool completely, but it is delicious!

LAYER ONE:

2 cups self-rising flour   1 cup chopped nuts
2 sticks margarine, melted

Spray a 9x13-inch casserole dish with vegetable cooking spray. Mix together flour, melted margarine, and chopped nuts. Spread in casserole dish, and bake at 350° for 15–20 minutes, until lightly browned. Cool completely.

LAYER TWO:

1 (8-ounce) package cream   1 (8-ounce) container frozen
  cheese, softened   nondairy whipped topping,
2½ cups confectioners' sugar   thawed

Mix cream cheese, confectioners' sugar, and whipped topping; spread over cooled crust, and refrigerate.

LAYER THREE:

4 cups sliced fresh peaches

Spread peaches over creamed mixture. Set aside.

LAYER FOUR:

1 cup sugar   4 tablespoons peach gelatin
4 tablespoons flour   1 cup water

Mix sugar, flour, gelatin, and water. Cook over medium heat until thick. Cool completely. When cool, pour over peaches and refrigerate. Flavor is better if it sits overnight.

South Carolina Ladies & Gents Love to Cook! (South Carolina)

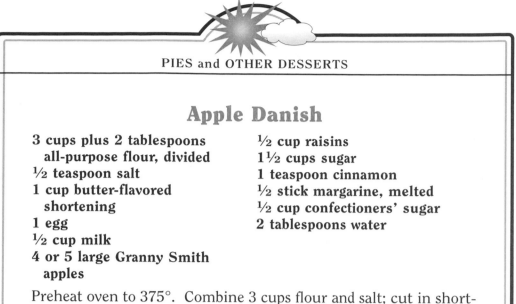

Apple Danish

3 cups plus 2 tablespoons
  all-purpose flour, divided
½ teaspoon salt
1 cup butter-flavored
  shortening
1 egg
½ cup milk
4 or 5 large Granny Smith
  apples

½ cup raisins
1½ cups sugar
1 teaspoon cinnamon
½ stick margarine, melted
½ cup confectioners' sugar
2 tablespoons water

Preheat oven to 375°. Combine 3 cups flour and salt; cut in short-ening. Separate egg and save white for top. Beat yolk with milk and add to flour mixture; mix well. Grease a 10x15-inch baking pan, and set aside. Divide dough into 2 pieces and roll each to fit pan. Dough will be very thin. Peel apples and slice very thin; add raisins, granulated sugar, cinnamon, melted margarine, and remaining 2 tablespoons flour; stir to mix well. Place first dough layer in pan, and top with apple filling. Cover with remaining layer of dough. Brush top crust with beaten egg white and bake 35–40 minutes, or until golden brown. Combine confectioners' sugar and water; drizzle over warm pastry. Best served warm or at room tem-perature.

A Carolina Country Collection II (South Carolina)

Timmy's Fireworks Trifle

1 (4-ounce) package vanilla
  pudding mix (not instant)
3 cups skim milk
2 pints blueberries, divided
⅓ cup plus 3 tablespoons
  sugar, divided
¼ cup plus 2 tablespoons
  orange juice, divided
1 pint strawberries, divided

1 (18¼-ounce) package
  Pillsbury Moist Supreme
  White Cake Mix
1¼ cups water
¼ cup oil
3 egg whites
1 cup whipping cream
2 tablespoons powdered sugar

In medium saucepan, combine pudding mix and milk. Prepare as directed on package. Cover; refrigerate until cool. Meanwhile, reserve ½ cup blueberries, ⅓ cup sugar, and ¼ orange juice; stir to mix, crushing berries slightly. Set aside. Reserve ½ cup strawberries for garnish. In another non-metal bowl, combine remaining 1½ cups strawberries, 3 tablespoons sugar, and 2 tablespoons orange juice; stir to mix, crushing berries slightly. Set aside.

Heat oven to 350°. Spray 2 (8- or 9-inch) round cake pans with nonstick cooking spray. Prepare cake mix as directed on package using water, oil, and egg whites. Pour batter evenly into sprayed pans. Bake at 350° for 30–40 minutes or until toothpick inserted in center comes out clean. Cool in pans on wire racks for 15 minutes. Remove cake from pans; cool 30 minutes or until completely cooled. Cut cakes in half horizontally to make 4 layers.

Place 1 layer in bottom of clear 2½-quart soufflé dish or glass trifle bowl, trimming sides of cake to fit, if necessary. Spread with half of crushed blueberry mixture; top with ⅓ of pudding. Top with second cake layer, trimmed if necessary, all the crushed strawberry mixture, and ⅓ pudding. Top with third cake layer, trimmed if necessary, remaining crushed blueberry mixture, and remaining pudding. Top with fourth cake layer. Cover; refrigerate at least 1 hour before serving. In medium bowl, whip cream until soft peaks form. Gradually add powdered sugar, beating until stiff peaks form. Top trifle with whipped cream. Sprinkle with reserved blueberries and strawberries. Store in refrigerator. Makes 12 servings.

Simply Florida...Strawberries (Florida)

The Best Bread Pudding

On September 20, 2000, Joanie Duke, one of the cutest little older ladies that I've had the pleasure of meeting, bounded into the restaurant (and when I say "bounded in," I really mean it). She told me how much she enjoyed my recipes and that she had one of hers to share with me and shoved something into my hand, wrapped in plastic wrap. It was the best bread pudding I had ever wrapped my lips around. This quickly became the favorite bread pudding recipe for The Lady & Sons.

2 cups granulated sugar
5 large eggs, beaten
2 cups milk
2 teaspoons pure vanilla extract
3 cups cubed Italian bread, cut
   and allowed to stale overnight
   in a bowl

1 cup packed light brown sugar
¼ cup (½ stick) butter,
   softened
1 cup chopped pecans

Preheat oven to 350°. Grease a 9x13x2-inch pan. Mix together granulated sugar, eggs, and milk in a bowl; add vanilla. Pour over cubed bread and let sit for 10 minutes. In another bowl, mix and crumble together brown sugar, butter, and pecans. Pour bread mixture into prepared pan. Sprinkle brown sugar mixture over the top and bake for 35–45 minutes, or until set. Remove from oven.

SAUCE:

1 cup granulated sugar
½ cup (1 stick) butter, melted
1 egg, beaten

2 teaspoons pure vanilla extract
1 cup brandy

Mix together granulated sugar, butter, egg, and vanilla in a saucepan. Over medium heat, stir together until sugar is melted. Add brandy, stirring well. Pour over bread pudding. Delicious served warm or cold.

The Lady & Sons Just Desserts (Georgia)

Lemon Mousse with Raspberry Sauce

MOUSSE:

1 (¼-ounce) envelope
  unflavored gelatin
2 tablespoons white wine
1½ tablespoons grated lemon
  rind

⅓ cup lemon juice
3 eggs, separated
8 tablespoons sugar, divided
1 cup heavy cream, whipped

Soften gelatin in wine in top of double boiler. Add lemon rind and lemon juice. Stir over simmering water until gelatin dissolves. Beat egg yolks with 3 tablespoons sugar. Slowly add whipped cream. Beat egg whites until stiff, gradually adding remaining 5 tablespoons sugar. Fold into lemon mixture. Pour into a 6–8 cup mold; chill at least 2 hours.

RASPBERRY SAUCE:

1 (10-ounce) package frozen
  raspberries, thawed
2 tablespoons sugar

1 tablespoon lemon juice
1 tablespoon Grand Marnier

Drain raspberries and reserve juice. Combine raspberries, sugar, and lemon juice; purée in processor or blender. Strain. Add liqueur and as much raspberry juice as needed for desired consistency. Unmold Mousse and serve with Raspberry Sauce.

Macon Sets a Fine Table (Georgia)

Quick Chocolate Mousse

10 ounces whipping cream
5 ounces semisweet Couverture or
  good-quality dark chocolate,
  broken into pieces

Heat whipping cream in a saucepan; do not boil. Add chocolate. Cook until blended, stirring frequently; do not boil. Let stand until cool. Chill, covered, for 24 hours.

   Beat chocolate mixture in a mixer bowl until firm. Dip a spoon in hot water and scoop the chocolate mousse into individual dessert bowls. Serves 4.

Note: May add one teaspoon Kahlúa or Grand Marnier to chocolate mixture before cooling.

Made in the Shade (Florida)

Orange Charlotte

A scrumptious orange cloud for dessert!

1⅓ tablespoons unflavored
   gelatin
⅓ cup cold water
⅓ cup boiling water
1 cup sugar
3 tablespoons fresh lemon
   juice

1 cup fresh orange juice
1 cup heavy cream
2 teaspoons vanilla flavoring
3 egg whites
Cherries and nuts, if desired for
   garnish

Soften gelatin in cold water. Dissolve in boiling water. Add sugar and stir until dissolved over low heat, if necessary. Add lemon juice and orange juice to mixture. Chill in refrigerator until mixture begins to congeal slightly. Whip cream, flavor with vanilla, and fold into juice mixture. Fold in beaten egg whites. Return to refrigerator until firm. Garnish with cherries and nuts, if desired. May be served in individual dishes or crystal bowl. Makes 6–8 servings.

Note: Use a sweet and juicy orange for best taste. Frozen concentrate may be used in place of fresh orange juice.

Puttin' on the Peachtree (Georgia)

PHOTO BY GWEN McKEE

The 50-foot-wide Tree of Life is the centerpiece of Disney's Animal Kingdom® Theme Park and part of Disney World in Orlando, Florida. This 14-story masterpiece with its tapestry of 325 animal carvings was sculpted by more than a dozen artisans. The Tree of Life is topped with more than 103,000 translucent, five-shades-of-green leaves that were individually placed and actually blow in the wind.

Charlotte Russe

1 pint whipping cream
1 teaspoon vanilla
½ cup sugar
Sherry to taste
½ tablespoon gelatin

¼ cup cold milk
¼ cup warm milk
5 egg whites, beaten
Lady fingers, split

Whip cream until stiff; add vanilla and sugar. Add sherry to taste. Soften gelatin in cold milk, then dissolve in warm milk. When cool, add to above mixture, beating cream all the time. Add beaten egg whites. Pour in bowl or dessert glasses lined with lady fingers. Serves 6.

Charleston Receipts (South Carolina)

Pineapple Charlotte Russe

2 tablespoons gelatin
2 cups sweet milk, divided
1 pint whipping cream
2 egg whites

1 cup sugar
1 (15-ounce) can crushed
  pineapple, drained

Dissolve gelatin in ½ cup milk. Bring 1½ cups milk to boiling point. Mix hot milk with dissolved gelatin; let cool. Whip cream and egg whites, then add milk and gelatin, whipping constantly. Then add sugar and pineapple. Rinse mold with cold water. Pour mixture into mold. Store in refrigerator until congealed.

Note: Sometimes in place of pineapple I substitute same amount of orange pulp.

The South Carolina Cook Book (South Carolina)

Mary Flannery O'Connor (March 25, 1925–August 3, 1964) was an American novelist, short-story writer, and essayist. Born in Savannah, Georgia, Flannery O'Connor was an important voice in American literature. O'Connor wrote two novels and thirty-two short stories, as well as a number of reviews and commentaries. She was a southern writer who often wrote in a Southern Gothic style. Her texts usually take place in the South and revolve around morally flawed characters. One of her trademarks is blunt foreshadowing, giving a reader an idea of what will happen far before it happens. Her two novels were *Wise Blood* (1952) and *The Violent Bear It Away* (1960). She also published two books of short stories: *A Good Man Is Hard to Find and Other Stories* (1955) and *Everything That Rises Must Converge* (published posthumously in 1965).

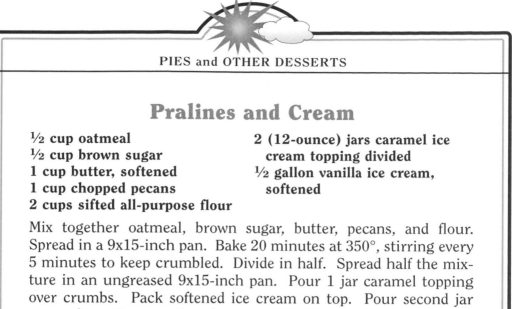

Pralines and Cream

½ cup oatmeal
½ cup brown sugar
1 cup butter, softened
1 cup chopped pecans
2 cups sifted all-purpose flour

2 (12-ounce) jars caramel ice
    cream topping divided
½ gallon vanilla ice cream,
    softened

Mix together oatmeal, brown sugar, butter, pecans, and flour. Spread in a 9x15-inch pan. Bake 20 minutes at 350°, stirring every 5 minutes to keep crumbled. Divide in half. Spread half the mixture in an ungreased 9x15-inch pan. Pour 1 jar caramel topping over crumbs. Pack softened ice cream on top. Pour second jar caramel topping over ice cream. Sprinkle remaining crumbs on top. Freeze. When ready to serve, cut into squares. Store in freezer. Serves 15.

Putting on the Grits (South Carolina)

Frozen Amaretto Parfaits

1 package macaroon cookies
6 egg yolks
2 eggs
¾ cup sugar

¾ cup amaretto liqueur
2 cups heavy cream, whipped
Additional whipped cream
Toasted almonds

Crumble macaroons coarsely and toast at 300° for 20 minutes until brown and crunchy but not too hard. Stir occasionally during baking; set aside. In a large bowl, combine egg yolks, eggs, and sugar. Beat on high speed of electric mixer until thick and fluffy and sugar is dissolved, about 6 minutes. Continue beating and gradually add liqueur. By hand fold in whipped cream and ¾ of macaroon crumbs. Gently spoon ½ mixture into parfait glasses. Layer a thin layer of crumbs and spoon in remaining soufflé. Freeze 4–6 hours (cover with foil if longer). To serve, top with whipped cream and toasted almonds. Serves 4–6.

Beyond the Bay (Florida)

Vanilla Ice Cream Crêpes with Strawberry Sauce

Crêpes are tissue-thin pancakes that can be used to make any number of delicious desserts. In this recipe, you will fill crêpes with ice cream and smother with Strawberry Sauce and whipped cream.

CRÊPE SHELLS:

¼ cup all-purpose flour
7 tablespoons milk
1 large egg
½ tablespoon vegetable oil
1 pinch salt
Vegetable spray or oil

Combine flour, milk, egg, oil, and salt in a blender or food processor. Blend into a smooth batter, stopping motor a few times to scrape down the sides of the bowl. Cover and refrigerate batter for 1 hour. Blend batter well before making crêpes.

Over moderate heat, lightly oil a preheated, 6-inch, nonstick sauté pan. Add enough batter to make a thin coat, tilt pan so batter forms a thin, even covering over bottom of saute pan. Cook each crêpe until it sets, about 45 seconds, flip over and cook other side for 30 seconds.

Place cooked crêpe on wax paper or clean, dry surface. Do not stack crêpes while hot. Cooled crêpes may be stacked, wrapped in aluminum foil, and refrigerated for a few days or frozen for a few months. If frozen, thaw in refrigerator for 6 hours before use.

STRAWBERRY SAUCE:

1 pint strawberries, washed
2 tablespoons granulated sugar
6 tablespoons water
3 cups vanilla ice cream
4 cups whipped cream

Pick stems off strawberries and slice; place in mixing bowl with sugar and water. Lay crêpes out flat and place a scoop of ice cream in middle. Roll up crêpes and place on plates. Smother with strawberries and sauce. Garnish with whipped cream, and serve immediately. Yields 4 servings.

Mastering the Art of Florida Seafood (Florida)

Mock Ice Cream

1 (8-ounce) package cream
  cheese, softened
1 (10-ounce) tub Cool Whip
1 (10-ounce) package frozen
  strawberries

½ cup sugar
1 (8-ounce) can crushed
  pineapple, drained

Blend cream cheese, Cool Whip, strawberries, sugar, and pineapple.
Freeze. Serve as ice cream or serve chilled as mousse.

Country Club Cooks (Florida)

Fresh Peach Ice Cream

1 quart mashed ripe fresh
  peaches
Juice of 1½ lemons
Pinch of salt

3 cups sugar
1 pint whipping cream,
  unwhipped
1 quart half-and-half

Mix ingredients; refrigerate for 1 day before actually making the ice
cream in an ice cream freezer.

The McClellanville Coast Cookbook (South Carolina)

Homemade Peach Ice Cream

3 cups sugar
4 eggs, beaten
1 quart milk
1 tablespoon vanilla
1 (5-ounce) can sweetened
  condensed milk
2 (12-ounce) cans evaporated
  milk

1 quart sweetened sliced
  peaches
Sugar to taste
Whole milk
Ice
Rock salt

Combine first 4 ingredients and cook on top of stove until it thickens some. Take off heat and cool. Add condensed milk and evaporated milk. Blend peaches in blender and add sugar to taste. Add
to milk mixture. Pour into 6-quart ice cream churn and finish filling with whole milk. Fill churn with ice and rock salt, and churn.

Red Oak Recipes (Georgia)

The Attic's Almond Amaretto Ice Cream

ALMOND CRUNCH TOPPING:

2 ounces slices almonds	1 cup sugar
2 tablespoons butter	1 tablespoon water

Spread sliced almonds in a buttered pan. In a small, heavy saucepan, stir together sugar with a tablespoon of water over low heat until sugar has melted. Then pour it over the almonds and let harden. When topping is completely cold, break it up with fingers or a kitchen hammer, and grind it in a blender into smaller bits. Store topping in a covered jar in the refrigerator.

½ gallon vanilla ice cream	Almond Crunch Topping
8 tablespoons amaretto liqueur	

Freeze parfait wine glasses. Just before serving spoon in ice cream, splash with amaretto and sprinkle with Almond Crunch Topping. Serves 8.

Georgia's Historic Restaurants (Georgia)

Gold Eagle Benne Delight

½ cup butter	1 cup marshmallows
1 cup evaporated milk	Benne seeds, toasted
1 (16-ounce) box light brown sugar	

Combine butter, evaporated milk, brown sugar, and marshmallows in double boiler. Cook until soft and marshmallows are melted. Store in refrigerator in jar and reheat as needed. Serve hot on vanilla ice cream with benne seeds sprinkled over the top. Makes 1 quart.

Sea Island Seasons (South Carolina)

PHOTO BY BARBARA MOSELEY.

Extending across the southern tip of the Florida peninsula and most of Florida Bay, Everglades National Park is the only subtropical preserve in North America and the only place in the world where alligators and crocodiles exist side by side.

Listed below are the cookbooks that have contributed recipes to this book, along with copyright, author, publisher, city, and state, when applicable.

An American Celebration ©2003 Celebration Women's Club, Celebration, FL

Apalachicola Cookbook ©1984 Philaco Woman's Club, Eastpoint, FL

Atlanta Cooknotes ©1982 The Junior League of Atlanta, GA

Bay Fêtes ©2003 Junior Service League of Panama City, FL

Bay Leaves ©1975 Panama City Junior Service League, Panama City, FL

Best for the Holidays ©2001 Dot Gibson Publications, Waycross, GA

Best Kept Secrets, Homeland Park Fire Department, Anderson, SC

The Best of Living in South Carolina, Electric Cooperatives of SC, Cayce, SC

The Best of Sophie Kay Cookbook ©1998 Sophie Kay, Daytona Beach, FL

Bethel Food Bazaar II ©1988 Bethel United Methodist Women, Spartanburg, SC

Betty Talmadge's Lovejoy Plantation Cookbook ©1983 Betty Talmadge, Atlanta, GA

Bevelyn Blair's Everyday Pies ©2000 Bevelyn Blair, Columbus, GA

Beyond the Bay ©1985 Panama City Junior Service League, Panama City, FL

The Bishop Family Heirloom Cookbook, JoAnn R. Pike, Greenville, SC

The Blue Willow Inn Bible of Southern Cooking ©2005 Louis and Billie Van Dyke, Social Circle, GA

Boarding House Reach ©1981 Dot Gibson Publications, Waycross, GA

Bountiful Blessings from the Bauknight Table, H. Felder & Margaret D. Bauknight Family, Central, SC

Bread of Life–Chef Curtis Watkins, Curtis Watkins, Douglasville, GA

Bread of Life–Salem Baptist Church ©2003 Salem Baptist Church Youth, Milledgeville, GA

Breads and Spreads ©1992 Carol Rees Publications, Dot Gibson Publications, Waycross, GA

Calypso Café ©1999 Wimmer Companies, Bob Epstein, Memphis, TN

Canopy Roads ©1979 Tallahassee Junior Woman's Club, Tallahassee, FL

A Carolina Country Collection I and II, Turner's Inc., Seneca, SC

Carolina Cuisine Encore! ©1981 The Junior Assembly of Anderson, SC

Catch-of-the Day ©1981 Ginny Lentz, Marshall, NC

Charleston Receipts ©1950 The Junior League of Charleston, SC

Charleston Receipts Repeats ©1950 The Junior League of Charleston, SC

Cherries Galore ©1984 Clara Eschmann, Macon, GA

Chilimania! ©1992 GSC Books Division, Herb and Chris Geltner, Merritt Island, FL

Christmas Memories ©2001 Jeannine Browning, Melbourne, FL

Citrus Lovers Cook Book ©1980 Golden West Publishers, Al and Mildred Fischer, Phoenix, AZ

Collard Greens and Sushi, Tamara Patridge, Morrow, GA

A Collection from Summerville Kitchens, Summerville Republican Women's Club, Summerville, SC

A Collection of Favorite Recipes, Deercreek Home and Garden Club, Jacksonville, FL

The Colonel's Inn Caterers'–Tallahassee Historical Cookbook ©1984 Colonel's Inn Caterers, Tallahassee, FL

Cook and Deal ©1982 D. J. Cook, Wimmer Companies, Memphis, TN

Cookin' in the Keys ©1985, 2003 William Flagg, Palm Island Press, Key West, FL

Cookin' on Island Time ©Palm Island Estates Association, Inc., Grove City, FL

Cooking . . . Done the Baptist Way, First Baptist Church, Abbeville, SC

Cooking Carley Style, McMaster Family Fund, Aiken, SC

Cooking for Two, No Nonsense Cookbook, James McNaughton, Quincy, FL

Cooking in Paradise, Key West Power Squadron, Summerland Key, FL

Cooking in the New South ©1984 Anne Byrn Phillips, Peachtree Publishers, Ltd., Atlanta, GA

Cooking on the Go ©1982 NTW Enterprises, Greer, SC

Cooking with Class, Park Maitland School, Maitland, FL

Cooking with Faith, Faith Baptist Church Women's Missionary Union, Summerville, SC

Cooking with Miracle Deliverance, Miracle Deliverance Mothers' Board, Columbia, SC

Cooking with 257, Boy Scout Troop 257, North Port, FL

Country Cakes ©1984 Blair of Columbus, GA

Country Club Cooks, Spanish Lakes Country Club Homeowners Association, Ft. Pierce, FL

Country Cookin': Recipes from Callaway Gardens ©1980 The Gardens Country Store, Pine Mountain, GA

Country Cupboard ©1985 Central High School Athletic Club, Thomasville, GA

Crab Island Cookbook, Edited by Chef Rebecca Watkins, Destin, FL

Cross Creek Kitchens ©1983 Sally Morrison, Triad Publishing, Co., Inc, Gainesville, FL

The Cruising K.I.S.S. Cookbook II ©2003 Corinne C. Kanter, SAILco Press, Inc., Marathon, FL

Culinary Arts & Crafts ©1984 The Park Maitland School, Maitland, FL

Culinary Classics ©1981 Young Matron's Circle for Tallulah Falls School, Roswell, GA

Culinary Memories of Merridun, Volume 1 ©2001 Peggy Waller, JD and White Dog Publications, Union, SC

Culinary Memories of Merridun, Volume 2 ©2003 Peggy Waller, JD and White Dog Publications, Union, SC

Cypress Gardens Cookbook ©1970 St. Agnes Guild, St. Paul's Episcopal Church, Winter Haven, FL

The Dapper Zapper ©1981 Carol Jean Wheeler, Alpharetta, GA

Dining Under the Carolina Moon ©2005 Debbi Covington, Beaufort, SC

"Don't Forget the Parsley . . . ." ©1982 O-C Tech Foundation, Orangeburg, SC

Down by the Water ©1997 Junior League of Columbus, SC

Educated Taste, LaGrange College Alumni Association, LaGrange, GA

Encore ©1981 Walker School Association, Dot Gibson Publications, Waycross, GA

The Enlightened Gourmet ©1984 CGW Enterprises, Charleston, SC

Entirely Entertaining in the Bonnet House Style, Bonnet House Alliance, Ft. Lauderdale, FL

The Essential Catfish Cookbook ©2001 Shannon Harper and Janet Cope, Pineapple Press, Inc., Sarasota, FL

Faithfully Charleston ©2001 St. Michael's Church, Charleston, SC

Family Collections ©1983 St. Matthew's Episcopal Church Woman, Snellville, GA

Famous Florida Recipes ©1972 Lowis Carlton, Great Outdoors Publishing Company, St. Petersburg, FL

Famous Recipes from Mrs. Wilkes' Boarding House ©1976 Mrs. L.H. Wilkes, Savannah, GA

Fare by the Sea ©1983 Junior League of Sarasota, FL

Feeding the Faithful, United Methodist Women of Mauldlin United Methodist Church, Maudlin, SC

Feeding the Flock, St. Joseph Catholic Church, Pensacola, FL

Fine Dining Georgia Style ©2005 John M. Bailey, Quail Ridge Bress, Brandon, MS

First Come, First Served . . . In Savannah ©2001 St. Andrew's School PTO, Savannah, GA

500 Favorite Recipes, The Ladies of Whispering Pines Mennonite Church, Honea Path, SC

Flavored with Tradition ©1979 Flavored with Tradition, Inc., Johns Island, SC

Flavors of the Gardens ©2000 Callaway Gardens, Pine Mountain, GA

Florida Cook Book ©2001 Golden West Publications, Phoenix, AZ

Florida Flavors ©1984 Environmental Studies Council, Inc., Jensen Beach, FL

Florida Seafood Cookery ©1991 Lowis Carlton, St. Petersburg, FL

Foresters' Favorite Foods, Pine Forest United Methodist Women's Organization, Dublin, GA

Frederica Fare, The Parents Association of Frederica Academy, St. Simons Island, GA

Friendly Feasts Act II, Friends of Riverside Theatre, Vero Beach, FL

From Black Tie to Blackeyed Peas ©2000 Dr. Irving Victor, M.D., Savannah, GA

Galley Gourmet III ©1984 Ferne Raveson, Boca Raton, FL

The Gasparilla Cookbook ©1961 The Junior League of Tampa, FL

Gator Country Cooks ©1975 The Junior League of Gainesville, FL

Georgia National Fair Blue Ribbon Cookbook ©2004 Georgia National Fair, Perry, GA

Georgia On My Menu ©1988 Junior League of Cobb-Marietta, Marietta, GA

Georgia's Historic Restaurants ©1987 Dawn O'Brien and Jean Spaugh, John F. Blair Publishers, Winston-Salem, NC

The Gingerbread House Cookbook ©2000 The Gingerbread House, Savannah, GA

Golden Isles Cuisine ©1978 Dot Gibson Publications, Waycross, GA

Good Cookin', Virginia B. Snell, Metter, GA

Good Cooking, Grand Lagoon Yacht Club, Pensacola, FL

Go-o-od Goodies from Good Hope's Good Cooks, Good Hope Baptist Church, Saluda, SC

Gourmet Cooking ©1982 Earl Peyroux, Pensacola, FL

Gourmet Cooking II ©1985 Earl Peyroux, Pensacola, FL

Gracious Goodness . . . Charleston! ©1991 BEHS Endowment Fund, Bishop England High School, Charleston, SC

Gracious Goodness: Christmas in Charleston ©1996 Bishop England High School, Charleston, SC

Grandma Mamie Jones' Family Favorites, Marilyn B. Jones, Climax, GA

Great Cooks Rise . . . with the May River Tide ©2001 The Church of the Cross, Bluffton, SC

Gulf Coast Cooking ©1991 Shearer Publishing, Fredericksburg, TX

Gulfshore Delights ©1984 Junior League of Fort Myers, FL

Gourmet Cooking II ©1985 Earl Peyroux, Pensacola, FL

Heart of the Palms ©1982 The Junior League of the Palm Beaches, Palm Beach, FL

Heaven in a Pot, Wesley United Methodist Women, Marco Island, FL

Historic Spanish Point: Cooking Then and Now, Gulf Coast Heritage Association, Inc., Osprey, FL

Holiday Favorites ©1991 Dot Gibson Publications, Waycross, GA

The Holiday Hostess ©Valdosta Junior Service League, Valdosta, GA

Home Sweet Habitat, Habitat for Humanity International, Shelton, CT

Hudson's Cookbook ©1982 Brian and Gloria Carmines, Hilton Head Island, SC

I Love to Cook Book ©1997 Medical University of South Carolina, Charleston, SC

INN the Kitchen at Abingdon Manor, Patty Griffey, Abingdon Manor, Latta, SC

Intercoastal Waterway Restaurant Guide & Recipe Book, Charles and Susan Eanes, Espichel Enterprises, Dunedin, FL

Island Events Cookbook ©1986 Island Events, Telluride, CO

Jacksonville & Company ©1982 Junior League of Jacksonville, FL

Jefferies Relay Team: Generating a Cure ©2005 Jeffries Relay for Life Team, Moncks Corner, SC

Juicy Miss Lucy Cookbook ©1982 Two Girls from Filly, Longwood, FL

The Lady & Sons Just Desserts ©2002 Paula H. Deen, Savannah, GA

The Lady & Sons Savannah Country Cookbook ©1997 Paula H. Deen, Savannah, GA

The Lady & Sons, Too! ©2000 Paula H. Deen, Savannah, GA

The Lazy Cook's Cookbook: A Greek Odyssey, Mary D. Angelakis, Spartanburg, SC

Les Soups Fantastiques ©1998 Strawberry Press, Monique Fisher, Sarasota, FL

Let's ACT Up in the Kitchen, Abuse Counseling and Treatment, Inc., Fort Myers, FL

Let's Talk Food from A to Z, Doris Reynolds, Naples, FL

The Life of the Party ©2003 The Junior League of Tampa, FL

Look Mom, I Can Cook ©1987 Dot Gibson Publications, Waycross, GA

Lost Tree Cook Book, Lost Tree Chapel, North Palm Beach, FL

Lowcountry Delights ©2002 Maxine Pinson and Malyssa Pinson, Savannah, GA

Lowcountry Delights II ©2003 Maxine Pinson and Malyssa, Pinson, Savannah, GA

Lowcountry Delights III ©2004 Maxine Pinson and Malyssa Pinson, Savannah, GA

Macon Sets a Fine Table ©1986 Middle Georgia Historical Society, Inc., Macon, GA

Made in the Shade ©1999 Junior League of Fort Lauderdale, FL

Main Street Winder, Winder Woman's Club, Winder, GA

Margaritaville Cookbook, Ruth Perez and Brenda Vidal, Key West, FL

Mastering the Art of Florida Seafood
©1999 Lonnie Lynch, Pineapple Press,
Inc., Sarasota, FL

Maurice's Tropical Fruit Cook Book ©1979
Maurice de Verteuil, St. Petersburg, FL

The McClellanville Coast Cookbook ©1992
McClellanville Arts Council,
McClellanville, SC

Meet Me at the Garden Gate ©2001 The
Junior League of Spartanburg, Inc., SC

The Mongo Mango Cookbook ©2001
Cynthia Thuma, Pineapple Press, Inc.,
Sarasota, FL

*Montezuma Amish Mennonite Cookbook
II,* Mrs. Ruth Yoder, Montezuma, GA

Mountain Folk, Mountain Food ©1997
Recovery Communications, Inc.,
Atlanta, GA

The Museum Cookbook, The Museum,
Greenwood, SC

Music, Menus & Magnolias ©1996
Charleston Symphony Orchestra
League, Charleston, SC

My Best to You, Carolyn Jackson, Winder,
GA

Nell Graydon's Cook Book ©1969 Nell S.
Graydon, Orangeburg, SC

NeNa's Garden ©2002 Kathy Boyd, Faith
Publishing, Hartsville, SC

Ode to the Oyster, Joan and Doug Adams,
Gulf Breeze, FL

Olivia's Favorite Menus and Recipes
©1984 Olivia H. Adams, Greenville, SC

One Course at a Time ©1988 Paddi B.
Childers, N. Myrtle Beach, SC

The Orange Bowl Cookbook ©1983 The
Orange Bowl Committee, Miami, FL

Our Best Home Cooking ©2001 Judith C.
Dyer, Norcross, GA

Palm Beach Entertains ©1978 Junior
League of the Palm Beaches, Inc., West
Palm Beach, FL

Palmetto Hospitality Inn Style ©1994
Tracy M. Winters and Phyllis Y.
Winters, Greensburg, IN

Par 3: Tea-Time at the Masters® ©2005
Junior League of Augusta, GA

The Peach Sampler ©1983 Eliza Mears
Horton, West Columbia, SC

Peachtree Bouquet ©1987 Junior League
of DeKalb County Georgia, Inc.,
Decatur, GA

Perennials ©1984 Gainesville-Hall County
Junior League, Gainesville, GA

A Pinch of Sunshine ©1982 Junior Service
League of Brooksville, FL

Please Don't Feed the Alligators ©1985
Hilton Head Elementary PTA, Hilton
Head Island, SC

'Pon Top Edisto ©1997 Trinity Episcopal
Church, Edisto Island, SC

Pool Bar Jim's Famous Frozen Drinks
©1979 James D. Lisenby, Hilton Head
Island, SC

Prescriptions for Good Eating ©1984
Greenville County Medical Society
Auxiliary, Greenville, SC

Preserving Our Italian Heritage ©1991
Sons of Italy Florida Foundation, Fort
Lauderdale, FL

The Prima Diner ©1981 Sarasota Opera
Gift Shop, Sarasota, FL

Puttin' on the Peachtree... ©1979 Junior
League of DeKalb County Georgia, Inc.,
Decatur, GA

Putting on the Grits ©1984 The Junior
League of Columbia, Inc. SC

Quail Country ©1983 The Junior League
of Albany, GA

Recipes & Memories ©1996 Lee McCaskill,
Fort Pierce, FL

Recipes and Remembrances, GFWC Santa
Rosa Women's Club, Gulf Breeze, FL

Recipes for Lori's Lighthouse, Lori's
Lighthouse Youth Center, Cantonment,
FL

Recipes from Pawleys Island ©1955
Church of Women of All Saints
Waccamaw Episcopal Church, Pawleys
Island, SC

Recipes from the Olde Pink House ©1981 Hershel S. McCallar, Jr. and D. Jeffery Keith, Savannah, GA

Red Oak Recipes, Frances G. Womack, Tifton, GA

Ridge Recipes, Ridge Spring Harvest Festival, Ridge Spring, SC

Roberts Ranch Museum Cookbook, Friends of the Collier County Museum, Naples, FL

The Sandlapper Cookbook ©1974 Sandlapper Publishing Co., Inc., Orangeburg, SC

The Sandlappers' Salvation Cookbook ©1988 Fairey Family Association, Burton, SC

Savannah Collection ©1986 Martha Giddens Nesbit, Savannah, GA

Savor Summerville, Summerville Family YMCA, Summerville, SC

Savor the Moment: Entertaining without Reservations ©2000 Junior League of Boca Raton, FL

Sawgrass and Pines, Perry Garden Club, Perry, FL

Sea Island Seasons ©1980 Beaufort County Open Land Trust, Beaufort, SC

Seasoned with Light, First Baptist Church, Hartsville, SC

Seasoned with Sunshine ©1982 P.A.C.E. Grace Lutheran School, Winter Haven, FL

Seasons in the Sun ©1976 The Lowe Art Museum, University of Miami, Coral Gables, FL

Second Round, Tea Time at the Masters® ©1988 Junior League of Augusta, GA

Secrets from the Galley ©1983 The Galley Kitchen Shoppe, Inc., Lake Park, FL

Seminole Savorings ©1982 Seminole Productions, Inc., Tallahassee, FL

Sherman Didn't Burn Our Recipes, Bartow's Still Cooking, Walter's Publishing, Bartow, GA

Simply Florida . . . Strawberries, Florida Strawberry Grower's Association, Plant City, FL

Sing for Your Supper, Venetian Harmony Chorus, Englewood, FL

A Slice of Paradise ©1996 Junior League of Palm Beaches, Inc., West Palm Beach, FL

Some Assembly Required ©2004 Lee J. Chadwick, Alpharetta, GA

Soups, Stews, Gumbos, Chilis, Chowders, and Bisques, Southern Island Publishing, John Colquhoun, Beaufort, SC

The South Carolina Cook Book ©1954 University of South Carolina Press, Columbia, SC

South Carolina Ladies & Gents Love to Cook! ©2003 SC Farm Bureau Women's Committee, Columbia, SC

Southeastern Wildlife Cookbook ©1989 University of South Carolina Press, Columbia, SC

Southern Bread Winners ©1996 Dot Gibson Publications, Linda G. Hatcher, Waycross, GA

Southern Cooking ©1975 Sandlapper Publishing, Co. Orangeburg, SC

Southern Manna ©1988 Dot Gibson Publications, Waycross, GA

Southern Vegetable Cooking ©1981 Sandlapper Publishing Co., Inc., Orangeburg, SC

Step-by-Step to Natural Food ©1979 Diane Campbell, Clearwater, FL

Stir Crazy! ©1986 Junior Welfare League of Florence, SC

Stirrin' the Pots on Daufuskie ©1985 Billie Burn, Daufuskie Island, SC

Strictly for Boys ©1980 Betty L. Waskiewicz, Beaufort, SC

The Stuffed Griffin ©1976 The Utility Club of Griffin, GA

Sugar Beach ©1984 Fort Walton Beach Junior Service League, Fort Walton, FL

Sunny Side Up ©1980 The Junior League of Fort Lauderdale, FL

Sweet Surrender with Advice à la Carte ©1985 McElyea Publications, Winter Park, FL

Tapestry ©2000 The Junior Welfare League of Rock Hill, SC

A Taste of Georgia ©1977 Newman Junior Service League, Newman, GA

A Taste of Georgia, Another Serving ©1994 Newman Junior Service League, Newman, GA

A Taste of Heaven, St. Francis of Assisi Church, Apopka, FL

A Taste of South Carolina ©1983 The Palmetto Cabinet of South Carolina, Sandlapper Publishing, Co., Inc., Orangeburg, SC

A Taste Through Time, Woodruff Community Center, Woodruff, SC

Tastes from Paradise, Naples Woman's Club, Naples, FL

Tastes from Paradise: A Garden of Eating, Sisterhood, Jewish Congregation of Marco Island, FL

Temptations ©1985 Junior Service League of Rome, GA

Thoroughbred Fare ©1984 Wimmer Brothers, Aiken, SC

Through Our Kitchen Windows ©1980 WMSC Council, Bahia Vista Mennonite Church, Sarasota, FL

Thyme Waves ©1981 Junior Museum of Bay County, Inc., Panama City, FL

Thymes Remembered ©1998 Junior League of Tallahassee, FL

Traditions ©1992 Carol Rees Publications, Tina Salser Rees, Dot Gibson Publications, Waycross, GA

Treasures of the Tropics, Hibiscus Children's Center, Jensen Beach, FL

Tried & True Recipes from Covington, Georgia ©2005 Covington, Georgia, East Metro Christian Women's Connection, Conyers, GA

Tropical Settings ©1995 The Junior League of Ft. Myers, FL

True Grits ©1995 Junior League of Atlanta, GA

Two Hundred Years of Charleston Cooking ©1976 University of South Carolina, Columbia, SC

Unbearably Good! ©1986 Americus Junior Service League, Americus, GA

Under the Canopy ©1995 GFWC–Tallahassee Junior Woman's Club, Tallahassee, FL

Uptown Down South ©1986 Greenville Junior League Publications, Greenville, SC

Vidalia Sweet Onion Lovers Cookbook ©1996 Bland Farms, Glennville, GA

Vincent Russo's Seafood Cookbook ©1984, 1988 Vincent Russo, Savannah, GA

Wanted: Quick Draw's Favorite Recipes ©2003 Harold "Quick Draw" Finch, McDonough, GA

What's Cooking? In King's Grant ©1998 King's Grant HOA, Summerville, SC

Wild Fare & Wise Words ©2005 Jim and Ann Canada, Rock Hill, SC

Windsor Academy Cookbook ©1988 Ponder's Inc., Windsor Academy, Thomasville, GA

The Woman's Exchange Classic Recipes ©2001 The Woman's Exchange of St. Augustine, FL

INDEX

PHOTO © GEORGIA DEPARTMENT OF ECONOMIC DEVELOPMENT.

Carved into Stone Mountain near Atlanta, Georgia, are the figures of three Confederate heroes of the Civil War: Stonewall Jackson, Jefferson Davis, and Robert E. Lee. The monument was designed as a memorial to the heroic struggle of the South during the Civil War.

The recipes included in the REGIONAL COOKBOOK SERIES have been collected from the

BEST OF THE BEST STATE COOKBOOK SERIES

Best of the Best from the

Southeast
Cookbook

Selected Recipes from the
Favorite Cookbooks of
South Carolina, Georgia, and Florida